KETO FOR CARB LOVERS

500+

Amazing Low-Carb, High-Fat Recipes & 21-Day Meal Plan

SUSAN MILTON

TABLE OF CONTANTS

DESCRIPTION

Are you a Keto Carb Lover looking to live a healthy? The ketogenic diet is a great way to watch pounds melt away, quickly and safely. Your own body turns into a fat-burning machine, using up stores of fat rather than glucose from the food you're eating for energy. At the same time, it protects your heart and other muscles from damage since you're feeding them nourishing, healthy oils, and lots of needed protein.

For the ketogenic diet to work, you don't need to count calories and weigh or measure your food necessarily, but as with all eating plans, you need to be honest with yourself about what you're eating and how much. I want you to remember though, no matter how much you try to lose that extra body fat, you must take your age into consideration. Especially if you have already passed middle age, you need to accept that you can no longer have the body you had when you were 20 or 30. Sometimes, in the quest to be our best, we may forget that we have a wholesome, working body – far more than a lot of people can say. But don't lose heart, while the time to look your "best" may have passed, the time to just shed a few pounds, enjoy your body, and live a healthier life is now!

This cookbook has the best collection of healthy recipes perfect for keto carb lovers to live a healthy and leaner lifestyle. Here are some of the recipes covered in this guide;

- Breakfast
- Mains
- Sides
- Seafood
- Poultry

- Meat
- Vegetables
- Pasta
- Soups and Stews
- Eggs and dairy

- Smoothies
- Salads
- Snacks and Desserts

Try your best to find a balance between living healthily and being happy with the body you have. Make sure to follow this simple cookbook guide to help you lose weight and live an overall healthier lifestyle.

INTRODUCTION

The Keto Diet is all about setting up your body to start burning fat instead of glucose when energy is needed by the body. The ketodiet comprises of low carb (carbohydrate), and high fat diets. The Keto Diet has become popular in most parts of the globe because people have now come to like it due to its numerous health benefits. Starting the Keto diet is very simple but some people do have some doubt in them asking themselves if the keto Diet can work in them as it works for others. Starting the Keto Diet also requires that you know what Keto Diet is so that kick start with ease. Kick starting Ketosis could include: cutting down carbohydrates' intake, eating high-quality fats, doing much exercise, maintaining your protein level.

One of the ways in which the body obtains calories is through carbohydrates being are macronutrients. Carbs is a short form of saying carbohydrate while calories also mean energy. Carbohydrates according to several studies show that carbohydrate is the main source of energy. Carbohydrate is a combination of carbon, hydrogen and oxygen. That is why they are called carbohydrate. Normally, the daily consumption of 1g of carbohydrate is equivalent to 4 calories. This means a diet of 1,800 calories per day will give about 202g and 292g for both low and high end.

A ketogenic diet helps in regulating the levels of blood sugar and lowers the blood pressure levels. Since it is low-carb and a high-fat diet, it leads to a reduction of triglycerides and cholesterol. This is because of the increase in the levels of HDL (good cholesterol) while reducing the levels of LDL (bad cholesterol). A high level of HDL indicates a lower risk of cardiac diseases.

For controlling the levels of high blood sugar, insulin is produced in the body. It assists the cells in making use of glucose and storing the rest for future use. People with diabetes, especially the ones suffering from Type-2 diabetes, are often trodden with a low carb diet. By minimizing the intake of carbs, the requirement for insulin decreases and this, in turn, reduces the levels of blood sugar.

Usually, by afternoon, the energy levels of an average man go down drastically and the craving for caffeine increase. While following this diet, you will feel fuller for longer and have more energy than usual. This is because the body is continually burning fats for providing energy and doesn't depend on glucose. Once in ketosis, a person can work tirelessly for longer than usual without worrying about any swings in energy levels.

A keto diet helps in strengthening fertility. Polycystic Ovarian Syndrome is a widespread hormonal disorder in women, and it can be treated and controlled by following the keto diet. This diet also helps in overcoming other symptoms like acne and obesity. It regularizes the menstrual cycle as well.

BREAKFAST

01. MUSHROOM AND CHORIZO MIX

Preparation time: 5 minutes
Cooking time: 6 hours
Servings: 2

Ingredients:

- 1 avocado, peeled, pitted and cubed
- ½ cup vegetable stock
- 1 pound chorizo, chopped
- 1 red bell pepper, chopped
- 8 mushrooms, chopped
- 1 small red onion, chopped
- 3 garlic cloves, minced
- ½ cup parsley, chopped
- 10 ounces beef, chopped

Directions:

1. Add all the ingredients to your slow cooker, except the avocado. Cover and cook on low for 6 hours.
2. Divide everything between plates, sprinkle avocado cubes on top and serve.

Nutrition Values: Calories 1563, fat 116,3, fiber 9,6, carbs 25,9, protein 103,6

02. SMOKED HAM AND BABY SPINACH MIX

Preparation time: 5 minutes
Cooking time: 4 hours and 5 minutes
Servings: 2

Ingredients:

- 2 tablespoons olive oil
- ¼ cup coconut milk
- 2 eggs, whisked
- 4 ounces cooked smoked ham, chopped
- 1 cup baby spinach
- A pinch of black pepper

Directions:

1. Heat up a pan with the oil over medium heat. Add the ham and black pepper, stir, cook for 5 minutes and transfer it to your slow cooker.
2. In a bowl, mix the eggs with the coconut milk, spinach and some more black pepper. Whisk well and pour over the ham.
3. Stir everything gently in the slow cooker, cover and cook on low for 4 hours.
4. Divide between plates and serve for breakfast.

Nutrition Values: Calories 348, fat 30,5, fiber 1,7, carbs 4,7, protein 16.1

03. APPLES AND WALNUT BOWLS

Preparation time: 5 minutes
Cooking time: 7 hours
Servings: 4

Ingredients:

- 1 cup walnuts, soaked in cold water for 12 hours and drained
- 3 apples, peeled, cored and cubed
- 1 teaspoon ground cinnamon
- 1 tablespoon date sugar
- ½ teaspoon ground nutmeg
- 1 cup almond milk

Directions:

1. In your slow cooker, mix all the ingredients.
2. Cover, cook on low for 7 hours, divide into bowls and serve for breakfast.

Nutrition Values: Calories 428, fat 33,2, fiber 8, carbs 31,8, protein 9,4

04. LEEK AND TURKEY BREAKFAST MIX

Preparation time: 5 minutes
Cooking time: 7 hours
Servings: 4

Ingredients:

- 2 cups leeks, chopped
- 2 tablespoons olive oil
- 1 cup mustard greens, torn
- 2 garlic cloves, minced
- 8 eggs, whisked
- 1 ½ cups turkey fillet, cooked and chopped

Directions:

1. Heat up a pan with the oil over medium heat, add the turkey, stir, and let it brown for 5 minutes then transfer to your slow cooker.
2. Add the rest of the ingredients to the slow cooker as well, toss them to combine well, cover and cook on low for 7 hours.
3. Divide everything between plates and serve for breakfast.

Nutrition Values: Calories 281, fat 16,2, fiber 1,3, carbs 8,2, protein 26

05. BANANA PORRIDGE

Preparation time: 5 minutes
Cooking time: 6 hours
Servings: 2

Ingredients:

- ½ cup walnuts, chopped
- 2 bananas, peeled and chopped
- 1 cup coconut milk
- 2 tablespoons coconut butter, softened
- ½ teaspoon ground cinnamon
- 2 teaspoons coconut sugar

Directions:
1. In your slow cooker, mix all the ingredients together, cover and cook on low for 6 hours.
2. Divide everything into bowls and serve for breakfast.

Nutrition Values: Calories 777, fat 65,5, fiber 13,1, carbs 48,4, protein 13,6

06. COCOA CHERRY BOWLS

Preparation time: 5 minutes
Cooking time: 3 hours
Servings: 4

Ingredients:
- 3 cups almond milk
- 2 tablespoons ground flaxseeds
- 2 tablespoons cocoa powder
- 1/3 cup cherries, pitted
- 3 tablespoons coconut sugar
- ½ teaspoon vanilla extract

Directions:
1. In your slow cooker, mix all the ingredients, cover and cook on high for 3 hours.
2. Divide everything into bowls and serve for breakfast.

Nutrition Values: Calories 461, fat 44,4, fiber 5,8, carbs 23, protein 5,3

07. CARDAMOM CARROTS MIX

Preparation time: 5 minutes
Cooking time: 4 hours
Servings: 4

Ingredients:
- 2 cups coconut milk
- 3 tablespoons flax meal
- 1 and ½ cups carrots, shredded
- 2 tablespoons coconut sugar
- 1 teaspoon cardamom, ground

Directions:
1. In your slow cooker, mix all the ingredients, cover and cook on High for 4 hours.
2. Divide into bowls and serve for breakfast.

Nutrition Values: Calories 332, fat 30,5, fiber 5,5, carbs 16,5, protein 4,3

08. CINNAMON CAULIFLOWER RICE

Preparation time: 4 minutes

Cooking time: 6 hours
Servings: 4

Ingredients:
- 6 ½ cups water
- ¾ cup coconut sugar
- 2 cups cauliflower rice
- 1 tablespoon ground cinnamon
- ½ cup coconut, grated

Directions:
1. In your slow cooker, mix all the ingredients, cover and cook on low for 6 hours.
2. Stir, divide into bowls and serve for breakfast.

Nutrition Values: Calories 236, fat 5,2, fiber 1,8, carbs 47,1, protein 4,3

09. APPLE CAULIFLOWER RICE

Preparation time: 5 minutes
Cooking time: 6 hours
Servings: 4

Ingredients:
- 1 ½ cups cauliflower rice
- 1 ½ teaspoons cinnamon powder
- 1/3 cup coconut sugar
- 2 tablespoons coconut oil, melted
- 2 apples, peeled, cored and sliced
- 3 cups almond milk

Directions:
1. In your slow cooker, mix all the ingredients, cover and cook on low for 6 hours.
2. Divide everything into bowls and serve.

Nutrition Values: Calories 642, fat 51,5, fiber 6,7, carbs 47,9, protein 7,8

10. ALMOND STRAWBERRY MIX

Preparation time: 5 minutes
Cooking time: 3 hours
Servings: 2

Ingredients:
- 3 tablespoons ground flaxseed
- ¼ cup strawberries, halved
- 2 cups almond milk
- ½ teaspoon coconut sugar

Directions:
1. In your slow cooker, mix all the ingredients, cover and cook on low for 3 hours.
2. Divide everything into bowls and serve for breakfast.

Nutrition Values: Calories 617, fat 60,6, fiber 8,5, carbs 18,7, protein 7,6

11. NUTS AND PEARS BREAKFAST MIX

Preparation time: 5 minutes

Cooking time: 7 hours

Servings: 4

Ingredients:

- ½ cup almonds, soaked for 12 hours and drained
- ½ cup walnuts, soaked for 12 hours and drained
- 2 pears peeled, cored and cubed
- 1 teaspoon ground cinnamon
- 1 tablespoon coconut sugar
- 1 cup almond milk

Directions:

1. In your slow cooker, mix all the ingredients, cover and cook on low for 7 hours.
2. Divide everything bowls and serve for breakfast.

Nutrition Values: Calories 361, fat 29,6, fiber 6,8, carbs 22,6, protein 8

12. MUSHROOM AND KALE FRITTATA

Preparation time: 10 minutes

Cooking time: 2 hours

Servings: 4

Ingredients:

- 6 eggs, whisked
- 4 ounces mushrooms, chopped
- 1 teaspoon garlic powder
- A pinch of salt and black pepper
- ½ cup kale, chopped
- 2 spring onions, chopped
- 1 teaspoon olive oil

Directions:

1. In a bowl, mix all the ingredients except the spring onions and the oil and whisk well.
2. Grease a slow cooker with the oil, add egg and kale mix and cook on High for 2 hours.
3. Divide the frittata between plates, sprinkle spring onions on top and serve.

Nutrition Values: Calories 119, fat 7,8, fiber 0,7, carbs 3,4, protein 9,7

13. SPICED BEEF BREAKFAST BOWLS

Preparation time: 5 minutes

Cooking time: 8 hours

Servings: 4

Ingredients:

- 1 pound beef, cut into strips
- 1 teaspoon ground coriander
- ¼ cup beef stock
- 1 tablespoon dried oregano
- 1 tablespoon cumin powder

- 2 tablespoons chili powder
- 2 yellow onions, chopped
- A pinch of salt and black pepper
- 1 teaspoon lime juice

Directions:

1. Combine all the ingredients in your slow cooker, mix, cover and cook on low for 8 hours.
2. Divide everything into bowls and serve for breakfast.

Nutrition Values: Calories 257, fat 8,3, fiber 3,2, carbs 9,5, protein 36,1

14. DELICIOUS TURKEY AND CAULIFLOWER MIX

Preparation time: 5 minutes

Cooking time: 5 hours

Servings: 3

Ingredients:

- 1 cauliflower head, florets separated
- ½ cup tomato sauce
- 12 ounces turkey fillet, cooked and sliced
- 2 garlic cloves, minced
- A pinch of sea salt and black pepper
- Olive oil

Directions:

1. Grease your slow cooker with the olive oil then add all the ingredients and toss them a bit. Cook on low for 5 hours.
2. Divide the mix into bowls and serve for breakfast.

Nutrition Values: Calories 175, fat 5,3, fiber 2,9, carbs 7,5, protein 24,4

15. SWEET POTATO AND SPRING ONIONS BOWLS

Preparation time: 5 minutes

Cooking time: 6 hours

Servings: 2

Ingredients:

- 1 ½ cups spring onions, chopped
- 2 tablespoons olive oil
- 2 teaspoons garlic, minced
- 4 eggs, whisked
- 1 cup sweet potato, peeled and grated

Directions:

1. Grease your slow cooker with the oil, add all the ingredients, mix together, cover and cook on low for 6 hours.
2. Divide the mix into bowls and serve for breakfast.

Nutrition Values: Calories 364, fat 23,1, fiber 5,3, carbs 27,8, protein 14,6

16. MUSHROOMS OMELET

Preparation time: 5 minutes
Cooking time: 7 hours
Servings: 4

Ingredients:

- 8 eggs, whisked
- 1 green bell pepper, chopped
- 1 yellow onion, chopped
- 8 ounces mushrooms, chopped
- A pinch of salt and black pepper
- Olive oil

Directions:

1. In a bowl, whisk together the eggs with the bell pepper, onion, mushrooms, salt and pepper.
2. Grease the slow cooker with the olive oil, add the eggs mixture, cover and cook on low for 7 hours.
3. Divide the omelet between plates and serve for breakfast.

Nutrition Values: Calories 188, fat 12,5, fiber 1,6, carbs 7,4, protein 13,5

17. BEEF CASSEROLE

Preparation time: 5 minutes
Cooking time: 8 hours
Servings: 4

Ingredients:

- 1 yellow onion, chopped
- 1 pound beef, cooked and chopped
- 1 red bell pepper, chopped
- 12 eggs, whisked
- 2 garlic cloves, minced
- 1 tablespoon olive oil
- 1 teaspoon fresh parsley, chopped
- 1 cup coconut milk
- A pinch of salt and black pepper

Directions:

1. Grease the slow cooker with the olive oil then add the onion, beef, bell pepper, garlic, salt and pepper and toss.
2. Add the eggs, parsley and the coconut milk over the beef mix, cover and cook on low for 8 hours.
3. Divide everything between plates and serve for breakfast.

Nutrition Values: Calories 590, fat 38,1, fiber 2,4, carbs 9,7, protein 53,1

18. BREAKFAST BEEF MEATLOAF

Preparation time: 5 minutes
Cooking time: 3 hours and 5 minutes
Servings: 4

Ingredients:

- 1 yellow onion, chopped
- 2 pounds beef, minced
- 1 teaspoon olive oil
- 3 garlic cloves, minced
- ¼ cup coconut flour
- 1 tablespoon fresh sage, minced
- A pinch of sea salt and black pepper
- 1 tablespoon sweet paprika
- 2 eggs, whisked

Directions:

1. Heat up a pan with half the oil over medium high heat. Add the onion and the garlic, stir, cook for 5 minutes and then transfer to a bowl.
2. Add all the other ingredients, stir everything well, and shape your meatloaf.
3. Grease the slow cooker with the remaining olive oil, add the meatloaf, cover and cook on high for 3 hours.
4. Slice, divide between plates and serve for breakfast.

Nutrition Values: Calories 559, fat 19,7, fiber 9, carbs 17,2, protein 74,8

19. GARLIC AND LEEK OMELET

Preparation time: 5 minutes
Cooking time: 6 hours
Servings: 4

Ingredients:

- 4 garlic cloves, minced
- 1 yellow onion, chopped
- 2 leeks, chopped
- 8 eggs, whisked
- 1 cup coconut milk
- Olive oil

Directions:

1. In a bowl, mix all the ingredients together except the olive oil.
2. Grease the slow cooker with the olive oil, pour the egg mixture in the slow cooker as well, cover and cook on low for 6 hours.
3. Divide the omelet between plates and serve it for breakfast.

Nutrition Values: Calories 336, fat 26,7, fiber 2,8, carbs 13,9, protein 13,6

20. OKRA BREAKFAST MIX

Preparation time: 5 minutes
Cooking time: 3 hours
Servings: 4

Ingredients:

- 1 yellow onion, chopped
- 3 cups okra, sliced
- 4 eggs, whisked
- 2 cups yellow bell pepper, chopped
- 2 tablespoons fresh basil, chopped
- 1 tablespoon olive oil
- A pinch of salt and black pepper

Directions:

1. In a bowl, whisk together all the ingredients except the olive oil.
2. Grease the slow cooker with the oil, pour the okra mix, even it, cover and cook on High for 3 hours.
3. Divide everything between plates and serve for breakfast.

Nutrition Values: Calories 153, fat 8,2, fiber 3,8, carbs 13, protein 7,9

21. BAKED EGGS WITH BACON AND DOUBLE CHEESE

Servings: 4
Preparation Time: 5
Cooking Time: 25

Ingredients

- 8 eggs from free-range chickens
- 1 Tbsp fresh parsley, finely chopped
- 1 tsp of basil, chopped

Salt to taste

- 1/4 cup of Gruyere cheese, grated
- 4 slices of bacon
- 2 Tbsp olive oil
- 1 scallion, cut into thin slices
- 3/4 cup of goat cheese, crumbled
- 2 cherry tomatoes, quartered

Directions

1. Preheat the oven to 400 F/200 C.
2. In a bowl, beat eggs, parsley, basil and salt.
3. Heat the oil in a skillet on high fire, pour the olive oil. Sauté the scallion and chopped bacon until get a nice color.
4. Add grated Gruyere cheese and cook, stirring, for further 2 - 3 minutes.
5. Pour the egg mixture and stir.
6. Transfer the egg/bacon mixture in a baking dish. Sprinkle crumbled goat cheese and cover with cherry tomatoes.
7. Bake for about 15 minutes or until cheese

melted. Serve hot.

Nutrition Values:
Calories: 177.6 Carbohydrates: 4g Proteins: 25g Fat: 45g Fiber: 1g

22. ZUCCHINI SPAGHETTI WITH MELTED CHEESE

Servings: 4
Preparation Time: 15 minutes
Cooking Time: 4 hours and 30

Ingredients

- 1 1/2 lbs. of zucchini sliced
- 1 lb Spaghetti
- 1/2 cup of olive oil
- 2 cloves of garlic
- 1 Tbsp fresh oregano
- 1 Tbsp fresh thyme
- 1/2 cup water
- 1 cup grated parmesan cheese
- Salt and pepper to taste

Directions

1. Clean and grate zucchini to make a zucchini spaghetti with the help of mandolin.
2. Pour the Olive oil on the bottom of your Crock Pot. Add the garlic, zucchini, oregano, thyme and water. Season with the salt and pepper and stir.
3. Cover and cook on LOW for 4 hours.
4. Open lid and add grated parmesan cheese.
5. Cover again and cook on HIGH for 30 minutes. Serve hot.

Nutrition Values:
Calories: 380 Carbohydrates: 6g Proteins: 15g Fat: 35g Fiber: 2g

23. COCONUT AND AVOCADO ALMOND MILKSHAKE

Servings: 3
Preparation Time: 5 minutes

Ingredients

- 2 1/2 cups coconut milk (canned
- 1/2 avocado, pitted and cut in half
- 1/4 cup coconut flakes (unsweetened
- 2 Tbsp ground nuts
- 2 Tbsp stevia granulated sweetener (optional
- Ice cubes

Directions

1. Place all ingredients in your high-speed blender; blend until smooth completely.
2. Serve in chilled glasses.

Nutrition Values:

Calories: 476 Carbohydrates: 8g Proteins: 6g Fat: 50g
Fiber: 3.2g

24. EGG WHITES OMELET WITH TURKEY AND MASCARPONE

Servings: 4
Preparation Time: 5 minutes
Cooking Time: 5 minutes

Ingredients

- 8 egg whites
- 4 slices of smoked turkey, finely chopped
- 1 grated tomato
- 1/2 cup of Greek yogurt
- 2 slices of Mascarpone cheese
- 2 Tbsp of olive oil

Directions

1. In a bowl, beat the egg whites with yogurt, smoked turkey, tomato and cheese.
2. Heat the oil in a non-stick frying pan and pour the egg white mixture.
3. Cook omelet for 2 minutes, flip and cook for 1 minute.
4. Serve immediately.

Nutrition Values:

Calories: 182 Carbohydrates: 5.2 Proteins: 10.5g Fat: 13.5g Fiber: 0.5g

25. EGGS STUFFED WITH SPINACH AND BACON

Servings: 6
Preparation Time: 15 minutes
Cooking Time: 10 minutes

Ingredients

- 6 large eggs, boiled (hard
- 1/2 cup of olive oil
- 2 slices bacon, chopped
- 1 lb fresh spinach chopped
- 1/2 cup of mayonnaise
- 2 Tbsp of yellow mustard
- 2 Tbsp of grated parmesan cheese
- Salt and pepper to taste

Directions

1. Place the eggs in a saucepan, cover completely with cold water.
2. Once the water begins to boil, turn off the heat and let cook for 10 minutes.
3. Transfer eggs into a bowl with cold water.
4. Peel eggs, halve and remove the yolks; reserve yolks.
5. Heat the olive oil in a frying skillet over medium-high heat and sauce the bacon and spinach.

6. In a meantime, in a large bowl stir the egg yolks, mayonnaise, mustard, parmesan and salt and pepper.
7. Add spinach with bacon mixture and stir again to combine thoroughly.
8. Fill the egg whites with the mixture and place on a platter.
9. Refrigerate for one hour and serve.

Nutrition Values:

Calories: 407 Carbohydrates: 7g Proteins: 12g Fat: 37.2g Fiber: 2g

26. EGGS WITH SMOKED PAPRIKA AND PECORINO

Servings: 4
Preparation Time: 5 minutes
Cooking Time: 15 minutes

Ingredients

- 1/4 cup of fresh butter
- 1 clove of garlic, sliced
- 1 fresh onion finely chopped
- 1 tomato grated
- Salt and freshly ground pepper to taste
- 8 eggs from free-range chickens
- 2 Tbsp smoked paprika
- 1 cup of Pecorino Romano grated
- 2 Tbsp of fresh basil, chopped

Directions

1. Heat butter in a frying skillet over medium heat; sauté the garlic, the onion, and the tomato.
2. Season with the salt and pepper to taste, and cook, stirring constantly, for about 5 minutes.
3. Add eggs, one at a time and stir; sprinkle with the smoked paprika and stir again.
4. Cook for further 2 - 3 minutes.
5. Sprinkle with grated Pecorino and fresh basil and serve.

Nutrition Values:

Calories: 427 Carbohydrates: 6.4g Proteins: 27g Fat: 33g Fiber: 2.6g

27. HOMEMADE KETO ALMOND SPREAD

Servings: 10
Preparation Time: 15
Cooking Time: 12 minutes

Ingredients

- 3 cups almonds, roasted
- 1 pinch of salt
- 1 tsp cinnamon
- 1 tsp almond or vanilla extract

- 2 Tbsp of natural granulated sweetener (Stevia, Truvia, Erythritol...etc.

Directions

1. Preheat the oven to 350 F/175 C.
2. Line one rimmed sheet with parchment paper and spread almonds.
3. Roast for 10 - 12 minutes. Remove almonds from the oven and let them cool for 5 - 10 minutes.
4. Place almonds in a food processor along with all remaining ingredients.
5. Process for 10 minutes or until completely smooth.
6. Store in a glass jar and keep refrigerated.

Nutrition Values:

Calories: 248 Carbohydrates: 8g Proteins: 9g Fat: 22g Fiber: 4.5g

28. KETO BREAKFAST WAFFLES WITH CRISPY BACON

Servings: 4
Preparation Time: 10 minutes
Cooking Time: 10 minutes

Ingredients

- 1/3 cup fresh butter melted
- 4 slices bacon
- 2 eggs from free-range chickens
- 3 cup of almond flour
- 1 1/2 tsp baking soda
- 2 tsp natural sweetener (Stevia, Truvia, Erythritol...etc.

Ingredients

1. Microwave the butter about 30 seconds; set aside.
2. Heat the frying skillet and brown bacon until crisp.
3. In a small bowl, combine flour, baking soda and sweetener.
4. Add eggs and stir thoroughly. Add melted butter and stir.
5. Preheat the waffle iron according to manufacture instruction.
6. Spoon the batter on the edges and place 2 slices of bacon over.
7. Cook waffles until golden brown; flip once.
8. Serve hot.

Nutrition Values:

Calories: 346 Carbohydrates: 1g Proteins: 8g Fat: 35g Fiber: 0g

29. KETO COCONUT WAFFLES

Servings: 6
Preparation Time: 10 minutes

Cooking Time: 10 minutes

Ingredients

- 4 eggs from free-range chickens
- 2 cup almond flour
- 1 Tbsp of coconut flour
- 1/2 tsp baking soda
- 1/2 tsp of sea salt
- 1/2 tsp ground cinnamon
- 1/4 cup coconut milk (canned
- 1 cup almond milk (unsweetened
- 1/4 cup shredded coconut, unsweetened
- 2 Tbsp of natural sweetener (Stevia, Erythritol...etc.
- 1 1/2 tsp vanilla extract

1. **Directions**
2. Preheat your waffle iron according to manufacturer instructions.
3. In a bowl, whisk the eggs yolks.
4. Add the almond flour, coconut flour, baking soda, pinch of salt, cinnamon, almond milk, coconut milk, shredded coconut, and sweetener; stir well.
5. In a separate bowl, beat the egg whites until become froth.
6. Add the egg whites to the egg yolk batter mixture and pour the vanilla extract; stir well.
7. Pour the batter in a waffle iron and cook according to your preference.
8. Serve hot.

Nutrition Values:

Calories: 55 Carbohydrates: 1.1g Proteins: 3.5g Fat: 4g Fiber: 0.3g

30. KETO DILLY - ZUCCHINI AND FETA MUFFINS

Servings: 12
Preparation Time: 10 minutes
Cooking Time: 25 minutes

Ingredients

- 1 1/2 cups almond flour
- 2 Tbs natural sweetener (Stevia, Truvia, Erythritol...etc.
- 2 tsp baking powder
- 1/2 tsp salt
- 3/4 tsp fresh dill
- 1/4 cup almond milk
- 1 butter stick softened
- 2 Eggs from free-range chickens
- 2/3 cup Feta cheese crumbled
- 3/4 cup shredded zucchini

Directions

1. Preheat oven to 400 F/200 C. Grease one muffin tin; set aside.
2. In a large bowl, combine the almond flour, sweetener, baking powder, salt and dill.
3. In a separate bowl, combine the almond milk, softened butter and eggs.
4. Stir the cheese and shredded zucchini and combined well.
5. Stir the almond milk mixture to the dry ingredients and gently stir.
6. Fill the prepared muffin cups about two-thirds full.
7. Bake for 20 to 25 minutes.
8. Serve warm or cold.

Nutrition Values:

Calories: 157 Carbohydrates: 1g Proteins: 2.5g Fat: 16.5g Fiber: 0.1g

31. LEMONITO ZUCCHINI MUFFINS

Servings: 12
Preparation Time: 10 minutes
Cooking Time: 25 minutes

Ingredients

- 2 cups of almond flour
- 1/2 cup of natural granulated sweetener (Stevia, Truvia, Erythritol...etc.
- 1 Tbsp baking powder
- 1 tsp salt
- Grated peel of 1/2 lemon
- 3/4 cup roasted almonds, finely chopped
- 2 eggs, beaten
- 1/2 cup almond milk
- 1/3 cup olive oil
- 1 cup zucchini, shredded and drained

Directions

1. Preheat the oven to 400 F/200 C.
2. Grease with the oil one 12-cup muffin tin.
3. In a bowl, combine together the flour, sweetener, baking powder, salt and lemon peel; stir. Add finely chopped almonds and stir again.
4. In a separate bowl, whisk the eggs, almond milk and olive oil.
5. Combine dry ingredients with egg mixture; stir until just combines and add shredded zucchini.
6. Spoon the batter into prepared muffin tin. Bake for 20 to 25 minutes.
7. Serve warm or cold.

Nutrition Values:

Calories: 118.5 g Carbohydrates: 2.2g Proteins: 3gFat: 12g Fiber: 1g

32. CREAMY EGGS AND ASPARAGUS

Preparation time: 10 minutes
Cooking time: 15 minutes
Servings: 4

Ingredients:

- 2 ounces butter
- 4 eggs, whisked
- 8 ounces coconut cream
- 3 ounces parmesan, grated
- A pinch of salt and black pepper
- A pinch of cayenne pepper
- 1 and ½ pounds green asparagus, trimmed and halved
- 1 and ½ tablespoon lemon juice
- 1 tablespoon olive oil

Directions:

1. Heat up a pan with the butter over medium-high heat, add the eggs and scramble them for 6-7 minutes.
2. Add parmesan, cream, salt, pepper and cayenne, stir, take off heat and divide between plates.
3. Heat up a pan with the oil over medium-high heat, add asparagus, a pinch of cayenne and the lemon juice, cook for 2-3 minutes on each side, divide next to the scrambled eggs and serve for breakfast.
4. Enjoy!

Nutrition Values: Calories 212, fat 8, fiber 5, carbs 15, protein 7

33. KETO BREAKFAST BURGER

Preparation time: 10 minutes
Cooking time: 15 minutes
Servings: 4

Ingredients:

- 1 pound beef, ground
- 1 teaspoon mustard
- ½ teaspoon onion powder
- ½ teaspoon garlic powder
- 2 tablespoons ghee
- A pinch of salt and black pepper
- ¼ cup homemade mayonnaise
- 1 teaspoon chili sauce

Directions:

1. In a bowl, combine the meat with mustard, onion and garlic powder, salt and pepper, stir and shape 4 burgers out of this mix.
2. Heat up a pan with the ghee over medium-high heat, add burgers, cook them for 4-5 minutes on each side, divide between plates

and serve with some chili sauce and mayo spread on top and in keto buns.

3. Enjoy!

Nutrition Values: Calories 200, fat 7, fiber 8, carbs 16, protein 29

34. BREAKFAST CAULIFLOWER MIX

Preparation time: 10 minutes
Cooking time: 25 minutes
Servings: 4

Ingredients:

- 2 tablespoons ghee
- 1 small yellow onion, chopped
- 2 garlic cloves, minced
- 3 jalapeno peppers, chopped
- 1 pound beef meat, lean and ground
- A pinch of salt and black pepper
- 1 cauliflower head, grated
- ½ cup water
- ½ cup homemade mayonnaise
- ¼ cup sunflower seed butter
- 1 teaspoon cumin, ground
- 1 tablespoons coconut aminos
- 4 eggs
- ½ avocado, peeled, cored and chopped
- 1 tablespoon parsley, chopped

Directions:

1. Heat up a pan with the ghee over medium-high heat, add jalapeno, onion and garlic, stir and cook for 3 minutes.
2. Add meat, salt and pepper, stir and brown for 5 minutes more.
3. Add cauliflower, stir and cook for 2 minutes.
4. Add sunflower seed butter, water, mayo, aminos and cumin, stir and cook everything for 5 more minutes.
5. Make 4 holes in this mix, crack and egg in each, sprinkle with salt and pepper, introduce in preheated broiler and cook for 10 minutes.
6. Divide this mix between plates, sprinkle parsley and top with avocado pieces and serve.
7. Enjoy!

Nutrition Values: Calories 288, fat 12, fiber 6, carbs 15, protein 38

35. AVOCADOS STUFFED WITH SALMON

Preparation time: 10 minutes
Cooking time: 0 minutes
Servings: 2

Ingredients:

- 1 big avocado, pitted and halved
- 2 ounces smoked salmon, flaked
- Juice of 1 lemon
- 2 tablespoons olive oil
- 1 ounce goat cheese, crumbled
- A pinch of salt and black pepper

Directions:

1. In your food processor, combine the salmon with the lemon juice, oil, cheese, salt and pepper and pulse well.
2. Divide this mix into avocado halves and serve.
3. Enjoy!

Nutrition Values: Calories 300m fat 15, fiber 5, carbs 8, protein 16

36. NUTRITIOUS BREAKFAST SALAD

Preparation time: 10 minutes
Cooking time: 6 minutes
Servings: 2

Ingredients:

- 3 cups kale, torn
- 1 teaspoon red vinegar
- A pinch of salt and black pepper
- 2 teaspoons olive oil
- 2 eggs
- 4 strips bacon, chopped
- 10 cherry tomatoes, halved
- 2 ounces avocado, pitted, peeled and sliced

Directions:

1. Put some water in a pot, bring to a boil over medium-high heat, add the eggs, boil them for 6 minutes, drain, rinse them, cool them down, peel and slice them.
2. In a salad bowl, combine the kale with the vinegar, salt, pepper, oil, eggs, bacon, tomatoes and avocado, toss well, divide between plates and serve for breakfast.
3. Enjoy!

Nutrition Values: Calories 292, fat 14, fiber 7, carbs 18, protein 16

37. BREAKFAST BROCCOLI MUFFINS

Preparation time: 10 minutes
Cooking time: 30 minutes
Servings: 4

Ingredients:

- 2 teaspoons ghee, soft
- 2 eggs
- 2 cups almond flour
- 1 cup broccoli florets, chopped

- 1 cup almond milk
- 2 tablespoons nutritional yeast
- 1 teaspoon baking powder

Directions:
1. In a bowl, mix the eggs with the flour, broccoli, milk, yeast and baking powder and stir really well.
2. Grease a muffin tray with the ghee, divide broccoli mix, introduce in the oven and cook at 350 degrees F for 30 minutes.
3. Serve these muffins for breakfast.
4. Enjoy!

Nutrition Values: Calories 204, fat 4, fiber 7, carbs 15, protein 11

38. BREAKFAST PORK BAGEL
Preparation time: 10 minutes
Cooking time: 40 minutes
Servings: 6

- **Ingredients:**
- 1 yellow onion, chopped
- 1 tablespoon ghee
- 2 pounds pork meat, ground
- 2 eggs
- 2/3 cup tomato sauce
- A pinch of salt and black pepper
- 1 teaspoon sweet paprika

Directions:
1. Heat up a pan with the ghee over medium heat, add onion, stir and cook for 3-4 minutes.
2. In a bowl, combine the meat with sautéed onions, eggs, tomato sauce, salt, pepper and paprika, stir well and shape 6 bagels using your hands.
3. Arrange the meat bagels on a lined baking sheet and cook them in the oven at 400 degrees F for 40 minutes.
4. Divide the bagels between plates and serve them for breakfast.
5. Enjoy!

Nutrition Values: Calories 300, fat 11, fiber 8, carbs 16, protein 12

39. EASY BAKED EGGS
Preparation time: 10 minutes
Cooking time: 20 minutes
Servings: 4
Ingredients:
- 1 cup baby spinach
- 4 ounces bacon, chopped
- 8 eggs, whisked

- A pinch of salt and black pepper

Directions:
1. Heat up a pan over medium-high heat, add bacon, stir and brown it for 4 minutes.
2. Add baby spinach, salt and pepper, toss, cook for 1 minute more, take off heat and divide into 4 ramekins.
3. Divide whisked eggs in each ramekin, introduce them all in the oven and cook at 400 degrees F for 15 minutes.
4. Serve the baked eggs for breakfast.
5. Enjoy!

Nutrition Values: Calories 281, fat 4, fiber 8, carbs 18, protein 6

40. BACON AND SHRIMP BREAKFAST
Preparation Time: 25 minutes
Servings: 4
Ingredients:
- 4 bacon slices; chopped.
- 4 ounces shrimp; deveined
- 1 cup mushrooms; sliced
- 1/2 cup coconut cream
- 4 ounces smoked salmon; chopped.
- Salt and black pepper to the taste.

Directions:
1. Heat up a pan over medium heat; add bacon; stir and cook for 5 minutes
2. Add mushrooms; stir and cook for 5 minutes more
3. Add salmon; stir and cook for 3 minutes
4. Add shrimp and cook for 2 minutes
5. Add salt, pepper and coconut cream; stir, cook for 1 minute, take off heat and divide between plates

Nutrition Values: Calories: 340; Fat: 23; Fiber: 1; Carbs: 4; Protein: 17

41. CHICKEN OMELET
Preparation Time: 20 minutes
Servings: 1
Ingredients:
- 2 bacon slices; cooked and crumbled
- 2 eggs
- 1 tablespoon homemade mayonnaise
- 1 tomato; chopped.
- 1 ounce rotisserie chicken; shredded
- 1 teaspoon mustard
- 1 small avocado; pitted, peeled and chopped.
- Salt and black pepper to the taste.

Directions:
1. In a bowl, mix eggs with some salt and pepper and whisk gently.

2. Heat up a pan over medium heat; spray with some cooking oil, add eggs and cook your omelet for 5 minutes
3. Add chicken, avocado, tomato, bacon, mayo and mustard on one half of the omelet.
4. Fold omelet, cover pan and cook for 5 minutes more
5. Transfer to a plate and serve

Nutrition Values: Calories: 400; Fat: 32; Fiber: 6; Carbs: 4; Protein: 25

42. KETO BREAKFAST MUFFINS

Preparation Time: 40 minutes
Servings: 4
Ingredients:
- 1/4 cup kale; chopped.
- 8 prosciutto slices
- 1 tablespoon coconut oil
- 1/4 cup chives; chopped.
- 1/2 cup almond milk
- 6 eggs
- Salt and black pepper to the taste.

Directions:
1. In a bowl, mix eggs with salt, pepper, milk, chives and kale and stir well.
2. Grease a muffin tray with melted coconut oil, line with prosciutto slices, pour eggs mix, introduce in the oven and bake at 350 degrees F for 30 minutes
3. Transfer muffins to a platter and serve for breakfast.

Nutrition Values: Calories: 140; Fat: 3; Fiber: 1; Carbs: 3; Protein: 10

43. KETO FRENCH TOAST

Preparation Time: 50 minutes
Servings: 18
Ingredients:
- 1 cup whey protein
- 12 egg whites
- 4 ounces cream cheese
- For the French toast:
- 1 teaspoon vanilla
- 1/2 cup coconut milk
- 2 eggs
- 1 teaspoon cinnamon; ground
- 1/2 cup almond milk
- 1/2 cup swerve
- 1/2 cup ghee; melted

Directions:
1. In a bowl, mix 12 egg whites with your mixer for a few minutes
2. Add protein and stir gently.

3. Add cream cheese and stir again.
4. Pour this into 2 greased bread pans, introduce in the oven at 325 degrees F and bake for 45 minutes
5. Leave breads to cool down and slice them into 18 pieces
6. In a bowl, mix 2 eggs with vanilla, cinnamon and coconut milk and whisk well.
7. Dip bread slices in this mix.
8. Heat up a pan with some coconut oil over medium heat; add bread slices, cook until they are golden on each side and divide between plates
9. Heat up a pan with the ghee over high heat; add almond milk and heat up well.
10. Add swerve; stir and take off heat.
11. Leave aside to cool down a bit and drizzle over French toasts

Nutrition Values: Calories: 200; Fat: 12; Fiber: 1; Carbs: 1; Protein: 7

44. ALMOND PANCAKES

Preparation Time: 20 minutes
Servings: 12
Ingredients:
- 6 eggs
- 1/4 cup almonds; toasted
- 2 ounces cocoa chocolate
- 1 teaspoon almond extract
- 1/3 cup coconut; shredded
- 1/2 teaspoon baking powder
- 1/4 cup coconut oil
- 1/2 cup coconut flour
- 1/4 cup stevia
- 1 cup almond milk
- Cooking spray
- A pinch of salt

Directions:
1. In a bowl, mix coconut flour with stevia, salt, baking powder and coconut and stir.
2. Add coconut oil, eggs, almond milk and the almond extract and stir well again.
3. Add chocolate and almonds and whisk well again.
4. Heat up a pan with cooking spray over medium heat; add 2 tablespoons batter, spread into a circle, cook until it's golden, flip, cook again until it's done and transfer to a pan.
5. Repeat with the rest of the batter and serve your pancakes right away.

Nutrition Values: Calories: 266; Fat: 13; Fiber: 8; Carbs: 10; Protein: 11

45. MASALA CHICKEN

Preparation time: 5 minutes
Cooking time: 7 hours
Servings: 6
Ingredients:

- 2 pounds chicken breasts, skinless, boneless, cubed
- ½ cup cashews, chopped
- 2 cups tomato puree
- 2 ½ tablespoons garam masala
- 2 garlic cloves, minced
- 1 yellow onion, chopped
- ½ cup cilantro, chopped

Directions:

1. In your slow cooker, combine all the ingredients, mix well, cover and cook on low for 7 hours.
2. Divide everything into bowls and serve.

Nutrition Values: Calories 394, fat 16,7, fiber 2,4, carbs 13,3, protein 47,2

46. PORK STRIPS AND SWEET POTATOES

Preparation time: 5 minutes
Cooking time: 8 hours
Servings: 4

Ingredients:

- 2 pounds pork stew meat, cut into strips
- 3 sweet potatoes, peeled and cubed
- 2 yellow onions, chopped
- 1 tablespoon garlic powder
- 1 tablespoon fresh sage, chopped
- ½ cup beef stock

Directions:

1. In your slow cooker, combine all the ingredients and mix well.
2. Cover and cook on low for 8 hours. Divide into bowls and serve while warm.

Nutrition Values: Calories 646, fat 22,3, fiber 6,2, carbs 38,4, protein 69,5

47. CARROTS AND CELERY STEW

Preparation time: 10 minutes
Cooking time: 5 hours
Servings: 4

Ingredients:

- 1 tablespoon olive oil
- 1 yellow onion, chopped
- 4 garlic cloves, minced
- 4 carrots, sliced
- 3 celery ribs, chopped
- 1 tablespoon fresh basil, chopped
- 1 tablespoon fresh cilantro, chopped
- 1 cup chicken stock
- 6 ounces fresh tomatoes, peeled, chopped
- 1 red bell pepper, cubed
- A pinch of salt and black pepper

Directions:

1. In your slow cooker, combine all the ingredients, mix, cover and cook on low for 5 hours.
2. Divide the stew into bowls and serve while warm.

Nutrition Values: Calories 98, fat 3,9, fiber 3,9, carbs 15,1, protein 2,2

48. SWEET POTATO CHILI

Preparation time: 10 minutes
Cooking time: 8 hours
Servings: 6

Ingredients:

- 2 pounds sweet potatoes, peeled and cubed
- 1 garlic clove, minced
- 1 red onion, chopped
- 25 ounces homemade tomato sauce
- 12 ounces fresh peeled, chopped tomatoes,
- 3 cups beef stock
- 2 tablespoons chili powder
- ¼ teaspoon oregano, dried

Directions:

1. In your slow cooker, combine all the ingredients, cover and cook on low for 8 hours.
2. Divide everything into bowls and serve.

Nutrition Values: Calories 260, fat 1,3, fiber 10,1, carbs 59,3, protein 6

49. CINNAMON PORK STEW

Preparation time: 5 minutes
Cooking time: 8 hours
Servings: 4

Ingredients:

- 1 pound pork stew meat, cubed
- 2 tablespoons coconut oil, melted
- 1 sweet potato, peeled and cubed
- 1 red onion, chopped

- ½ tablespoon ground cinnamon
- A pinch of salt and black pepper

Directions:
1. Grease your slow cooker with the coconut oil then add all the ingredients, cover and cook on low for 8 hours.
2. Divide the stew into bowls and serve warm.

Nutrition Values: Calories 338, fat 17,8, fiber 2, carbs 9,2, protein 34,1

50. TOMATO PORK CHOPS

Preparation time: 5 minutes
Cooking time: 7 hours
Servings: 4

Ingredients:
- 1 teaspoon fresh ginger, grated
- 2 garlic cloves, minced
- 1 yellow onion, chopped
- 1 ½ cups fresh tomato sauce
- 1 tablespoon olive oil
- 2 tablespoons balsamic vinegar
- A pinch of salt and black pepper
- 4 pork chops, bone-in

Directions:
1. In your slow cooker, combine all the ingredients, mix, cover and cook on low for 7 hours.
2. Divide everything between plates and serve.

Nutrition Values: Calories 324, fat 23,6, fiber 2,1, carbs 8,4, protein 19,6

51. CLAM SOUP

Preparation time: 5 minutes
Cooking time: 4 hours
Servings: 6

Ingredients:
- 1 yellow onion, chopped
- 20 ounces cooked clams
- 1 cup chicken stock
- ½ teaspoon dried thyme
- A pinch of salt and black pepper
- 2 tablespoons olive oil
- 1 cup coconut cream
- 1 cup coconut milk

Directions:
1. Grease your slow cooker with the olive oil then add all the ingredients, cover and cook on high for 4 hours.
2. Divide into bowls and serve.

Nutrition Values: Calories 455, fat 32,1, fiber 2,7, carbs 42,9, protein 3,3

52. TOMATO SHRIMP

Preparation time: 5 minutes
Cooking time: 1 hour and 30 minutes
Servings: 4

Ingredients:
- 2 tablespoons avocado oil
- 2 pounds shrimp, peeled and deveined
- 2 teaspoons garlic, minced
- 1 cup fresh tomato sauce
- A pinch of salt and black pepper

Directions:
1. In your slow cooker, combine all the ingredients then cover and cook on low for 1 hour and 30 minutes.
2. Divide everything into bowls and serve while hot.

Nutrition Values: Calories 296, fat 4,9, fiber 1,3, carbs 7,6, protein 52,7

53. SHRIMP CURRY

Preparation time: 5 minutes
Cooking time: 1 hour and 30 minutes
Servings: 4

Ingredients:
- 1 tablespoon olive oil
- 2 hot green chilies, chopped
- 1 yellow onion, chopped
- 2 garlic cloves, minced
- 1 teaspoon fresh ginger, grated
- 1 tablespoon ground cumin
- 2 tomatoes, chopped
- 2 teaspoons turmeric powder
- 1 ½ pounds shrimp, peeled and deveined
- 1 tablespoon fresh cilantro, chopped

Directions:
1. Grease your slow cooker with the olive oil then add all the ingredients except the cilantro to the slow cooker.
2. Cover and cook on low for 1 hour and 30 minutes.
3. Divide the curry into bowls, sprinkle the cilantro on top and serve.

Nutrition Values: Calories 277, fat 7,1, fiber 2,2, carbs 11,9, protein 40,5

54. COD AND FENNEL

Preparation time: 5 minutes
Cooking time: 2 hours
Servings: 4

Ingredients:
- 4 cod fillets, skinless and boneless

- A pinch of salt and black pepper
- ½ teaspoon ground coriander
- 1 tablespoon lime juice
- 2 fennel bulbs, chopped
- 1 tablespoon chives, chopped
- 1 ½ cups fish stock

Directions:
1. In your slow cooker, combine all the ingredients except the chives then cover and cook on low for 2 hours.
2. Divide the fish and fennel mix between four plates, sprinkle the chives on top and serve.

Nutrition Values: Calories 142, fat 2, fiber 3,7, carbs 8,9, protein 23,5

55. EGGPLANT SOUP
Preparation time: 5 minutes
Cooking time: 3 hours
Servings: 4

Ingredients:
- 1 pound eggplant, cubed
- 2 yellow onions, chopped
- 2 garlic cloves, minced
- 4 tomatoes, sliced
- 6 cups chicken stock
- 1 tablespoon olive oil
- A pinch of salt and black pepper

Directions:
1. In your slow cooker, combine all the ingredients, cover and cook on high for 3 hours.
2. Divide everything into bowls and serve.

Nutrition Values: Calories 119, fat 4,9, fiber 6,7, carbs 18,2, protein 3,9

56. COD AND BELL PEPPERS
Preparation time: 5 minutes
Cooking time: 2 hours
Servings: 4

Ingredients:
- 14 ounces chicken stock
- 3 carrots, chopped
- 1 red onion, chopped
- 2 garlic cloves, minced
- ¼ cup parsley, chopped
- ¼ teaspoon turmeric
- 1 pound cod, skinless, boneless, cubed
- 2 red bell peppers, seeds removed, chopped

Directions:
1. In your slow cooker, combine all the ingredients, cover and cook on low for 2

hours.
2. Divide between plates and serve.

Nutrition Values: Calories 176, fat 1,4, fiber 2,7, carbs 12,7, protein 27,7

57. MUSHROOM STEW
Preparation time: 10 minutes
Cooking time: 6 hours
Servings: 4

Ingredients:
1. 1 pound mushrooms, sliced
2. 1 tablespoon fresh ginger, grated
3. 2 cups chicken stock
4. 1 yellow onion, chopped
5. 1 cup chopped carrots
6. 5 garlic cloves, minced
7. A pinch of salt and black pepper
8. 12 ounces fresh tomatoes, peeled, chopped
9. ¼ cup cilantro, chopped

Directions:
1. In your slow cooker, combine all the ingredients except the cilantro. Mix together, cover and cook on low for 6 hours.
2. Divide the stew into bowls and garnish with the cilantro then serve.

Nutrition Values: Calories 77, fat 0,9, fiber 3,7, carbs 14,9, protein 5,6

58. BROCCOLI CREAM SOUP
Preparation time: 5 minutes
Cooking time: 5 hours
Servings: 4

Ingredients:
- 1 tablespoon fresh ginger, grated
- 3 garlic cloves, minced
- 1 yellow onion, chopped
- 3 cups vegetable stock
- 1 tablespoon curry powder
- 1 big broccoli head, florets separated
- 14 ounces coconut milk
- A pinch of salt and black pepper

Directions:
1. In your slow cooker, combine all the ingredients except the coconut milk.Cover and cook on low for 5 hours.
2. Add the coconut milk then blend the soup using an immersion blender. Divide into bowls and serve.

Nutrition Values: Calories 299, fat 25,9, fiber 6,5, carbs 19,7, protein 6,2

59. SALMON AND SPRING ONIONS
Preparation time: 5 minutes

Cooking time: 2 hours
Servings: 4

Ingredients:

- 6 spring onions, chopped
- 1 teaspoon fresh ginger, grated
- 1 tablespoon olive oil
- 4 salmon fillets, boneless
- Juice of 1 lime
- Zest of 1 lime, grated
- A pinch of salt and black pepper
- ½ cup vegetable stock

Directions:

1. In your slow cooker, combine all the ingredients, cover and cook on low for 2 hours.
2. Divide between plates and serve hot.

Nutrition Values: Calories 237, fat 5, fiber 2, carbs 15, protein 8

60. SHRIMP AND OLIVES

Preparation time: 5 minutes
Cooking time: 2 hours
Servings: 4

Ingredients:

- 1 garlic clove, minced
- 1 tablespoon olive oil
- ¼ cup chicken stock
- 14 ounces cherry tomatoes, halved
- 1 pound shrimp, peeled and deveined
- 1 cup pitted, chopped black olives
- A pinch of salt and black pepper
- 1 tablespoon cilantro, chopped

Directions:

1. Grease your slow cooker with the olive oil then add all the ingredients except the cilantro. Mix together, cover and cook on low for 2 hours.
2. Divide the shrimp mix into bowls and serve with fresh cilantro sprinkled on top.

Nutrition Values: Calories 228, fat 9,2, fiber 1,2, carbs 7,6, protein 26,8

61. COD AND ASPARAGUS MIX

Preparation time: 10 minutes
Cooking time: 2 hours
Servings: 4

Ingredients:

- 1 teaspoon olive oil
- 5 ounces tomato sauce
- 4 cod fillets, boneless
- 1 bunch asparagus, trimmed and halved

- ½ tablespoon sweet paprika

Directions:

1. Grease your slow cooker with the oil, add all the ingredients, cover and cook on low for 2 hours.
2. Divide the cod and asparagus between plates and serve.

Nutrition Values: Calories 112, fat 2,4, fiber 1, carbs 2,6, protein 20,7

62. TOMATO HALIBUT MIX

Preparation time: 5 minutes
Cooking time: 2 hours and 30 minutes
Servings: 4

Ingredients:

- 1 pound halibut, skinless, boneless, cubed
- 2 tablespoons olive oil
- 2 garlic cloves, minced
- 1 tablespoon cilantro, chopped
- 12 ounces fresh tomatoes, peeled, chopped

Directions:

1. Grease your slow cooker with the oil, add all the remaining ingredients, cover and cook on low for 2 hours and 30 minutes.
2. Divide everything into bowls and serve.

Nutrition Values: Calories 475, fat 15,6, fiber 1,1, carbs 3,8, protein 76,5

63. LEMONY SHRIMP

Preparation time: 5 minutes
Cooking time: 1 hour and 30 minutes
Servings: 6

Ingredients:

- 2 pounds large shrimp, peeled and deveined
- Juice of 1 lemon
- 1 tablespoon lemon zest, grated
- 1 teaspoon olive oil
- ¼ teaspoon hot pepper sauce

Directions:

1. In your slow cooker, combine all the ingredients, cover and cook on low for 1 hour and 30 minutes.
2. Divide everything into bowls and serve.

Nutrition Values: Calories 131, fat 0,8, fiber 0,1, carbs 3,6, protein 28,4

64. BALSAMIC SHRIMP

Preparation time: 5 minutes
Cooking time: 1 hour and 30 minutes
Servings: 4

Ingredients:

- 1 pound shrimp, peeled and deveined

- 1 cup chicken stock
- 3 tablespoons coconut sugar
- 3 tablespoons balsamic vinegar

Directions:

1. In your slow cooker, combine all the ingredients, cover and cook on low for 1 hour and 30 minutes.
2. Divide everything into bowls and serve.

Nutrition Values: Calories 159, fat 2,1, fiber 0, carbs 7,3, protein 26

65. CLAM BOWLS

Preparation time: 5 minutes
Cooking time: 4 hours
Servings: 6

Ingredients:

- 3 garlic cloves, minced
- 1 yellow onion, chopped
- 1 tablespoon olive oil
- 1 tablespoon fresh parsley, chopped
- ½ cup chicken stock
- 1 teaspoon red pepper flakes
- 24 ounces fresh tomatoes, peeled, chopped
- 2 pounds clams

Directions:

1. In your slow cooker, combine all the ingredients, mix together, cover and cook on high for 4 hours.
2. Divide the clam mixture into bowls and serve.

Nutrition Values: Calories 125, fat 3, fiber 2,5, carbs 23,5, protein 2,3

66. RICE BOWL

Preparation Time: 55 minutes
Servings: 4

Ingredients

- ¼ cup cucumber, sliced
- 1 tsp. salt
- 1 tbsp. stevia
- 7 tbsp. Japanese rice vinegar
- 3 medium-sized eggplants, sliced
- 3 tbsp. sweet white miso paste
- 1 tbsp. mirin rice wine
- 4 cups sushi rice, cooked
- 4 spring onions
- 1 tbsp. sesame seeds, toasted

Directions:

1. Coat the cucumber slices with the rice wine vinegar, salt, and stevia.
2. Place a dish on top of the bowl to weight it down completely.

3. Pre-heat the Air Fryer at 400°F.
4. In a bowl, mix together the eggplants, mirin rice wine, and miso paste. Allow to marinate for half an hour.
5. Cook the eggplant in the fryer for 10 minutes.
6. Place the eggplant slices in the Air Fryer and cook for 10 minutes.
7. Fill the bottom of a serving bowl with rice and top with the eggplants and pickled cucumbers. Add the spring onions and sesame seeds for garnish.

67. ASIAN TOFU BITES

Preparation Time: 20 minutes
Servings: 4

Ingredients

- 1 packaged firm tofu, cubed and pressed to remove excess water
- 1 tbsp. soy sauce
- 1 tbsp. ketchup
- 1 tbsp. maple syrup
- ½ tsp. vinegar
- 1 tsp. liquid smoke
- 1 tsp. hot sauce
- 2 tbsp. sesame seeds
- 1 tsp. garlic powder
- Salt and pepper to taste

Directions:

1. Pre-heat the Air Fryer at 375°F.
2. Take a baking dish small enough to fit inside the fryer and spritz it with cooking spray.
3. Combine all the ingredients to coat the tofu completely and allow the marinade to absorb for half an hour.
4. Transfer the tofu to the baking dish, then cook for 15 minutes. Flip the tofu over and cook for another 15 minute on the other side.

68. CHICKPEAS

Preparation Time: 20 minutes
Servings: 4

Ingredients

- 1 15-oz. can chickpeas, drained but not rinsed
- 2 tbsp. olive oil
- 1 tsp. salt
- 2 tbsp. lemon juice

Directions:

1. Pre-heat the Air Fryer at 400°F.
2. Add all the ingredients together in a bowl and mix. Transfer this mixture to the basket of the fryer.
3. Cook for 15 minutes, ensuring the chickpeas become nice and crispy.

69. CAULIFLOWER CHEESE TATER TOTS

Preparation Time: 25 minutes
Servings: 12

Ingredients

- 1 lb. cauliflower, steamed and chopped
- ½ cup nutritional yeast
- 1 tbsp. oats
- 1 flax egg [1 tbsp. desiccated coconuts + 3 tbsp. flaxseed meal
- + 3 tbsp. water]
- 1 onion, chopped
- 1 tsp. garlic, minced
- 1 tsp. parsley, chopped
- 1 tsp. oregano, chopped
- 1 tsp. chives, chopped
- Salt and pepper to taste
- ½ cup keto bread crumbs

Directions:

1. Pre-heat the Air Fryer at 390°F.
2. Drain any excess water out of the cauliflower by wringing it with a paper towel.
3. In a bowl, combine the cauliflower with the remaining ingredients, save the keto bread crumbs. Using your hands, shape the mixture into several small balls.
4. Coat the balls in the bread crumbs and transfer to the basket of your fryer. Allow to cook for 6 minutes, after which you should raise the temperature to 400°F and then leave to cook for an additional 10 minutes.

70. SWEET ONIONS & POTATOES

Preparation Time: 30 minutes
Servings: 6

Ingredients

- 2 large sweet potatoes, peeled and cut into chunks
- 2 medium sweet onions, cut into chunks
- 3 tbsp. olive oil
- 1 tsp. dried thyme
- Salt and pepper to taste
- ¼ cup almonds, sliced and toasted

Directions:

1. Pre-heat the Air Fryer at 425°F.
2. In a bowl, combine all of the ingredients, except for the sliced almonds.
3. Transfer the vegetables and dressing to a ramekin and cook in the fryer for 20 minutes.
4. When ready to serve, add the almonds on top.

71. MUSHROOM PIZZA SQUARES

Preparation Time: 20 minutes
Servings: 10

Ingredients

- 1 vegan pizza dough
- 1 cup oyster mushrooms, chopped
- 1 shallot, chopped
- ¼ red bell pepper, chopped
- 2 tbsp. parsley
- Salt and pepper

Directions:

1. Pre-heat the Air Fryer at 400°F.
2. Cut the vegan pizza dough into squares.
3. In a bowl, combine the oyster mushrooms, shallot, bell pepper and parsley. Sprinkle some salt and pepper as desired.
4. Spread this mixture on top of the pizza squares.
5. Cook in the Air Fryer for 10 minutes.

72. TOFU & SWEET POTATOES

Preparation Time: 50 minutes
Servings: 8

Ingredients

- 8 sweet potatoes, scrubbed
- 2 tbsp. olive oil
- 1 large onion, chopped
- 2 green chilies, deseeded and chopped
- ½ lb. tofu, crumbled
- 2 tbsp. Cajun seasoning
- cup tomatoes
- 1 can kidney beans, drained and rinsed
- Salt and pepper to taste

Directions:

1. Pre-heat the Air Fryer at 400°F.
2. With a knife, pierce the skin of the sweet potatoes in numerous places and cook in the fryer for half an hour, making sure they become soft. Remove from the fryer, halve each potato, and set to one side.
3. Over a medium heat, fry the onions and chilis in a little oil for 2 minutes until fragrant.
4. Add in the tofu and Cajun seasoning and allow to cook for a further 3 minutes before incorporating the kidney beans and tomatoes. Sprinkle some salt and pepper as desire.
5. Top each sweet potato halve with a spoonful of the tofu mixture and serve.

73. RISOTTO

Preparation Time: 40 minutes
Servings: 2

Ingredients

- 1 onion, diced
- 2 cups chicken stock, boiling
- ½ cup parmesan cheese or cheddar cheese, grated
- 1 clove garlic, minced
- ¾ cup arborio rice
- 1 tbsp. olive oil
- 1 tbsp. butter, unsalted

Directions:

1. Turn the Air Fryer to 390°F and set for 5 minutes to warm.
2. Grease a round baking tin with oil and stir in the butter, garlic, and onion.
3. Put the tin in the fryer and allow to cook for 4 minutes.
4. Pour in the rice and cook for a further 4 minutes, stirring three times throughout the cooking time.
5. Turn the temperature down to 320°F.
6. Add the chicken stock and give the dish a gentle stir. Cook for 22 minutes, leaving the fryer uncovered.
7. Pour in the cheese, stir once more and serve.

74. CHICKPEA & AVOCADO MASH

Preparation Time: 30 minutes
Servings: 4

Ingredients

- 1 medium-sized head of cauliflower, cut into florets
- 1 can chickpeas, drained and rinsed
- 1 tbsp. extra-virgin olive oil
- 2 tbsp. lemon juice
- Salt and pepper to taste
- 4 keto flatbreads, toasted
- 2 ripe avocados, mashed

Directions:

1. Pre-heat the Air Fryer at 425°F.
2. In a bowl, mix together the chickpeas, cauliflower, lemon juice and olive oil. Sprinkle salt and pepper as desired.
3. Put inside the Air Fryer basket and cook for 25 minutes.
4. Spread on top of the flatbread along with the mashed avocado. Sprinkle on more pepper and salt as desired and enjoy with hot sauce.

75. FRIED POTATOES

Preparation Time: 55 minutes
Servings: 1

Ingredients

- 1 medium russet potatoes, scrubbed and peeled

- 1 tsp. olive oil
- ¼ tsp. onion powder
- 1/8 tsp. salt
- A dollop of vegan butter
- A dollop of vegan cream cheese
- 1 tbsp. Kalamata olives
- 1 tbsp. chives, chopped

Directions:

1. Pre-heat the Air Fryer at 400°F.
2. In a bowl, coat the potatoes with the onion powder, salt, olive oil, and vegan butter.
3. Transfer to the fryer and allow to cook for 40 minutes, turning the potatoes over at the halfway point.
4. Take care when removing the potatoes from the fryer and enjoy with the vegan cream cheese, Kalamata olives and chives on top, plus any other vegan sides you desire.

76. FRENCH GREEN BEANS

Preparation Time: 20 minutes
Servings: 4

Ingredients

- 1 ½ lb. French green beans, stems removed and blanched
- 1 tbsp. salt
- ½ lb. shallots, peeled and cut into quarters
- ½ tsp. ground white pepper
- 2 tbsp. olive oil
- ¼ cup slivered almonds, toasted

Directions:

1. Pre-heat the Air Fryer at 400°F.
2. Coat the vegetables with the rest of the ingredients in a bowl.
3. Transfer to the basket of your fryer and cook for 10 minutes, making sure the green beans achieve a light brown color.

77. BLACK BEAN CHILI

Preparation Time: 25 minutes
Servings: 6

Ingredients

- 1 tbsp. olive oil
- 1 medium onion, diced
- 3 cloves of garlic, minced
- 1 cup vegetable broth
- 3 cans black beans, drained and rinsed
- 2 cans diced tomatoes
- 2 chipotle peppers, chopped
- 2 tsp. cumin
- 2 tsp. chili powder
- 1 tsp. dried oregano

- ½ tsp. salt

Directions:

1. Over a medium heat, fry the garlic and onions in a little oil for 3 minutes.
2. Add in the remaining ingredients, stirring constantly and scraping the bottom to prevent sticking.
3. Pre-heat your Air Fryer at 400°F.
4. Take a heat-resistant dish small enough to fit inside the fryer and place the mixture inside. Put a sheet of aluminum foil on top.
5. Transfer to the air fryer and cook for 20 minutes.
6. When ready, plate up and serve with diced avocado, chopped cilantro, and chopped tomatoes.

78. CAULIFLOWER

Preparation Time: 20 minutes
Servings: 4
Ingredients

- 1 head cauliflower, cut into florets
- 1 tbsp. extra-virgin olive oil
- 2 scallions, chopped
- 5 cloves of garlic, sliced
- 1 ½ tbsp. tamari
- 1 tbsp. rice vinegar
- ½ tsp. stevia
- 1 tbsp. sriracha

Directions:

1. Pre-heat the Air Fryer to 400°F.
2. Put the cauliflower florets in the Air Fryer and drizzle some oil over them before cooking for 10 minutes.
3. Turn the cauliflower over, throw in the onions and garlic, and stir. Cook for another 10 minutes.
4. Mix together the rest of the ingredients in a bowl.
5. Remove the cooked cauliflower from the fryer and coat it in the sauce.
6. Return to the Air Fryer and allow to cook for another 5 minutes. Enjoy with a side of rice.

79. TOFU BITES

Preparation Time: 65 minutes
Servings: 3

Ingredients

- 2 tbsp. sesame oil
- ¼ cup maple syrup
- 3 tbsp. peanut butter
- ¼ cup liquid aminos
- 3tbsp. chili garlic sauce

- 2 tbsp. rice wine vinegar
- 2 cloves of garlic, minced
- 1 inch fresh ginger, peeled and grated
- 1 tsp. red pepper flakes
- 1 block extra firm tofu, pressed to remove excess water and cubed
- Toasted peanuts, chopped
- 1 tsp. sesame seeds
- 1 sprig cilantro, chopped

Directions:

1. Whisk together the first 9 ingredients in a large bowl to well combine.
2. Transfer to an airtight bag along with the cubed tofu. Allow to marinate for a minimum of a half hour.
3. Pre-heat the Air Fryer to 425°F.
4. Put the tofu cubes in the fryer, keep any excess marinade for the sauce. Cook for 15 minutes.
5. In the meantime, heat the marinade over a medium heat to reduce by half.
6. Plate up the cooked tofu with some cooked rice and serve with the sauce. Complete the dish with the sesame seeds, cilantro and peanuts.

80. FAUX RICE

Preparation Time: 60 minutes
Servings: 8

Ingredients

- 1 medium-to-large head of cauliflower
- ½ lemon, juiced
- garlic cloves, minced
- 2 cans mushrooms, 8 oz. each
- 1 can water chestnuts, 8 oz.
- ¾ cup peas
- ½ cup egg substitute or 1 egg, beaten
- 4 tbsp. soy sauce
- 1 tbsp. peanut oil
- 1 tbsp. sesame oil
- 1 tbsp. ginger, fresh and minced
- High quality cooking spray

Directions:

1. Mix together the peanut oil, soy sauce, sesame oil, minced ginger, lemon juice, and minced garlic to combine well.
2. Peel and wash the cauliflower head before cutting it into small florets.
3. In a food processor, pulse the florets in small batches to break them down to resemble rice grains.
4. Pour into your Air Fryer basket.

5. Drain the can of water chestnuts and roughly chop them. Pour into the basket.

6. Cook at 350°F for 20 minutes.

7. In the meantime, drain the mushrooms. When the 20 minutes are up, add the mushrooms and the peas to the fryer and continue to cook for another 15 minutes.

8. Lightly spritz a frying pan with cooking spray. Prepare an omelet with the egg substitute or the beaten egg, ensuring it is firm. Lay on a cutting board and slice it up.

9. When the cauliflower is ready, throw in the omelet and cook for an additional 5 minutes. Serve hot.

81. POTATO CROQUETTES

Preparation Time: 25 minutes
Servings: 10

Ingredients

- ¼ cup nutritional yeast
- 2 cups boiled potatoes, mashed
- 1 flax egg [1 tbsp. flaxseed meal + 3 tbsp. water]
- 1 tbsp. keto almond flour
- 2 tbsp. chives, chopped
- Salt and pepper to taste
- 2 tbsp. vegetable oil
- ¼ cup keto bread crumbs

Directions:

1. Pre-heat the Air Fryer to 400°F.

2. In a bowl, combine together the nutritional yeast, potatoes, flax eggs, keto almond flour, and chives. Sprinkle with salt and pepper as desired.

3. In separate bowl mix together the vegetable oil and bread crumbs to achieve a crumbly consistency.

4. Use your hands to shape the potato mixture into small balls and dip each one into the breadcrumb mixture.

5. Place the croquettes inside the air fryer and cook for 15 minutes, ensuring the croquettes turn golden brown.

82. SWEET & SOUR TOFU

Preparation Time: 55 minutes
Servings: 2

Ingredients

- 2 tsp. apple cider vinegar
- 1 tbsp. stevia
- 1 tbsp. soy sauce
- 3 tsp. lime juice
- 1 tsp. ground ginger

- 1 tsp. garlic powder
- ½ block firm tofu, pressed to remove excess liquid and cut into cubes
- 1 tsp. cornstarch
- 2 green onions, chopped
- Toasted sesame seeds for garnish

Directions:

1. In a bowl, thoroughly combine the apple cider vinegar, stevia, soy sauce, lime juice, ground ginger, and garlic powder.

2. Cover the tofu with this mixture and leave to marinate for at least 30 minutes.

3. Transfer the tofu to the Air Fryer, keeping any excess marinade for the sauce. Cook at 400°F for 20 minutes or until crispy.

4. In the meantime, thicken the sauce with the cornstarch over a medium-low heat.

5. Serve the cooked tofu with the sauce, green onions, sesame seeds, and some rice.

83. VEGETABLE SALAD

Preparation Time: 20 minutes
Servings: 4

Ingredients

- 6 plum tomatoes, halved
- 2 large red onions, sliced
- 4 long red pepper, sliced
- 2 yellow pepper, sliced
- 6 cloves of garlic, crushed
- 1 tbsp. extra-virgin olive oil
- 1 tsp. paprika
- ½ lemon, juiced
- Salt and pepper to taste
- 1 tbsp. baby capers

Directions:

1. Pre-heat the Air Fryer at 420°F.

2. Put the tomatoes, onions, peppers, and garlic in a large bowl and cover with the extra virgin olive oil, paprika, and lemon juice. Sprinkle with salt and pepper as desired.

3. Line the inside of your fryer with aluminum foil. Place the vegetables inside and allow to cook for 10 minutes, ensuring the edges turn brown.

4. Serve in a salad bowl with the baby capers. Make sure all the ingredients are well combined.

84. MEDITERRANEAN VEGETABLES

Preparation Time: 30 minutes
Servings: 4

Ingredients

- 1 cup cherry tomatoes, halved

- 1 large zucchini, sliced
- 1 green pepper, sliced
- 1 parsnip, sliced
- 1 carrot, sliced
- 1 tsp. mixed herbs
- 1 tsp. mustard
- 1 tsp. garlic puree
- 6 tbsp. olive oil
- Salt and pepper to taste

Directions:
1. Pre-heat the Air Fryer at 400°F.
2. Combine all the ingredients in a bowl, making sure to coat the vegetables well.
3. Transfer to the fryer and cook for 6 minutes, ensuring the vegetables are tender and browned.

85. SWEET POTATOES

Preparation Time: 55 minutes
Servings: 4

Ingredients

- 2 potatoes, peeled and cubed
- 4 carrots, cut into chunks
- 1 head broccoli, cut into florets
- 4 zucchinis, sliced thickly
- Salt and pepper to taste
- ¼ cup olive oil
- 1 tbsp. dry onion powder

Directions:
1. Pre-heat the Air Fryer to 400°F.
2. In a baking dish small enough to fit inside the fryer, add all the ingredients and combine well.
3. Cook for 45 minutes in the fryer, ensuring the vegetables are soft and the sides have browned before serving.

86. SAGE CHICKEN ESCALLOPS

Preparation Time: 45 minutes
Servings: 4

Ingredients

- 4 skinless chicken breasts
- 2 eggs, beaten
- ½ cup keto almond flour
- 6 sage leaves
- ¼ cup keto bread crumbs
- ¼ cup parmesan cheese
- Cooking spray

Directions:
1. Cut the chicken breasts into thin, flat slices.
2. In a bowl, combine the parmesan with the

sage.
3. Add in the keto almond flour and eggs and sprinkle with salt and pepper as desired. Mix well.
4. Dip chicken in the flour-egg mixture.
5. Coat the chicken in the panko bread crumbs.
6. Spritz the inside of the Air Fryer with cooking spray and set it to 390°F, allowing it to warm.
7. Cook the chicken for 20 minutes.
8. When golden, serve with fried rice.

87. FRIED PICKLES

Preparation Time: 30 minutes
Servings: 4

Ingredients

- 14 dill pickles, sliced
- ¼ cup keto almond flour
- 1/8 tsp. baking powder
- Pinch of salt
- 2 tbsp. cornstarch + 3 tbsp. water
- 6 tbsp. keto bread crumbs
- ½ tsp. paprika
- Cooking spray

Directions:
1. Pre-heat your Air Fryer at 400°F.
2. Drain any excess moisture out of the dill pickles on a paper towel.
3. In a bowl, combine the keto almond flour, baking powder and salt.
4. Throw in the cornstarch and water mixture and combine well with a whisk.
5. Put the panko bread crumbs in a shallow dish along with the paprika. Mix thoroughly.
6. Dip the pickles in the flour batter, before coating in the bread crumbs. Spritz all the pickles with the cooking spray.
7. Transfer to the fryer and cook for 15 minutes, until a golden brown color is achieved.

88. CAULIFLOWER BITES

Preparation Time: 30 minutes
Servings: 4

Ingredients

1. 1 cup keto almond flour
2. ⅓ cup desiccated coconut
3. Salt and pepper to taste
4. 1 flax egg [1 tbsp. flaxseed meal + 3 tbsp. water]
5. 1 small cauliflower, cut into florets
6. 1 tsp. mixed spice
7. ½ tsp. mustard powder
8. 2 tbsp. maple syrup
9. 1 clove of garlic, minced
10. 2 tbsp. soy sauce

Directions:

1. Pre-heat the Air Fryer to 400°F.
2. In a bowl, mix together the oats, keto almond flour, and desiccated coconut, sprinkling with some salt and pepper as desired.
3. In a separate bowl, season the flax egg with a pinch of salt.
4. Coat the cauliflower with mixed spice and mustard powder.
5. Dip the florets into the flax egg, then into the flour mixture. Cook for 15 minutes in the fryer.
6. In the meantime, place a saucepan over medium heat and add in the maple syrup, garlic, and soy sauce. Boil first, before reducing the heat to allow the sauce to thicken.
7. Remove the florets from the Air Fryer and transfer to the saucepan. Coat the florets in the sauce before returning to the fryer and allowing to cook for an additional 5 minutes.

89. CHICKEN & VEGGIES

Preparation Time: 30 minutes
Servings: 4

Ingredients

- 8 chicken thighs
- 5 oz. mushrooms, sliced
- 1 red onion, diced
- Fresh black pepper, to taste
- 10 medium asparagus
- ½ cup carrots, diced
- ¼ cup balsamic vinegar
- 2 red bell peppers, diced
- ½ tsp. stevia
- 2 tbsp. extra-virgin olive oil
- 1 ½ tbsp. fresh rosemary
- 2 cloves garlic, chopped
- ½ tbsp. dried oregano
- 1 tsp. kosher salt
- 2 fresh sage, chopped

Directions:

1. Pre-heat the Air Fryer to 400°F.
2. Grease the inside of a baking tray with the oil.
3. Season the chicken with salt and pepper.
4. Put all of the vegetables in a large bowl and throw in the oregano, garlic, stevia, mushrooms, vinegar, and sage. Combine everything well before transferring to the baking tray.
5. Put the chicken thighs in the baking tray. Cook in the Air Fryer for about 20 minutes.
6. Serve hot.

90. FALAFEL

Preparation Time: 30 minutes
Servings: 8

Ingredients

- 1 tsp. cumin seeds
- ½ tsp. coriander seeds
- 2 cups chickpeas from can, drained and rinsed
- ½ tsp. red pepper flakes
- 3 cloves garlic
- ¼ cup parsley, chopped
- ¼ cup coriander, chopped
- ½ onion, diced
- 1 tbsp. juice from freshly squeezed lemon
- 3 tbsp. keto almond flour
- ½ tsp. salt cooking spray

Directions:

1. Fry the cumin and coriander seeds over medium heat until fragrant.
2. Grind using a mortar and pestle.
3. Put all of ingredients, except for the cooking spray, in a food processor and blend until a fine consistency is achieved.
4. Use your hands to mold the mixture into falafels and spritz with the cooking spray.
5. Preheat your Air Fryer at 400°F.
6. Transfer the falafels to the fryer in one single layer.
7. Cook for 15 minutes, serving when they turn golden brown.

91. EASY ASPARAGUS

Preparation Time: 10 minutes
Servings: 4

Ingredients

- 1 lb. fresh asparagus spears, trimmed
- 1 tbsp. olive oil
- Salt and pepper to taste

Directions:

1. Pre-heat the Air Fryer at 375°F.
2. Combine all of the ingredients and transfer to the Air Fryer.
3. Cook for 5 minutes until soft.

92. CAULIFLOWER STEAK

Preparation Time: 30 minutes
Servings: 2

Ingredients

- 1 cauliflower, sliced into two
- 1 tbsp. olive oil
- 2 tbsp. onion, chopped
- ¼ tsp. vegetable stock powder
- ¼ cup almond milk

- Salt and pepper to taste

Directions:
1. Place the cauliflower in a bowl of salted water and allow to absorb for at least 2 hours.
2. Pre-heat the Air Fryer to 400°F.
3. Rinse off the cauliflower, put inside the fryer and cook for 15 minutes.
4. In the meantime, fry the onions over medium heat, stirring constantly, until they turn translucent. Pour in the vegetable stock powder and milk. Bring to a boil and then lower the heat.
5. Let the sauce reduce and add in salt and pepper.
6. Plate up the cauliflower steak and top with the sauce.

93. ROCKET SALAD
Preparation Time: 35 minutes
Servings: 4

Ingredients
- 8 fresh figs, halved
- 1 ½ cups chickpeas, cooked
- 1 tsp. cumin seeds, roasted then crushed
- 4 tbsp. balsamic vinegar
- 2 tbsp. extra-virgin olive oil
- Salt and pepper to taste
- 3 cups arugula rocket, washed and dried

Directions:
1. Pre-heat the Air Fryer to 375°F.
2. Cover the Air Fryer basket with aluminum foil and grease lightly with oil. Put the figs in the fryer and allow to cook for 10 minutes.
3. In a bowl, combine the chickpeas and cumin seeds.
4. Remove the cooked figs from the fryer and replace with chickpeas. Cook for 10 minutes. Leave to cool.
5. In the meantime, prepare the dressing. Mix together the balsamic vinegar, olive oil, salt and pepper.
6. In a salad bowl combine the arugula rocket with the cooled figs and chickpeas.
7. Toss with the sauce and serve right away.

94. VEGAN RAVIOLI
Preparation Time: 15 minutes
Servings: 4

Ingredients
- ½ cup keto bread crumbs
- 2 tsp. nutritional yeast
- 1 tsp. dried basil
- 1 tsp. dried oregano
- 1 tsp. garlic powder
- Salt and pepper to taste
- ¼ cup aquafaba
- 8 oz. vegan ravioli
- Cooking spray

Directions:
1. Cover the Air Fryer basket with aluminum foil and coat with a light brushing of oil.
2. Pre-heat the Air Fryer to 400°F. Combine together the panko breadcrumbs, nutritional yeast, basil, oregano, and garlic powder. Sprinkle on salt and pepper to taste.
3. Put the aquafaba in a separate bowl. Dip the ravioli in the aquafaba before coating it in the panko mixture. Spritz with cooking spray and transfer to the Air Fryer.
4. Cook for 6 minutes ensuring to shake the Air Fryer basket halfway.

95. THANKSGIVING SPROUTS
Preparation Time: 20 minutes
Servings: 6

Ingredients
- 1 ½ lb. Brussels sprouts, cleaned and trimmed
- 3 tbsp. olive oil
- 1 tsp. salt
- 1 tsp. black pepper

Directions:
1. Pre-heat the Air Fryer to 375°F. Cover the basket with aluminum foil and coat with a light brushing of oil.
2. In a mixing bowl, combine all ingredients, coating the sprouts well.
3. Put in the fryer basket and cook for 10 minutes. Shake the Air Fryer basket throughout the duration to ensure even cooking.

96. BALSAMIC CHICKEN AND VEGETABLES
Servings:2
Preparation Time: 15 minutes
Cooking Time: 25 minutes

Ingredients:
- 4 chicken thigh, boneless and skinless
- 5 stalks of asparagus, halved
- 1 pepper, cut in chunks
- 1/2 red onion, diced
- ½ cup carrots, sliced
- 1 garlic cloves, minced
- 2-ounces mushrooms, diced
- ¼ cup balsamic vinegar

- 1 tablespoon olive oil
- ½ teaspoon stevia
- ½ tablespoon oregano
- Sunflower seeds and pepper as needed

Directions:
1. Pre-heat your oven to 425 degrees F.
2. Take a bowl and add all of the vegetables and mix.
3. Add spices and oil and mix.
4. Dip the chicken pieces into spice mix and coat them well.
5. Place the veggies and chicken onto a pan in a single layer.
6. Cook for 25 minutes.
7. Serve and enjoy!

Nutrition Values:
Calories: 401
Fat: 17g
Net Carbohydrates: 11g
Protein: 48g

97. CREAM DREDGED CORN PLATTER

Servings:3
Preparation Time: 10 minutes
Cooking Time: 4 hours

Ingredients:
- 3 cups corn
- 2 ounces cream cheese, cubed
- 2 tablespoons milk
- 2 tablespoons whipping cream
- 2 tablespoons butter, melted
- Salt and pepper as needed
- 1 tablespoon green onion, chopped

Directions:
1. Add corn, cream cheese, milk, whipping cream, butter, salt and pepper to your Slow Cooker.
2. Give it a nice toss to mix everything well.
3. Place lid and cook on LOW for 4 hours.
4. Divide the mix amongst serving platters.
5. Serve and enjoy!

Nutrition Values:
Calories: 261
Fat: 11g
Carbohydrates: 17g
Protein: 6g

98. EXUBERANT SWEET POTATOES

Servings:4
Preparation Time: 5 minutes
Cooking Time: 7-8 hours

Ingredients:
- 6 sweet potatoes, washed and dried

Directions:
1. Loosely ball up 7-8 pieces of aluminum foil in the bottom of your Slow Cooker, covering about half of the surface area.
2. Prick each potato 6-8 times using a fork.
3. Wrap each potato with foil and seal them.
4. Place wrapped potatoes in the cooker on top of the foil bed.
5. Place lid and cook on LOW for 7-8 hours.
6. Use tongs to remove the potatoes and unwrap them.
7. Serve and enjoy!

Nutrition Values:
Calories: 129
Fat: 0g
Carbohydrates: 30g
Protein: 2g

99. ETHIOPIAN CABBAGE DELIGHT

Servings:6
Preparation Time: 15 minutes
Cooking Time: 6- 8 hours

Ingredients:
- ½ cup water
- 1 head green cabbage, cored and chopped
- 1 pound sweet potatoes, peeled and chopped
- 3 carrots, peeled and chopped
- 1 onion, sliced
- 1 teaspoon extra virgin olive oil
- ½ teaspoon ground turmeric
- ½ teaspoon ground cumin
- ¼ teaspoon ground ginger

Directions:
1. Add water to your Slow Cooker.
2. Take a medium bowl and add cabbage, carrots, sweet potatoes, onion and mix.
3. Add olive oil, turmeric, ginger, cumin and toss until the veggies are fully coated.
4. Transfer veggie mix to your Slow Cooker.
5. Cover and cook on LOW for 6-8 hours.
6. Serve and enjoy!

Nutrition Values:
Calories: 155
Fat: 2g
Carbohydrates: 35g
Protein: 4g

100. THE VEGAN LOVERS REFRIED BEANS

Servings:12
Preparation Time: 5 minutes
Cooking Time: 10 hours

Ingredients:

- 4 cups vegetable broth
- 4 cups water
- 3 cups dried pinto beans
- 1 onion, chopped
- 2 jalapeno peppers, minced
- 4 garlic cloves, minced
- 1 tablespoon chili powder
- 2 teaspoon ground cumin
- 1 teaspoon sweet paprika
- 1 teaspoon salt
- ½ teaspoon fresh ground black pepper

Directions:
1. Add the listed ingredients to your Slow Cooker.
2. Cover and cook on HIGH for 10 hours .
3. If there's any extra liquid, ladle the liquid up and reserve it in a bowl .
4. Use an immersion blender to blend the mixture (in the Slow Cookeruntil smooth.
5. Add the reserved liquid.
6. Serve hot and enjoy!

Nutrition Values:
Calories: 91
Fat: 0g
Carbohydrates: 16g
Protein: 5g

101. COOL APPLE AND CARROT HARMONY

Servings:6
Preparation Time: 10 minutes
Cooking Time: 10 minutes

Ingredients:
- 1 cup apple juice
- 1 pound baby carrots
- 1 tablespoon cornstarch
- 1 tablespoon mint, chopped

Directions:
1. Add apple juice, carrots, cornstarch and mint to your Instant Pot.
2. Stir and lock the lid.
3. Cook on HIGH pressure for 10 minutes.
4. Perform a quick release.
5. Divide the mix amongst plates and serve.
6. Enjoy!

Nutrition Values:
Calories:161
Fat: 2g
Carbohydrates: 9g
Protein: 8g

102. MAC AND CHOKES

Servings:6
Preparation Time: 5 minutes
Cooking Time: 20 minutes

Ingredients:
- 1 tablespoon of olive oil
- 1 large sized diced onion
- 10 minced garlic cloves
- 1 can artichoke hearts
- 1 pound uncooked macaroni shells
- 12 ounce baby spinach
- 4 cups vegetable broth
- 1 teaspoon red pepper flakes
- 4 ounces vegan cheese
- ¼ cup cashew cream

Directions:
1. Set the pot to Sauté mode and add oil, allow the oil to heat up and add onions.
2. Cook for 2 minutes.
3. Add garlic and stir well.
4. Add artichoke hearts and sauté for 1 minute more.
5. Add uncooked pasta and 3 cups of broth alongside 2 cups of water.
6. Mix well.
7. Lock the lid and cook on HIGH pressure for 4 minutes.
8. Quick release the pressure.
9. Open the pot and stir.
10. Add extra water, fold in spinach and cook on Sauté mode for a few minutes.
11. Add cashew cream and grated vegan cheese.
12. Add pepper flakes and mix well.
13. Enjoy!

Nutrition Values:
Calories:649
Fat: 29g
Carbohydrates: 64g
Protein: 34g

103. BLACK EYED PEAS AND SPINACH PLATTER

Servings:4
Preparation Time: 10 minutes
Cooking Time: 8 hours

Ingredients:
- 1 cup black eyed peas, soaked overnight and drained
- 2 cups low-sodium vegetable broth
- 1 can (15 ouncestomatoes, diced with juice
- 8 ounces ham, chopped
- 1 onion, chopped
- 2 garlic cloves, minced

- 1 teaspoon dried oregano
- 1 teaspoon salt
- ½ teaspoon freshly ground black pepper
- ½ teaspoon ground mustard
- 1 bay leaf

Directions:
1. Add the listed ingredients to your Slow Cooker and stir.
2. Place lid and cook on LOW for 8 hours.
3. Discard the bay leaf.
4. Serve and enjoy!

Nutrition Values:
Calories: 209
Fat: 6g
Carbohydrates: 22g
Protein: 17g

104. HUMBLE MUSHROOM RICE

Servings:3
Preparation Time: 10 minutes
Cooking Time: 3 hours

Ingredients:
- ½ cup rice
- 2 green onions chopped
- 1 garlic clove, minced
- ¼ pound baby Portobello mushrooms, sliced
- 1 cup vegetable stock

Directions:
1. Add rice, onions, garlic, mushrooms, stock to your Slow Cooker.
2. Stir well and place lid.
3. Cook on LOW for 3 hours..
4. Stir and divide amongst serving platters.
5. Enjoy!

Nutrition Values:
Calories: 200
Fat: 6g
Carbohydrates: 28g
Protein: 5g

105. SWEET AND SOUR CABBAGE AND APPLES

Servings:4
Preparation Time: 15 minutes
Cooking Time: 8 hours

Ingredients:
- ¼ cup honey
- ¼ cup apple cider vinegar
- 2 tablespoons Orange Chili-Garlic Sauce
- 1 teaspoon sea salt
- 3 sweet tart apples, peeled, cored and sliced
- 2 heads green cabbage, cored and shredded
- 1 sweet red onion, thinly sliced

Directions:
1. Take a small bowl and whisk in honey, orange-chili garlic sauce, vinegar.
2. Stir well.
3. Add honey mix, apples, onion and cabbage to your Slow Cooker and stir.
4. Close lid and cook on LOW for 8 hours.
5. Serve and enjoy!

Nutrition Values:
Calories: 164
Fat: 1g
Carbohydrates: 41g
Protein: 4g

106. DELICIOUS ALOOPALAK

Servings:6
Preparation Time: 10 minutes
Cooking Time: 6-8 hours

Ingredients:
- 2 pounds red potatoes, chopped
- 1 small onion, diced
- 1 red bell pepper, seeded and diced
- ¼ cup fresh cilantro, chopped
- 1/3 cup low-sodium veggie broth
- 1 teaspoon salt
- ½ teaspoon Garam masala
- ½ teaspoon ground cumin
- ¼ teaspoon ground turmeric
- ¼ teaspoon ground coriander
- ¼ teaspoon freshly ground black pepper
- 2 pounds fresh spinach, chopped

Directions:
1. Add potatoes, bell pepper, onion, cilantro, broth and seasoning to your Slow Cooker.
2. Mix well.
3. Add spinach on top.
4. Place lid and cook on LOW for 6-8 hours.
5. Stir and serve.
6. Enjoy!

Nutrition Values:
Calories: 205
Fat: 1g
Carbohydrates: 44g
Protein: 9g

107. ORANGE AND CHILI GARLIC SAUCE

Servings:5 cups
Preparation Time: 15 minutes
Cooking Time: 8 hours

Ingredients:

- ½ cup apple cider vinegar
- 4 pounds red jalapeno peppers, stems, seeds and ribs removed, chopped
- 10 garlic cloves, chopped
- ½ cup tomato paste
- Juice of 1 orange zest
- ½ cup honey
- 2 tablespoons soy sauce
- 2 teaspoons salt

Directions:

1. Add vinegar, garlic, peppers, tomato paste, orange juice, honey, zest, soy sauce and salt to your Slow Cooker.
2. Stir and close lid.
3. Cook on LOW for 8 hours.
4. Use as needed!

Nutrition Values:
Calories: 33
Fat: 1g
Carbohydrates: 8g
Protein: 1g

108. TANTALIZING MUSHROOM GRAVY

Servings:2 cups
Preparation Time: 5 minutes
Cooking Time: 5-8 hours

Ingredients:

- 1 cup button mushrooms, sliced
- ¾ cup low-fat buttermilk
- 1/3 cup water
- 1 medium onion, finely diced
- 2 garlic cloves, minced
- 2 tablespoons extra virgin olive oil
- 2 tablespoons all-purpose flour
- 1 tablespoon fresh rosemary, minced
- Freshly ground black pepper

Directions:

1. Add the listed ingredients to your Slow Cooker.
2. Place lid and cook on LOW for 5-8 hours.
3. Serve warm and use as needed!

Nutrition Values:
Calories: 54
Fat: 4g
Carbohydrates: 4g
Protein: 2g

109. EVERYDAY VEGETABLE STOCK

Servings:10 cups
Preparation Time: 5 minutes
Cooking Time: 8-12 hours

Ingredients:

- 2 celery stalks (with leaves), quartered
- 4 ounces mushrooms, with stems
- 2 carrots, unpeeled and quartered
- 1 onion, unpeeled, quartered from pole to pole
- 1 garlic head, unpeeled, halved across middle
- 2 fresh thyme sprigs
- 10 peppercorns
- ½ teaspoon salt
- Enough water to fill 3 quarters of Slow Cooker

Directions:

1. Add celery, mushrooms, onion, carrots, garlic, thyme, salt, peppercorn and water to your Slow Cooker.
2. Stir and cover .
3. Cook on LOW for 8-12 hours.
4. Strain the stock through a fine mesh cloth/metal mesh and discard solids.
5. Use as needed.

Nutrition Values:
Calories: 38
Fat: 5g
Carbohydrates: 1g
Protein: 0g

110. GRILLED CHICKEN WITH LEMON AND FENNEL

Servings:4
Preparation Time: 5 minutes
Cooking Time: 25 minutes

Ingredients:

- 2 cups chicken fillets , cut and skewed
- 1 large fennel bulb
- 2 garlic cloves
- 1 jar green olives
- 1 lemon

Directions:

1. Pre-heat your grill to medium-high.
2. Crush garlic cloves.
3. Take a bowl and addolive oil and season with sunflower seeds and pepper.
4. Coat chicken skewers with the marinade.
5. Transfer them under the grill and grill for 20 minutes, making sure to turn them halfway through until golden.
6. Zest half of the lemon and cut the other half into quarters.
7. Cut the fennel bulb into similarly sized segments.
8. Brush olive oil all over the garlic clove

9. Chop them and add them to the bowl with the marinade.
10. Add lemon zest and olives.
11. Once the meat is ready, serve with the vegetable mix.
12. Enjoy!

Nutrition Values:
Calories: 649
Fat: 16g
Carbohydrates: 33g
Protein: 18g

111. CARAMELIZED PORK CHOPS AND ONION

Servings:4
Preparation Time: 5 minutes
Cooking Time: 40 minutes

Ingredients:
1. 4-pound chuck roast
2. 4 ounces green Chili, chopped
3. 2 tablespoons of chili powder
4. ½ teaspoon of dried oregano
5. ½ teaspoon of cumin, ground
6. 2 garlic cloves, minced

Directions:
1. Rub the chops with a seasoning of 1 teaspoon of pepper and 2 teaspoons of sunflower seeds.
2. Take a skillet and place it over medium heat, add oil and allow the oil to heat up
3. Brown the seasoned chop both sides.
4. Add water and onion to the skillet and cover, lower the heat to low and simmer for 20 minutes.
5. Turn the chops over and season with more sunflower seeds and pepper.
6. Cover and cook until the water fully evaporates and the beer shows a slightly brown texture.
7. Remove the chops and serve with a topping of the caramelized onion.
8. Serve and enjoy!

Nutrition Values:
Calorie: 47
Fat:4g
Carbohydrates: 4g
Protein: 0.5g

112. HEARTY PORK BELLY CASSEROLE

Servings:4
Preparation Time: 5 minutes
Cooking Time: 25 minutes

Ingredients:

- 8 pork belly slices, cut into small pieces
- 3 large onions, chopped
- 4 tablespoons lemon
- Juice of 1 lemon
- Seasoning as you needed

Directions:
1. Take a large pressure cooker and place it over medium heat.
2. Add onions and sweat them for 5 minutes.
3. Add pork belly slices and cook until the meat browns and onions become golden.
4. Cover with water and add honey, lemon zest, sunflower seeds, pepper, and close the pressure seal.
5. Pressure cook for 40 minutes.
6. Serve and enjoy with a garnish of fresh chopped parsley if you prefer.

Nutrition Values:
Calories: 753
Fat: 41g
Carbohydrates: 68g
Protein: 30g

113. APPLE PIE CRACKERS

Servings:100 crackers
Preparation Time: 10 minutes
Cooking Time: 120 minutes

Ingredients:

- 2 tablespoons + 2 teaspoons avocado oil
- 1 medium Granny Smith apple, roughly chopped
- ¼ cup Erythritol
- 1/4 cup sunflower seeds, ground
- 1 ¾ cups roughly ground flax seeds
- 1/8 teaspoon Ground cloves
- 1/8 teaspoon ground cardamom
- 3 tablespoons nutmeg
- ¼ teaspoon ground ginger

Directions:
1. Pre-heat your oven to 225 degrees F.
2. Line two baking sheets with parchment paper and keep them on the side.
3. Add oil, apple, Erythritol to a bowl and mix.
4. Transfer to food processor and add remaining ingredients, process until combined.
5. Transfer batter to baking sheets, spread evenly and cut into crackers.
6. Bake for 1 hour, flip and bake for another hour.
7. Let them cool and serve.
8. Enjoy!

Nutrition Values:

Total Carbs: 0.9g (%
Fiber: 0.5g
Protein: 0.4g (%
Fat: 2.1g (%

114. PAPRIKA LAMB CHOPS

Servings:4
Preparation Time: 10 minutes
Cooking Time: 15 minutes

Ingredients:

- 1 lamb rack, cut into chops
- pepper to taste
- 1 tablespoon paprika
- 1/2 cup cumin powder
- 1/2 teaspoon chili powder

Directions:

1. Take a bowl and add paprika, cumin, chili, pepper, and stir.
2. Add lamb chops and rub the mixture.
3. Heat grill over medium-temperature and add lamb chops, cook for 5 minutes.
4. Flip and cook for 5 minutes more, flip again.
5. Cook for 2 minutes, flip and cook for 2 minutes more.
6. Serve and enjoy!

Nutrition Values:

Calories: 200
Fat: 5g
Carbohydrates: 4g
Protein: 8g

115. SPICY CHARD MIX

Preparation time: 5 minutes
Cooking time: 2 hours and 30 minutes
Servings: 4

Ingredients:

- 12 cups torn Swiss chard
- 3 tablespoons olive oil
- 2 garlic cloves, minced
- 1 red chili pepper, chopped
- ½ teaspoon smoked paprika
- 1 cup vegetable stock

Directions:

1. In your slow cooker, combine all the ingredients, cover and cook on low for 2 hours and 30 minutes.
2. Divide between plates and serve as a side dish.

Nutrition Values: Calories 114, fat 10,9, fiber 2, carbs 4,8, protein 2,1

116. OREGANO CAULIFLOWER

Preparation time: 5 minutes
Cooking time: 5 hours
Servings: 4

Ingredients:

- 2 celery stalks, chopped
- 1 yellow onion, chopped
- 3 garlic cloves, minced
- 2 teaspoons dried oregano
- A pinch of salt and black pepper
- 1 pound cauliflower florets
- ½ cup vegetable stock

Directions:

1. In your slow cooker, combine all the ingredients, cover and cook on low for 5 hours.
2. Divide between plates and serve as a side dish.

Nutrition Values: Calories 48, fat 0,5, fiber 3,9, carbs 10,3, protein 2,8

117. RED CABBAGE SAUTÉ

Preparation time: 5 minutes
Cooking time: 5 hours
Servings: 4

Ingredients:

- 1 red onion, sliced
- 1 red cabbage, shredded

- A pinch of salt and black pepper
- 1 cup chicken stock
- 3 tablespoons mustard
- 1 tablespoon olive oil

Directions:

1. Grease your slow cooker with the oil, add all the ingredients, mix, cover and cook on low for 5 hours.
2. Divide between plates and serve as a side dish.

Nutrition Values: Calories 127, fat 6,3, fiber 6,3, carbs 16, protein 4,8

118. ORANGE CABBAGE MIX

Preparation time: 5 minutes
Cooking time: 5 hours
Servings: 4

Ingredients:

- ½ cup orange juice
- 1 big red cabbage, shredded
- ½ teaspoon dried thyme
- ½ teaspoon dried sage
- A pinch of salt and black pepper
- 2 tablespoons olive oil

Directions:

1. Grease the slow cooker with the olive oil, add all the ingredients, mix, cover and cook on low for 5 hours.
2. Divide between plates and serve as a side dish.

Nutrition Values: Calories 153, fat 7,4, fiber 7,9, carbs 21,5, protein 4,2

119. HONEY CABBAGE

Preparation time: 5 minutes
Cooking time: 5 hours
Servings: 4

Ingredients:

- 1 big red cabbage, shredded
- ½ cup chicken stock
- ½ cup raw honey
- A pinch of salt and white pepper

Directions:

1. In a bowl, mix the chicken stock with the honey, salt and pepper, and whisk together. Add this mix to the slow cooker.
2. Add the cabbage to the slow cooker and toss with the sauce. Cover and cook on low for 5 hours.

3. Divide between plates and serve.

Nutrition Values: Calories 208, fat 0,4, fiber 7,9, carbs 53,1, protein 4,2

120. GARLIC CARROTS

Preparation time: 10 minutes
Cooking time: 5 hours
Servings: 4

Ingredients:

- 4 garlic cloves, minced
- 1 pound baby carrots
- ¼ teaspoon dried thyme
- ½ teaspoon dried basil
- ½ cup vegetable stock
- A pinch of salt and black pepper
- 2 tablespoons olive oil
- 2 tablespoons chopped chives

Directions:

1. Grease your slow cooker with the olive oil, add all the ingredients, cover and cook on low for 5 hours.
2. Divide between plates and serve as a side dish.

Nutrition Values: Calories 106, fat 7,4, fiber 3,4, carbs 10,7, protein 1

121. MAPLE BRUSSEL SPROUTS

Preparation time: 10 minutes
Cooking time: 3 hours
Servings: 4

Ingredients:

- 1 cup red onion, sliced
- 2 pounds Brussel sprouts, halved
- A pinch of salt and black pepper
- 2 tablespoons coconut oil, melted
- ¼ cup maple syrup
- 1 tablespoon chopped rosemary

Directions:

1. In your slow cooker, combine all the ingredients, mix, cover and cook on high for 3 hours.
2. Divide between plates and serve as a side dish.

Nutrition Values: Calories 222, fat 7,8, fiber 9,5, carbs 37,1, protein 8,1

122. GINGER CARROTS

Preparation time: 5 minutes
Cooking time: 6 hours
Servings: 4

Ingredients:

- ¾ cup chicken stock

- A pinch of salt and black pepper
- 2 teaspoons fresh grated ginger
- 1 pound baby carrots, halved

Directions:

1. In your slow cooker, combine all the ingredients, cover and cook on low for 6 hours.
2. Divide between plates and serve as a side dish.

Nutrition Values: Calories 45, fat 0,3, fiber 3,4, carbs 10,1, protein 0,9

123. SQUASH WEDGES

Preparation time: 5 minutes
Cooking time: 7 hours
Servings: 4

Ingredients:

- 2 acorn squash, peeled, seeds removed and cut into wedges
- 1 cup chicken stock
- ¼ teaspoon sweet paprika
- A pinch of salt and black pepper

Directions:

1. In your slow cooker, mix all the ingredients, cover and cook on low for 7 hours.
2. Divide between plates and serve as a side dish.

Nutrition Values: Calories 89, fat 0,4, fiber 3,3, carbs 22,7, protein 1,9

124. CAYENNE EGGPLANT

Preparation time: 5 minutes
Cooking time: 6 hours
Servings: 4

Ingredients:

- 2 eggplants, cubed
- 1 tablespoon olive oil
- 2 garlic cloves, minced
- 1 yellow onion, chopped
- 2 cups fresh tomatoes, peeled, roughly chopped
- A pinch of cayenne pepper
- A handful cilantro, chopped

Directions:

1. Grease your slow cooker with the olive oil.
2. Add all the ingredients to the bowl, mix, cover and cook on low for 6 hours.
3. Divide between plates and serve.

Nutrition Values: Calories 130, fat 4,2, fiber 11,6, carbs 23.2, protein 4,1

125. ITALIAN EGGPLANT

Preparation time: 5 minutes
Cooking time: 6 hours
Servings: 4

Ingredients:

- 1 pound eggplant, cubed
- 1 teaspoon Italian seasoning
- A pinch of salt and black pepper
- 1 teaspoon minced garlic
- 2 tablespoons coconut oil, melted

Directions:

1. Grease your slow cooker with the coconut oil.
2. Add all the ingredients, cover and cook on low for 6 hours.
3. Divide between plates and serve.

Nutrition Values: Calories 92, fat 7,4, fiber 4, carbs 7, protein 1,2

126. CELERY MASH

Preparation time: 5 minutes
Cooking time: 5 hours
Servings: 6

Ingredients:

- ¼ cup coconut oil, melted
- 3 pounds celery root, cut into wedges
- 2 cups vegetable stock
- A pinch of salt and black pepper

Directions:

1. In your slow cooker, mix the vegetable stock with the celery root, salt and pepper, cover and cook on low for 5 hours.
2. Transfer to a bowl, add the coconut oil and mash well using an immersion blender. Divide between plates and serve as a side dish.

Nutrition Values: Calories 177, fat 10,4, fiber 4,1, carbs 21,5, protein 3,4

127. BALSAMIC BEETS

Preparation time: 5 minutes
Cooking time: 7 hours
Servings: 4

Ingredients:

- 2 tablespoons balsamic vinegar
- 8 beets, cut into quarters
- 1 tablespoon olive oil
- A pinch of salt and black pepper
- ¼ cup vegetable stock

Directions:

1. In your slow cooker, mix all the ingredients, cover and cook on low for 7 hours.
2. Divide between plates and serve.

Nutrition Values: Calories 120, fat 4, fiber 4, carbs 20,1, protein 3,4

128. BEEF AND SPINACH MIX

Preparation time: 5 minutes
Cooking time: 2 hours
Servings: 4

Ingredients:

- 3 ounces beef, cooked and chopped
- 1 pound baby spinach
- ½ cup chicken stock
- 1 tablespoon lime juice
- 1 garlic clove, minced
- A pinch of salt and black pepper

Directions:

1. In your slow cooker, combine all the ingredients, mix, cover and cook on low for 2 hours.
2. Divide everything between plates and serve as a side dish.

Nutrition Values: Calories 69, fat 1,8, fiber 2,5, carbs 4,8, protein 9,9

129. SRIRACHA ZUCCHINI

Preparation time: 5 minutes
Cooking time: 5 hours
Servings: 4

Ingredients:

- 1 pound zucchini, sliced
- 1 tablespoon sriracha sauce
- 1 tablespoon olive oil
- ¼ cup vegetable stock

Directions:

1. In your slow cooker, combine all the ingredients, cover and cook on low for 5 hours.
2. Divide between plates and serve as a side dish.

Nutrition Values: Calories 74, fat 6,3, fiber 1,3, carbs 4,2, protein 1,4

130. SPICY PUMPKIN MIX

Preparation time: 5 minutes
Cooking time: 6 hours
Servings: 4

Ingredients:

- 2 tablespoons olive oil
- 3 tablespoons coconut aminos
- 1 teaspoon fresh grated ginger
- A pinch of red pepper flakes
- 2 garlic cloves, minced
- 1 pumpkin, peeled, deseeded and sliced

- 1 tablespoon sesame seeds, toasted

Directions:
1. In your slow cooker, combine all the ingredients, cover and cook on low for 6 hours.
2. Divide between plates and serve as a side dish.

Nutrition Values: Calories 138, fat 8,4, fiber 1,4, carbs 16,3, protein 2,6

131. CARROTS MASH

Preparation time: 5 minutes
Cooking time: 5 hours
Servings: 4

Ingredients:
- 1 teaspoon sweet paprika
- 1 pound carrots, peeled and halved
- 1 cup vegetable stock
- 1/4 cup coconut oil, melted
- A pinch of salt and black pepper

Directions:
1. In your slow cooker, mix all the ingredients except the coconut oil, cover and cook on Low for 5 hours.
2. Transfer the carrots to a bowl, mash well, add the oil, whisk and serve as a side dish.

Nutrition Values: Calories 168, fat 14,2, fiber 3, carbs 12, protein 1

132. SPINACH SIDE SALAD

Preparation time: 5 minutes
Cooking time: 2 hours
Servings: 4

Ingredients:
- 1 tablespoon honey
- 2 tablespoons olive oil
- 1 pound baby spinach
- 1 pound cherry tomatoes, halved
- ¼ cup vegetable stock
- 2 teaspoons sesame seeds
- 1 tablespoon lime juice
- 2 tablespoons pine nuts, toasted
- A pinch of salt and black pepper

Directions:
1. In your slow cooker, combine all the ingredients except the pine nuts and the sesame seeds. Cover and cook on low for 2 hours.
2. Transfer the mix to a bowl, cool it down, and add the sesame seeds and the pine nuts. Mix and serve as a side dish.

Nutrition Values: Calories 162, fat 11,5, fiber 4,2, carbs 14,2, protein 5,1

133. ORANGE CELERY

Preparation time: 5 minutes
Cooking time: 5 hours
Servings: 4

Ingredients:
- 1 tablespoon orange juice
- Zest of 2 oranges, grated
- ¼ cup vegetable stock
- 1 pound celery root, cut into wedges
- 2 tablespoons olive oil
- 1 tablespoon chopped rosemary
- A pinch of salt and black pepper

Directions:
1. In your slow cooker, combine all the ingredients, cover and cook on low for 5 hours.
2. Divide between plates and serve as a side dish.

Nutrition Values: Calories 113, fat 7,6, fiber 2,5, carbs 11,6, protein 1,8

134. PARSLEY SWEET POTATOES

Preparation time: 5 minutes
Cooking time: 5 hours
Servings: 4

Ingredients:
- 3 tablespoons lemon juice
- 1 pound sweet potatoes, peeled, cubed
- A pinch of salt and black pepper
- 2 tablespoons olive oil
- 1 tablespoon parsley, chopped

Directions:
1. In your slow cooker, combine all the ingredients, cover and cook on low for 5 hours.
2. Divide between plates and serve as a side dish.

Nutrition Values: Calories 197, fat 7,3, fiber 4,7, carbs 31,9, protein 1,9

135. HERBED BRUSSEL SPROUTS

Preparation time: 5 minutes
Cooking time: 3 hours
Servings: 4

Ingredients:
- 8 garlic cloves, minced
- 2 tablespoons olive oil
- 1 pound Brussel sprouts, trimmed and halved
- ¼ cup chicken stock

- Zest of 1 lemon, grated
- ¼ cup chopped parsley
- ¼ cup fresh chopped basil
- ¼ cup fresh chopped rosemary
- A pinch of sea salt and black pepper

Directions:
1. In your slow cooker, combine all the ingredients, cover and cook on low for 3 hours.
2. Divide between plates and serve as a side dish.

Nutrition Values: Calories 132, fat 8,1, fiber 6,1, carbs 15, protein 4,6

136. ONION WALNUT SAUTÉ

Preparation time: 5 minutes
Cooking time: 3 hours
Servings: 2

Ingredients:
- 2 cups arugula
- 1 tablespoon olive oil
- 1 tablespoon balsamic vinegar
- 2 cups red onion, sliced
- ¼ cup chicken stock
- 1 avocado, pitted, peeled and cubed
- ½ cup chopped walnuts

Directions:
1. In your slow cooker, combine the onion with the chicken stock and half of the oil. Cover and cook on high for 3 hours.
2. In a separate bowl, mix the arugula with the vinegar, avocado and the walnuts. Add drained onion, mix together and divide between plates and serve as a side dish.

Nutrition Values: Calories 512, fat 45,4, fiber 11,6, carbs 23,4, protein 11,3

137. ROSEMARY GREEN BEANS

Preparation Time: 10 minutes
Servings: 1

Ingredients
- 1 tbsp. butter, melted
- 2 tbsp. rosemary
- ½ tsp. salt
- 3 cloves garlic, minced
- ¾ cup green beans, chopped

Directions:
1. Pre-heat your fryer at 390°F.
2. Combine the melted butter with the rosemary, salt, and minced garlic. Toss in the green beans, making sure to coat them well.

3. Cook in the fryer for five minutes.

138. CARROT CROQUETTES

Preparation Time: 10 minutes
Servings: 4

Ingredients
- 2 medium-sized carrots, trimmed and grated
- 2 medium-sized celery stalks, trimmed and grated
- ½ cup of leek, finely chopped
- 1 tbsp. garlic paste
- ¼ tsp. freshly cracked black pepper
- 1 tsp. fine sea salt
- 1 tbsp. fresh dill, finely chopped
- 1 egg, lightly whisked
- ¼ cup keto almond flour
- ¼ tsp. baking powder
- ½ cup keto bread crumbs [seasoned or regular]
- Chive mayo to serve

Directions:
1. Drain any excess liquid from the carrots and celery by placing them on a paper towel.
2. Stir together the vegetables with all of the other ingredients, save for the bread crumbs and chive mayo.
3. Use your hands to mold 1 tablespoon of the vegetable mixture into a ball and repeat until all of the mixture has been used up. Press down on each ball with your hand or a palette knife. Cover completely with bread crumbs. Spritz the croquettes with a non-stick cooking spray.
4. Arrange the croquettes in a single layer in your Air Fryer and fry for 6 minutes at 360°F.
5. Serve warm with the chive mayo on the side.

139. PEPPERED PUFF PASTRY

Preparation Time: 25 minutes
Servings: 4

Ingredients
1. 1 ½ tbsp. sesame oil
2. 1 cup white mushrooms, sliced
3. 2 cloves garlic, minced
4. 1 bell pepper, seeded and chopped
5. ¼ tsp. sea salt
6. ¼ tsp. dried rosemary
7. ½ tsp. ground black pepper, or more to taste
8. 11 oz. puff pastry sheets
9. ½ cup crème fraiche
10. 1 egg, well whisked
11. ½ cup parmesan cheese, preferably freshly grated

Directions:

1. Pre-heat your Air Fryer to 400°F.
2. In a skillet, heat the sesame oil over a moderate heat and fry the mushrooms, garlic, and pepper until soft and fragrant.
3. Sprinkle on the salt, rosemary, and pepper.
4. In the meantime, unroll the puff pastry and slice it into 4-inch squares.
5. Spread the crème fraiche across each square.
6. Spoon equal amounts of the vegetables into the puff pastry squares. Enclose each square around the filling in a triangle shape, pressing the edges with your fingertips.
7. Brush each triangle with some whisked egg and cover with grated Parmesan.
8. Cook for 22-25 minutes.

140. SAUTÉED GREEN BEANS

Preparation Time: 12 minutes
Servings: 4

Ingredients

- ¾ lb. green beans, cleaned
- 1 tbsp. balsamic vinegar
- ¼ tsp. kosher salt
- ½ tsp. mixed peppercorns, freshly cracked
- 1 tbsp. butter
- Sesame seeds to serve

Directions:

1. Pre-heat your Air Fryer at 390°F.
2. Combine the green beans with the rest of the ingredients, except for the sesame seeds. Transfer to the fryer and cook for 10 minutes.
3. In the meantime, heat the sesame seeds in a small skillet to toast all over, stirring constantly to prevent burning.
4. Serve the green beans accompanied by the toasted sesame seeds.

141. HORSERADISH MAYO & GORGONZOLA MUSHROOMS

Preparation Time: 15 minutes
Servings: 5

Ingredients

1. ½ cup of keto bread crumbs
2. 2 cloves garlic, pressed
3. 2 tbsp. fresh coriander, chopped
4. ⅓tsp. kosher salt
5. ½ tsp. crushed red pepper flakes
6. 1 ½ tbsp. olive oil
7. 20 medium-sized mushrooms, stems removed
8. ½ cup Gorgonzola cheese, grated
9. ¼ cup low-fat mayonnaise
10. 1 tsp. prepared horseradish, well-drained
11. tbsp. fresh parsley, finely chopped

Directions:

1. Combine the bread crumbs together with the garlic, coriander, salt, red pepper, and the olive oil.
2. Take equal-sized amounts of the bread crumb mixture and use them to stuff the mushroom caps. Add the grated Gorgonzola on top of each.
3. Put the mushrooms in the Air Fryer grill pan and transfer to the fryer.
4. Grill them at 380°F for 8-12 minutes, ensuring the stuffing is warm throughout.
5. In the meantime, prepare the horseradish mayo. Mix together the mayonnaise, horseradish and parsley.
6. When the mushrooms are ready, serve with the mayo.

142. SCALLION & RICOTTA POTATOES

Preparation Time: 15 minutes
Servings: 4

Ingredients

- 4 baking potatoes
- 2 tbsp. olive oil
- ½ cup Ricotta cheese, room temperature
- 2 tbsp. scallions, chopped
- 1 heaped tbsp. fresh parsley, roughly chopped
- 1 heaped tbsp. coriander, minced
- 2 oz. Cheddar cheese, preferably freshly grated
- 1 tsp. celery seeds
- ½ tsp. salt
- ½ tsp. garlic pepper

Directions:

1. Pierce the skin of the potatoes with a knife.
2. Cook in the Air Fryer basket for roughly 13 minutes at 350°F. If they are not cooked through by this time, leave for 2 – 3 minutes longer.
3. In the meantime, make the stuffing by combining all the other ingredients.
4. Cut halfway into the cooked potatoes to open them.
5. Spoon equal amounts of the stuffing into each potato and serve hot.

143. CRUMBED BEANS

Preparation Time: 10 minutes
Servings: 4

Ingredients

- ½ cup keto almond flour
- 1 tsp. smoky chipotle powder
- ½ tsp. ground black pepper

- 1 tsp. sea salt flakes
- 2 eggs, beaten
- ½ cup crushed saltines
- 10 oz. wax beans

Directions:
1. Combine the keto almond flour, chipotle powder, black pepper, and salt in a bowl. Put the eggs in a second bowl. Place the crushed saltines in a third bowl.
2. Wash the beans with cold water and discard any tough strings.
3. Coat the beans with the flour mixture, before dipping them into the beaten egg. Lastly cover them with the crushed saltines.
4. Spritz the beans with a cooking spray.
5. Air-fry at 360°F for 4 minutes. Give the cooking basket a good shake and continue to cook for 3 minutes. Serve hot.

144. COLBY POTATO PATTIES

Preparation Time: 15 minutes
Servings: 8

Ingredients
- 2 lb. white potatoes, peeled and grated
- ½ cup scallions, finely chopped
- ½ tsp. freshly ground black pepper, or more to taste
- 1 tbsp. fine sea salt
- ½ tsp. hot paprika
- 2 cups Colby cheese, shredded
- ¼ cup canola oil
- 1 cup crushed crackers

Directions:
1. Boil the potatoes until soft. Dry them off and peel them before mashing thoroughly, leaving no lumps.
2. Combine the mashed potatoes with scallions, pepper, salt, paprika, and cheese.
3. Mold the mixture into balls with your hands and press with your palm to flatten them into patties.
4. In a shallow dish, combine the canola oil and crushed crackers. Coat the patties in the crumb mixture.
5. Cook the patties at 360°F for about 10 minutes, in multiple batches if necessary.
6. Serve with tabasco mayo or the sauce of your choice.

145. TURKEY GARLIC POTATOES

Preparation Time: 45 minutes
Servings: 2

Ingredients

- 3 unsmoked turkey strips
- 6 small potatoes
- 1 tsp. garlic, minced
- 2 tsp. olive oil
- Salt to taste
- Pepper to taste

Directions:
1. Peel the potatoes and cube them finely.
2. Coat in 1 teaspoon of oil and cook in the Air Fryer for 10 minutes at 350°F.
3. In a separate bowl, slice the turkey finely and combine with the garlic, oil, salt and pepper. Pour the potatoes into the bowl and mix well.
4. Lay the mixture on some silver aluminum foil, transfer to the fryer and cook for about 10 minutes.
5. Serve with raita.

146. KETO CROUTONS

Preparation Time: 25 minutes
Servings: 4

Ingredients
- 2 slices keto friendly bread
- 1 tbsp. olive oil

Directions:
1. Cut the slices of bread into medium-size chunks.
2. Coat the inside of the Air Fryer with the oil. Set it to 390°F and allow it to heat up.
3. Place the chunks inside and shallow fry for at least 8 minutes.
4. Serve with hot soup.

147. GARLIC STUFFED MUSHROOMS

Preparation Time: 25 minutes
Servings: 4

Ingredients
- 6 small mushrooms
- 1 oz. onion, peeled and diced
- 1 tbsp. keto friendly bread crumbs
- 1 tbsp. olive oil
- 1 tsp. garlic, pureed
- 1 tsp. parsley
- Salt and pepper to taste

Directions:
1. Combine the keto bread crumbs, oil, onion, parsley, salt, pepper and garlic in a bowl. Cut out the mushrooms' stalks and stuff each cap with the crumb mixture.
2. Cook in the Air Fryer for 10 minutes at 350°F.
3. Serve with a side of mayo dip.

148. ZUCCHINI SWEET POTATOES

Preparation Time: 20 minutes
Servings: 4

Ingredients

- 2 large-sized sweet potatoes, peeled and quartered
- 1 medium-sized zucchini, sliced
- 1 Serrano pepper, deveined and thinly sliced
- 1 bell pepper, deveined and thinly sliced
- 1 – 2 carrots, cut into matchsticks
- ¼ cup olive oil
- 1 ½ tbsp. maple syrup
- ½ tsp. porcini powder
- ¼ tsp. mustard powder
- ½ tsp. fennel seeds
- 1 tbsp. garlic powder
- ½ tsp. fine sea salt
- ¼ tsp. ground black pepper
- Tomato ketchup to serve

Directions:

1. Put the sweet potatoes, zucchini, peppers, and the carrot into the basket of your Air Fryer. Coat with a drizzling of olive oil.
2. Pre-heat the fryer at 350°F.
3. Cook the vegetables for 15 minutes.
4. In the meantime, prepare the sauce by vigorously combining the other ingredients, save for the tomato ketchup, with a whisk.
5. Lightly grease a baking dish small enough to fit inside your fryer.
6. Move the cooked vegetables to the baking dish, pour over the sauce and make sure to coat the vegetables well.
7. Raise the temperature to 390°F and cook the vegetables for an additional 5 minutes.
8. Serve warm with a side of ketchup.

149. CHEESE LINGS

Preparation Time: 25 minutes
Servings: 6

Ingredients

- 1 cup keto almond flour
- small cubes cheese, grated
- ¼ tsp. chili powder
- 1 tsp. butter
- Salt to taste
- 1 tsp. baking powder

Directions:

1. Combine all the ingredients to form a dough, along with a small amount water as necessary.
2. Divide the dough into equal portions and roll

each one into a ball.
3. Pre-heat Air Fryer at 360°F.
4. Transfer the balls to the fryer and air fry for 5 minutes, stirring periodically.

150. POTATO SIDE DISH

Preparation Time: 30 minutes
Servings: 2

Ingredients

- 2 medium potatoes
- 1 tsp. butter
- 3 tbsp. sour cream
- 1 tsp. chives
- 1 ½ tbsp. cheese, grated
- Salt and pepper to taste

Directions:

1. Pierce the potatoes with a fork and boil them in water until they are cooked.
2. Transfer to the Air Fryer and cook for 15 minutes at 350°F.
3. In the meantime, combine the sour cream, cheese and chives in a bowl. Cut the potatoes halfway to open them up and fill with the butter and toppings.
4. Serve with salad.

151. ROASTED POTATOES & CHEESE

Preparation Time: 55 minutes
Servings: 4

Ingredients

- 4 medium potatoes
- 1 asparagus bunch
- ⅓cup cottage cheese
- ⅓cup low-fat crème fraiche
- 1 tbsp. wholegrain mustard

Directions:

1. Pour some oil into your Air Fryer and pre-heat to 390°F.
2. Cook potatoes for 20 minutes.
3. Boil the asparagus in salted water for 3 minutes.
4. Remove the potatoes and mash them with rest of ingredients. Sprinkle on salt and pepper.
5. Serve with rice.

152. VEGETABLE & CHEESE OMELET

Preparation Time: 15 minutes
Servings: 2

Ingredients

- 3 tbsp. plain milk
- 4 eggs, whisked
- 1 tsp. melted butter

- Kosher salt and freshly ground black pepper, to taste
- 1 red bell pepper, deveined and chopped
- 1 green bell pepper, deveined and chopped
- 1 white onion, finely chopped
- ½ cup baby spinach leaves, roughly chopped
- ½ cup Halloumi cheese, shaved

Directions:

1. Grease the Air Fryer baking pan with some canola oil.
2. Place all of the ingredients in the baking pan and stir well.
3. Transfer to the fryer and cook at 350°F for 13 minutes.
4. Serve warm.

153. SCRAMBLED EGGS

Preparation Time: 15 minutes
Servings: 2

Ingredients

- 2 tbsp. olive oil, melted
- 4 eggs, whisked
- 5 oz. fresh spinach, chopped
- 1 medium-sized tomato, chopped
- 1 tsp. fresh lemon juice
- ½ tsp. coarse salt
- ½ tsp. ground black pepper
- ½ cup of fresh basil, roughly chopped

Directions:

1. Grease the Air Fryer baking pan with the oil, tilting it to spread the oil around. Pre-heat the fryer at 280°F.
2. Mix the remaining ingredients, apart from the basil leaves, whisking well until everything is completely combined.
3. Cook in the fryer for 8 - 12 minutes.
4. Top with fresh basil leaves before serving with a little sour cream if desired.

154. SWEET CORN FRITTERS

Preparation Time: 20 minutes
Servings: 4

Ingredients

- 1 medium-sized carrot, grated
- 1 yellow onion, finely chopped
- 4 oz. canned sweet corn kernels, drained
- 1 tsp. sea salt flakes
- 1 heaping tbsp. fresh cilantro, chopped
- 1 medium-sized egg, whisked
- 2 tbsp. plain milk
- 1 cup of Parmesan cheese, grated
- ¼ cup keto almond flour

- ⅓ tsp. baking powder
- ⅓ tsp. stevia

Directions:

1. Place the grated carrot in a colander and press down to squeeze out any excess moisture. Dry it with a paper towel.
2. Combine the carrots with the remaining ingredients.
3. Mold 1 tablespoon of the mixture into a ball and press it down with your hand or a spoon to flatten it. Repeat until the rest of the mixture is used up.
4. Spritz the balls with cooking spray.
5. Arrange in the basket of your Air Fryer, taking care not to overlap any balls. Cook at 350°F for 8 to 11 minutes or until they're firm.
6. Serve warm.

155. ROSEMARY CORNBREAD

Preparation Time: 1 hr.
Servings: 6

Ingredients

- 1 cup cornmeal
- 1 ½ cups keto almond flour
- ½ tsp. baking soda
- ½ tsp. baking powder
- ¼ tsp. kosher salt
- 1 tsp. dried rosemary
- ¼ tsp. garlic powder
- 2 tbsp. stevia
- 2 eggs
- ¼ cup melted butter
- 1 cup buttermilk
- ½ cup corn kernels

Directions:

1. In a bowl, combine all the dry ingredients. In a separate bowl, mix together all the wet ingredients. Combine the two.
2. Fold in the corn kernels and stir vigorously.
3. Pour the batter into a lightly greased round loaf pan that is lightly greased.
4. Cook for 1 hour at 380°F.

156. VEGGIE ROLLS

Preparation Time: 30 minutes
Servings: 6

Ingredients

- 2 potatoes, mashed
- ¼ cup peas
- ¼ cup carrots, mashed
- 1 small cabbage, sliced

- ¼ beans
- 2 tbsp. sweetcorn
- 1 small onion, chopped
- 1 tsp. capsicum
- 1 tsp. coriander
- 2 tbsp. butter
- Ginger
- Garlic to taste
- ½ tsp. masala powder
- ½ tsp. chili powder
- ½ cup keto bread crumbs
- 1 packet spring roll sheets
- ½ cup cornstarch slurry

Directions:
1. Boil all the vegetables in water over a low heat. Rinse and allow to dry.
2. Unroll the spring roll sheets and spoon equal amounts of vegetable onto the center of each one. Fold into spring rolls and coat each one with the slurry and bread crumbs.
3. Pre-heat the Air Fryer to 390°F. Cook the rolls for 10 minutes.
4. Serve with a side of boiled rice.

157. GRILLED CHEESE
Preparation Time: 25 minutes
Servings: 2

Ingredients
- 4 slices keto bread
- ½ cup sharp cheddar cheese
- ¼ cup butter, melted

Directions:
1. Pre-heat the Air Fryer at 360°F.
2. Put cheese and butter in separate bowls.
3. Apply the butter to each side of the bread slices with a brush.
4. Spread the cheese across two of the slices of bread and make two sandwiches. Transfer both to the fryer.
5. Cook for 5 – 7 minutes or until a golden brown color is achieved and the cheese is melted.

158. POTATO GRATIN
Preparation Time: 55 minutes
Servings: 6

Ingredients
- ½ cup milk
- 7 medium russet potatoes, peeled
- 1 tsp. black pepper
- ½ cup cream
- ½ cup semi-mature cheese, grated

- ½ tsp. nutmeg

Directions:
1. Pre-heat the Air Fryer to 390°F.
2. Cut the potatoes into wafer-thin slices.
3. In a bowl, combine the milk and cream and sprinkle with salt, pepper, and nutmeg as desired.
4. Use the milk mixture to coat the slices of potatoes. Place in an 8" heat-resistant baking dish. Top the potatoes with the rest of the cream mixture.
5. Put the baking dish into the basket of the fryer and cook for 25 minutes.
6. Pour the cheese over the potatoes.
7. Cook for an additional 10 minutes, ensuring the top is nicely browned before serving.

159. ROASTED VEGETABLES
Preparation Time: 30 minutes
Servings: 6
Ingredients
- 1 ⅓ cup small parsnips
- 1 ⅓ cup celery [3 – 4 stalks]
- 2 red onions
- 1 ⅓ cup small butternut squash
- 1 tbsp. fresh thyme needles
- 1 tbsp. olive oil
- Salt and pepper to taste

Directions:
1. Pre-heat the Air Fryer to 390°F.
2. Peel the parsnips and onions and cut them into 2-cm cubes. Slice the onions into wedges.
3. Do not peel the butternut squash. Cut it in half, de-seed it, and cube.
4. Combine the cut vegetables with the thyme, olive oil, salt and pepper.
5. Put the vegetables in the basket and transfer the basket to the Air Fryer.
6. Cook for 20 minutes, stirring once throughout the cooking time, until the vegetables are nicely browned and cooked through.

160. SWEET POTATO CURRY FRIES
Preparation Time: 55 minutes
Servings: 4

Ingredients
- o lb. sweet potatoes
- 1 tsp. curry powder
- 2 tbsp. olive oil
- Salt to taste

Directions:
1. Pre-heat Air Fryer to 390°F.

2. Wash the sweet potatoes before slicing them into matchsticks.
3. Drizzle the oil in the pan, place the fries inside and bake for 25 minutes.
4. Sprinkle with curry and salt before serving with ketchup if desired.

161. CRUSTED SALMON

Preparation Time: 25 minutes

Servings: 4

Ingredients:

- 2 pounds salmon fillet
- 3 garlic cloves; minced
- 1/2 cup parmesan; grated
- 1/4 cup parsley; chopped.
- Salt and black pepper to the taste.

Directions:

1. Place salmon on a lined baking sheet, season with salt and pepper, cover with a parchment paper, introduce in the oven at 425 degrees F and bake for 10 minutes
2. Take fish out of the oven, sprinkle parmesan, parsley and garlic over fish, introduce in the oven again and cook for 5 minutes more
3. Divide between plates and serve

Nutrition Values: Calories: 240; Fat: 12; Fiber: 1; Carbs: 0.6; Protein: 25

162. SOUR CREAM SALMON

Preparation Time: 25 minutes

Servings: 4

Ingredients:

- 4 salmon fillets
- A drizzle of olive oil
- 1/3 cup parmesan; grated
- 1½ teaspoon mustard
- 1/2 cup sour cream
- Salt and black pepper to the taste.

Directions:

1. Place salmon on a lined baking sheet, season with salt and pepper and drizzle the oil.
2. In a bowl, mix sour cream with parmesan, mustard, salt and pepper and stir well.
3. Spoon this sour cream mix over salmon, introduce in the oven at 350 degrees F and bake for 15 minutes
4. Divide between plates and serve

Nutrition Values: Calories: 200; Fat: 6; Fiber: 1; Carbs: 4; Protein: 20

163. DELICIOUS ROASTED SALMON

Preparation Time: 22 minutes

Servings: 4

Ingredients:

- 1¼ pound salmon fillet

- 2 ounces Kimchi, finely chopped.
- 2 tablespoons ghee, soft
- Salt and black pepper to the taste.

Directions:

1. In your food processor, mix ghee with Kimchi and blend well.
2. Rub salmon with salt, pepper and Kimchi mix and place into a baking dish.
3. Introduce in the oven at 425 degrees F and bake for 15 minutes
4. Divide between plates and serve with a side salad.

Nutrition Values: Calories: 200; Fat: 12; Fiber: 0; Carbs: 3; Protein: 21

164. BAKED HALIBUT AND VEGGIES

Preparation Time: 45 minutes

Servings: 2

Ingredients:

- 2 halibut fillets
- 2 cups baby spinach
- 1 red bell pepper; roughly chopped.
- 1 yellow bell pepper; roughly chopped.
- 1 teaspoon cumin
- 1 teaspoon balsamic vinegar
- 1 tablespoon olive oil
- Salt and black pepper to the taste.

Directions:

1. In a bowl, mix bell peppers with salt, pepper, half of the oil and the vinegar, toss to coat well and transfer to a baking dish.
2. Introduce in the oven at 400 degrees F and bake for 20 minutes
3. Heat up a pan with the rest of the oil over medium heat; add fish, season with salt, pepper and cumin and brown on all sides
4. Take the baking dish out of the oven, add spinach; stir gently and divide the whole mix between plates
5. Add fish on the side, sprinkle some more salt and pepper and serve

Nutrition Values: Calories: 230; Fat: 12; Fiber: 1; Carbs: 4; Protein: 9

165. KETO FISH PIE

Preparation Time: 1 hour 20 minutes

Servings: 6

Ingredients:

- 1 red onion, chopped.

- 2 salmon fillets, skinless and cut into medium pieces
- 2 mackerel fillets, skinless and cut into medium pieces
- 3 haddock fillets and cut into medium pieces
- 2 bay leaves
- 1/4 cup ghee+ 2 tablespoons ghee
- 1 cauliflower head, florets separated
- 4 eggs
- 4 cloves
- 1 cup whipping cream
- 1/2 cup water
- A pinch of nutmeg, ground
- 1 teaspoon Dijon mustard
- 1 cup cheddar cheese, shredded+ 1/2 cup cheddar cheese, shredded
- Some chopped parsley
- Salt and black pepper to the taste.
- 4 tablespoons chives, chopped.

Directions:

1. Put some water in a pan, add some salt, bring to a boil over medium heat; add eggs, , cook them for 10 minutes, take off heat; drain, leave them to cool down, peel and cut them into quarters
2. Put water in another pot, bring to a boil, add cauliflower florets, cook for 10 minutes, drain them, transfer to your blender, add 1/4 cup ghee, pulse well and transfer to a bowl.
3. Put cream and 1/2 cup water in a pan, add fish, toss to coat and heat up over medium heat.
4. Add onion, cloves and bay leaves, bring to a boil, reduce heat and simmer for 10 minutes
5. Take off heat; transfer fish to a baking dish and leave aside
6. return pan with fish sauce to heat; add nutmeg; stir and cook for 5 minutes
7. Take off heat; discard cloves and bay leaves, add 1 cup cheddar cheese and 2 tablespoons ghee and stir well.
8. Place egg quarters on top of the fish in the baking dish.
9. Add cream and cheese sauce over them, top with cauliflower mash, sprinkle the rest of the cheddar cheese, chives and parsley, introduce in the oven at 400 degrees F for 30 minutes
10. Leave the pie to cool down a bit before slicing and serving.

Nutrition Values: Calories: 300; Fat: 45; Fiber: 3; Carbs: 5; Protein: 26

166. COD WITH ARUGULA

Preparation Time: 30 minutes
Servings: 2

Ingredients:

- 2 cod fillets
- 1 tablespoon olive oil
- Juice of 1 lemon
- 3 cup arugula
- 1/2 cup black olives; pitted and sliced
- 2 tablespoons capers
- 1 garlic clove; chopped.
- Salt and black pepper to the taste.

Directions:

1. Arrange fish fillets in a heatproof dish, season with salt, pepper, drizzle the oil and lemon juice, toss to coat, introduce in the oven at 450 degrees F and bake for 20 minutes
2. In your food processor, mix arugula with salt, pepper, capers, olives and garlic and blend a bit.
3. Arrange fish on plates, top with arugula tapenade and serve

Nutrition Values: Calories: 240; Fat: 5; Fiber: 3; Carbs: 3; Protein: 10

167. SALMON MEATBALLS

Preparation Time: 40 minutes
Servings: 4

Ingredients:

- 1 pound wild salmon, boneless and minced
- 1/4 cup chives, chopped.
- 1 egg
- 2 tablespoons Dijon mustard
- 1 tablespoon coconut flour
- 2 tablespoons ghee
- 2 garlic cloves, minced
- 1/3 cup onion, chopped.
- Salt and black pepper to the taste.

For the sauce:

- 4 garlic cloves, minced
- 2 cups coconut cream
- 2 tablespoons chives, chopped.
- 2 tablespoons ghee
- 2 tablespoons Dijon mustard
- Juice and zest of 1 lemon

Directions:

1. Heat up a pan with 2 tablespoons ghee over medium heat; add onion and 2 garlic cloves; stir, cook for 3 minutes and transfer to a bowl.
2. In another bowl, mix onion and garlic with salmon, chives, coconut flour, salt, pepper, 2

tablespoons mustard and egg and stir well.

3. Shape meatballs from the salmon mix, place on a baking sheet, introduce in the oven at 350 degrees F and bake for 25 minutes
4. Meanwhile; heat up a pan with 2 tablespoons ghee over medium heat; add 4 garlic cloves; stir and cook for 1 minute
5. Add coconut cream, 2 tablespoons Dijon mustard, lemon juice and zest and chives; stir and cook for 3 minutes
6. Take salmon meatballs out of the oven, drop them into the Dijon sauce, toss, cook for 1 minute and take off heat.
7. Divide into bowls and serve

Nutrition Values: Calories: 171; Fat: 5; Fiber: 1; Carbs: 6; Protein: 23

168. TUNA CAKES

Preparation Time: 20 minutes
Servings: 12

Ingredients:

- 15 ounces canned tuna; drain well and flaked
- 3 eggs
- 1 teaspoon parsley; dried
- 1/2 cup red onion; chopped.
- Oil for frying
- 1 teaspoon garlic powder
- 1/2 teaspoon dill; dried
- Salt and black pepper to the taste.

Directions:

1. In a bowl, mix tuna with salt, pepper, dill, parsley, onion, garlic powder and eggs and stir well.
2. Shape your cakes and place on a plate
3. Heat up a pan with some oil over medium high heat; add tuna cakes, cook for 5 minutes on each side
4. Divide between plates and serve

Nutrition Values: Calories: 140; Fat: 2; Fiber: 1; Carbs: 0.6; Protein: 6

169. SALMON WITH CAPER SAUCE

Preparation Time: 30 minutes
Servings: 3

Ingredients:

- 3 salmon fillets
- 1 tablespoon olive oil
- 1 tablespoon Italian seasoning
- 2 tablespoons capers
- 3 tablespoons lemon juice
- 4 garlic cloves, minced
- 2 tablespoons ghee

- Salt and black pepper to the taste.

Directions:

1. Heat up a pan with the olive oil over medium heat; add fish fillets skin side up, season them with salt, pepper and Italian seasoning, cook for 2 minutes, flip and cook for 2 more minutes, take off heat; cover pan and leave aside for 15 minutes
2. Transfer fish to a plate and leave them aside
3. Heat up the same pan over medium heat; add capers, lemon juice and garlic; stir and cook for 2 minutes
4. Take the pan off the heat; add ghee and stir very well.
5. Return fish to pan and toss to coat with the sauce
6. Divide between plates and serve

Nutrition Values: Calories: 245; Fat: 12; Fiber: 1; Carbs: 3; Protein: 23

170. TROUT AND SPECIAL SAUCE

Preparation Time: 20 minutes
Servings: 1

Ingredients:

- 1 big trout fillet
- 1 tablespoon olive oil
- 1 tablespoon ghee
- Zest and juice from 1 orange
- A handful parsley, chopped.
- 1/2 cup pecans, chopped.
- Salt and black pepper to the taste.

Directions:

1. Heat up a pan with the oil over medium high heat; add the fish fillet, season with salt and pepper, cook for 4 minutes on each side, transfer to a plate and keep warm for now.
2. Heat up the same pan with the ghee over medium heat; add pecans; stir and toast for 1 minutes
3. Add orange juice and zest, some salt and pepper and chopped parsley; stir, cook for 1 minute and pour over fish fillet.
4. Serve right away.

Nutrition Values: Calories: 200; Fat: 10; Fiber: 2; Carbs: 1; Protein: 14

171. BAKED FISH

Preparation Time: 50 minutes
Servings: 4

Ingredients:

- 1 pound haddock
- 3 teaspoons water

- 2 tablespoons lemon juice
- 2 tablespoons mayonnaise
- 1 teaspoon dill weed
- Cooking spray
- A pinch of old bay seasoning
- Salt and black pepper to the taste.

Directions:
1. Spray a baking dish with some cooking oil.
2. Add lemon juice, water and fish and toss to coat a bit.
3. Add salt, pepper, old bay seasoning and dill weed and toss again.
4. Add mayo and spread well.
5. Introduce in the oven at 350 degrees F and bake for 30 minutes
6. Divide between plates and serve

Nutrition Values: Calories: 104; Fat: 12; Fiber: 1; Carbs: 0.5; Protein: 20

172. BAKED HALIBUT

Preparation Time: 20 minutes
Servings: 4

Ingredients:
- 4 halibut fillets
- 1/2 cup parmesan; grated
- 1/4 cup ghee
- 1/4 cup mayonnaise
- 2 tablespoons green onions; chopped.
- 6 garlic cloves; minced
- Juice of 1/2 lemon
- A dash of Tabasco sauce
- Salt and black pepper to the taste.

Directions:
1. Season halibut with salt, pepper and some of the lemon juice, place in a baking dish and cook in the oven at 450 degrees F for 6 minutes
2. Meanwhile; heat up a pan with the ghee over medium heat; add parmesan, mayo, green onions, Tabasco sauce, garlic and the rest of the lemon juice and stir well.
3. Take fish out of the oven, drizzle parmesan sauce all over, turn oven to broil and broil your fish for 3 minutes
4. Divide between plates and serve

Nutrition Values: Calories: 240; Fat: 12; Fiber: 1; Carbs: 5; Protein: 23

173. TROUT AND GHEE SAUCE

Preparation Time: 20 minutes
Servings: 4

Ingredients:

- 4 trout fillets
- 3 teaspoons lemon zest, grated
- 3 tablespoons chives, chopped.
- 6 tablespoons ghee
- 2 tablespoons olive oil
- 2 teaspoons lemon juice
- Salt and black pepper to the taste.

Directions:
1. Season trout with salt and pepper, drizzle the olive oil and massage a bit.
2. Heat up your kitchen grill over medium high heat; add fish fillets, cook for 4 minutes, flip and cook for 4 minutes more
3. Meanwhile; heat up a pan with the ghee over medium heat; add salt, pepper, chives, lemon juice and zest and stir well.
4. Divide fish fillets on plates, drizzle the ghee sauce over them and serve

Nutrition Values: Calories: 320; Fat: 12; Fiber: 1; Carbs: 2; Protein: 24

174. CRAB LEGS

Preparation Time: 20 minutes
Servings: 3

Ingredients
- 3 lb. crab legs
- ¼ cup salted butter, melted and divided
- ½ lemon, juiced
- ¼ tsp. garlic powder

Directions:
1. In a bowl, toss the crab legs and two tablespoons of the melted butter together. Place the crab legs in the basket of the fryer.
2. Cook at 400°F for fifteen minutes, giving the basket a good shake halfway through.
3. Combine the remaining butter with the lemon juice and garlic powder.
4. Crack open the cooked crab legs and remove the meat. Serve with the butter dip on the side and enjoy!

175. CRUSTY PESTO SALMON

Preparation Time: 15 minutes
Servings: 2

Ingredients
- ¼ cup almonds, roughly chopped
- ¼ cup pesto
- 2 x 4-oz. salmon fillets
- 2 tbsp. unsalted butter, melted

Directions:
1. Mix the almonds and pesto together.
2. Place the salmon fillets in a round baking

dish, roughly six inches in diameter.

3. Brush the fillets with butter, followed by the pesto mixture, ensuring to coat both the top and bottom. Put the baking dish inside the fryer.
4. Cook for twelve minutes at 390°F.
5. The salmon is ready when it flakes easily when prodded with a fork. Serve warm.

176. BUTTERY COD
Preparation Time: 12 minutes
Servings: 2

Ingredients
- 2 x 4-oz. cod fillets
- 2 tbsp. salted butter, melted
- 1 tsp. Old Bay seasoning
- ½ medium lemon, sliced

Directions:
1. Place the cod fillets in a baking dish.
2. Brush with melted butter, season with Old Bay, and top with some lemon slices.
3. Wrap the fish in aluminum foil and put into your fryer.
4. Cook for eight minutes at 350°F.
5. The cod is ready when it flakes easily. Serve hot.

177. SESAME TUNA STEAK
Preparation Time: 12 minutes
Servings: 2

Ingredients
- 1 tbsp. coconut oil, melted
- 2 x 6-oz. tuna steaks
- ½ tsp. garlic powder
- 2 tsp. black sesame seeds
- 2 tsp. white sesame seeds

Directions:
1. Apply the coconut oil to the tuna steaks with a brunch, then season with garlic powder.
2. Combine the black and white sesame seeds. Embed them in the tuna steaks, covering the fish all over. Place the tuna into your air fryer.
3. Cook for eight minutes at 400°F, turning the fish halfway through.
4. The tuna steaks are ready when they have reached a temperature of 145°F. Serve straightaway.

178. LEMON GARLIC SHRIMP
Preparation Time: 15 minutes
Servings: 2

Ingredients
- 1 medium lemon
- ½ lb. medium shrimp, shelled and deveined

- ½ tsp. Old Bay seasoning
- 2 tbsp. unsalted butter, melted
- ½ tsp. minced garlic

Directions:
1. Grate the rind of the lemon into a bowl. Cut the lemon in half and juice it over the same bowl. Toss in the shrimp, Old Bay, and butter, mixing everything to make sure the shrimp is completely covered.
2. Transfer to a round baking dish roughly six inches wide, then place this dish in your fryer.
3. Cook at 400°F for six minutes. The shrimp is cooked when it turns a bright pink color.
4. Serve hot, drizzling any leftover sauce over the shrimp.

179. FOIL PACKET SALMON
Preparation Time: 15 minutes
Servings: 2

Ingredients
- 2 x 4-oz. skinless salmon fillets
- 2 tbsp. unsalted butter, melted
- ½ tsp. garlic powder
- 1 medium lemon
- ½ tsp. dried dill

Directions:
1. Take a sheet of aluminum foil and cut into two squares measuring roughly 5" x 5". Lay each of the salmon fillets at the center of each piece. Brush both fillets with a tablespoon of bullet and season with a quarter-teaspoon of garlic powder.
2. Halve the lemon and grate the skin of one half over the fish. Cut four half-slices of lemon, using two to top each fillet. Season each fillet with a quarter-teaspoon of dill.
3. Fold the tops and sides of the aluminum foil over the fish to create a kind of packet. Place each one in the fryer.
4. Cook for twelve minutes at 400°F.
5. The salmon is ready when it flakes easily. Serve hot.

180. FOIL PACKET LOBSTER TAIL
Preparation Time: 15 minutes
Servings: 2

Ingredients
- 2 x 6-oz. lobster tail halves
- 2 tbsp. salted butter, melted
- ½ medium lemon, juiced
- ½ tsp. Old Bay seasoning
- 1 tsp. dried parsley

Directions:

1. Lay each lobster on a sheet of aluminum foil. Pour a light drizzle of melted butter and lemon juice over each one, and season with Old Bay.
2. Fold down the sides and ends of the foil to seal the lobster. Place each one in the fryer.
3. Cook at 375°F for twelve minutes.
4. Just before serving, top the lobster with dried parsley.

181. AVOCADO SHRIMP

Preparation Time: 20 minutes
Servings: 2

Ingredients

- ½ cup onion, chopped
- 2 lb. shrimp
- 1 tbsp. seasoned salt
- 1 avocado
- ½ cup pecans, chopped

Directions:

1. Pre-heat the fryer at 400°F.
2. Put the chopped onion in the basket of the fryer and spritz with some cooking spray. Leave to cook for five minutes.
3. Add the shrimp and set the timer for a further five minutes. Sprinkle with some seasoned salt, then allow to cook for an additional five minutes.
4. During these last five minutes, halve your avocado and remove the pit. Cube each half, then scoop out the flesh.
5. Take care when removing the shrimp from the fryer. Place it on a dish and top with the avocado and the chopped pecans.

182. LEMON BUTTER SCALLOPS

Preparation Time: 30 minutes
Servings: 1

Ingredients

- 1 lemon
- 1 lb. scallops
- ½ cup butter
- ¼ cup parsley, chopped

Directions:

1. Juice the lemon into a Ziploc bag.
2. Wash your scallops, dry them, and season to taste. Put them in the bag with the lemon juice. Refrigerate for an hour.
3. Remove the bag from the refrigerator and leave for about twenty minutes until it returns to room temperature. Transfer the scallops into a foil pan that is small enough to be placed inside the fryer.
4. Pre-heat the fryer at 400°F and put the rack

inside.
5. Place the foil pan on the rack and cook for five minutes.
6. In the meantime, melt the butter in a saucepan over a medium heat. Zest the lemon over the saucepan, then add in the chopped parsley. Mix well.
7. Take care when removing the pan from the fryer. Transfer the contents to a plate and drizzle with the lemon-butter mixture. Serve hot.

183. CHEESY LEMON HALIBUT

Preparation Time: 20 minutes
Servings: 2

Ingredients

- 1 lb. halibut fillet
- ½ cup butter
- 2 ½ tbsp. mayonnaise
- 2 ½ tbsp. lemon juice
- ¾ cup parmesan cheese, grated

Directions:

1. Pre-heat your fryer at 375°F.
2. Spritz the halibut fillets with cooking spray and season as desired.
3. Put the halibut in the fryer and cook for twelve minutes.
4. In the meantime, combine the butter, mayonnaise, and lemon juice in a bowl with a hand mixer. Ensure a creamy texture is achieved.
5. Stir in the grated parmesan.
6. When the halibut is ready, open the drawer and spread the butter over the fish with a butter knife. Allow to cook for a further two minutes, then serve hot.

184. SPICY MACKEREL

Preparation Time: 20 minutes
Servings: 2

Ingredients

- 2 mackerel fillets
- 2 tbsp. red chili flakes
- 2 tsp. garlic, minced
- 1 tsp. lemon juice

Directions:

1. Season the mackerel fillets with the red pepper flakes, minced garlic, and a drizzle of lemon juice. Allow to sit for five minutes.
2. Preheat your fryer at 350°F.
3. Cook the mackerel for five minutes, before opening the drawer, flipping the fillets, and allowing to cook on the other side for another five minutes.

4. Plate the fillets, making sure to spoon any remaining juice over them before serving.

185. THYME SCALLOPS

Preparation Time: 12 minutes
Servings: 1

Ingredients

- 1 lb. scallops
- Salt and pepper
- ½ tbsp. butter
- ½ cup thyme, chopped

Directions:

1. Wash the scallops and dry them completely. Season with pepper and salt, then set aside while you prepare the pan.
2. Grease a foil pan in several spots with the butter and cover the bottom with the thyme. Place the scallops on top.
3. Pre-heat the fryer at 400°F and set the rack inside.
4. Place the foil pan on the rack and allow to cook for seven minutes.
5. Take care when removing the pan from the fryer and transfer the scallops to a serving dish. Spoon any remaining butter in the pan over the fish and enjoy.

186. CRISPY CALAMARI

Preparation Time: 15 minutes
Servings: 4

Ingredients

- 1 lb. fresh squid
- Salt and pepper
- 2 cups keto almond flour
- 1 cup water
- 2 cloves garlic, minced
- ½ cup mayonnaise

Directions:

1. Remove the skin from the squid and discard any ink. Slice the squid into rings and season with some salt and pepper.
2. Put the keto almond flour and water in separate bowls. Dip the squid firstly in the flour, then into the water, then into the almond flour again, ensuring that it is entirely covered with flour.
3. Pre-heat the fryer at 400°F. Put the squid inside and cook for six minutes.
4. In the meantime, prepare the aioli by combining the garlic with the mayonnaise in a bowl.
5. Once the squid is ready, plate up and serve with the aioli.

187. FILIPINO BISTEK

Preparation Time: 10 minutes + marinating time
Servings: 4

Ingredients

- 2 milkfish bellies, deboned and sliced into 4 portions
- ¾ tsp. salt
- ¼ tsp. ground black pepper
- ¼ tsp. cumin powder
- 2 tbsp. calamansi juice
- 2 lemongrass, trimmed and cut crosswise into small pieces
- ½ cup tamari sauce
- 2 tbsp. fish sauce [Patis]
- 2 tbsp. stevia
- 1 tsp. garlic powder
- ½ cup chicken broth
- 2 tbsp. olive oil

Directions:

1. Dry the fish using some paper towels.
2. Put the fish in a large bowl and coat with the rest of the ingredients. Allow to marinate for 3 hours in the refrigerator.
3. Cook the fish steaks on an Air Fryer grill basket at 340°F for 5 minutes.
4. Turn the steaks over and allow to grill for an additional 4 minutes. Cook until medium brown.
5. Serve with steamed white rice.

188. SALTINE FISH FILLETS

Preparation Time: 15 minutes
Servings: 4

Ingredients

- 1 cup crushed saltines
- ¼ cup extra-virgin olive oil
- 1 tsp. garlic powder
- ½ tsp. shallot powder
- 1 egg, well whisked
- 4 white fish fillets
- Salt and ground black pepper to taste
- Fresh Italian parsley to serve

Directions:

1. In a shallow bowl, combine the crushed saltines and olive oil.
2. In a separate bowl, mix together the garlic powder, shallot powder, and the beaten egg.
3. Sprinkle a good amount of salt and pepper over the fish, before dipping each fillet into the egg mixture.
4. Coat the fillets with the crumb mixture.

5. Air fry the fish at 370°F for 10 - 12 minutes.
6. Serve with fresh parsley.

189. COD NUGGETS

Preparation Time: 25 minutes
Servings: 4

Ingredients

- 1 lb. cod fillet, cut into chunks
- 1 tbsp. olive oil
- 1 cup cracker crumbs
- 1 tbsp. egg and water
- ½ cup keto almond flour
- Salt and pepper

Directions:

1. Place the cracker crumbs and oil in food processor and pulse together. Sprinkle the cod pieces with salt and pepper.
2. Roll the cod pieces in the flour before dredging them in egg and coating them in the cracker crumbs.
3. Pre-heat the Air Fryer to 350°F.
4. Put the fish in the basket and air fry to 350°F for 15 minutes or until a light golden-brown color is achieved.
5. Serve hot.

190. SWEET POTATOES & SALMON

Preparation Time: 45 minutes
Servings: 4

Ingredients

For the Salmon Fillets:

- 4 x 6-oz. skin-on salmon fillets
- 1 tbsp. extra-virgin olive oil
- 1 tsp. celery salt
- ¼ tsp. ground black pepper, or more to taste
- 2 tbsp. capers
- Pinch of dry mustard
- Pinch of ground mace
- 1 tsp. smoked cayenne pepper

For the Potatoes:

- 4 sweet potatoes, peeled and cut into wedges
- 1 tbsp. sesame oil
- Kosher salt and pepper, to taste

Directions:

1. Coat all sides of the salmon filets with a brushing of oil. Cover with all the seasonings for the fillets.
2. Air-fry at 360°F for 5 minutes, flip them over, and proceed to cook for 5 more minutes.
3. In the meantime, coat the sweet potatoes with the sesame oil, salt, and pepper.
4. Cook the potatoes at 380°F for 15 minutes.
5. Turn the potatoes over and cook for another

15 - 20 minutes.
6. Serve the potatoes and salmon together.

191. GRILLED SHRIMP

Preparation Time: 35 minutes
Servings: 4

Ingredients

- 18 shrimps, shelled and deveined
- 2 tbsp. freshly squeezed lemon juice
- ½ tsp. hot paprika
- ½ tsp. salt
- 1 tsp. lemon-pepper seasoning
- 2 tbsp. extra-virgin olive oil
- 2 garlic cloves, peeled and minced
- 1 tsp. onion powder
- ¼ tsp. cumin powder
- ½ cup fresh parsley, coarsely chopped

Directions:

1. Put all the ingredients in a bowl, making sure to coat the shrimp well. Refrigerate for 30 minutes.
2. Pre-heat the Air Fryer at 400°F
3. Air-fry the shrimp for 5 minutes, ensuring that the shrimps turn pink.
4. Serve with pasta or rice.

192. HOMEMADE COD FILLETS

Preparation Time: 15 minutes
Servings: 4

Ingredients

- 4 cod fillets
- ¼ tsp. fine sea salt
- ¼ tsp. ground black pepper, or more to taste
- 1 tsp. cayenne pepper
- ½ cup non-dairy milk
- ½ cup fresh Italian parsley, coarsely chopped
- 1 tsp. dried basil
- ½ tsp. dried oregano
- 1 Italian pepper, chopped
- 4 garlic cloves, minced

1. **Directions:**
2. Lightly grease a baking dish with some vegetable oil.
3. Coat the cod fillets with salt, pepper, and cayenne pepper.
4. Blend the rest of the ingredients in a food processor. Cover the fish fillets in this mixture.
5. Transfer the fillets to the Air Fryer and cook at 380°F for 10 to 12 minutes, ensure the cod is flaky before serving.

193. CHRISTMAS FLOUNDER

Preparation Time: 15 minutes + marinating time
Servings: 4

Ingredients

- 4 flounder fillets
- Sea salt and freshly cracked mixed peppercorns, to taste
- 1 ½ tbsp. dark sesame oil
- 2 tbsp. sake
- ¼ cup soy sauce
- 1 tbsp. grated lemon rind
- 2 garlic cloves, minced
- 1 tsp. stevia
- Fresh chopped chives, to serve

Directions:

1. Put all of the ingredients, except for the chives, in a large bowl. Coat the fillets well with the seasoning.
2. Refrigerate for 2 hours to let it marinate.
3. Place the fish fillets in the Air Fryer cooking basket and cook at 360°F for 10 to 12 minutes, turning once during the cooking time.
4. Simmer the rest of the marinade over a medium-to-low heat, stirring constantly, allowing it to thicken.
5. Plate up the flounder and add the glaze on top. Serve with fresh chives.

194. COCONUT PRAWNS

Preparation Time: 10 minutes
Servings: 4

Ingredients

- 12 prawns, cleaned and deveined
- Salt and ground black pepper, to taste
- ½ tsp. cumin powder
- 1 tsp. fresh lemon juice
- 1 medium egg, whisked
- ⅓ cup of beer
- ½ cup keto almond flour
- 1 tsp. baking powder
- 1 tbsp. curry powder
- ½ tsp. grated fresh ginger
- 1 cup flaked coconut

Directions:

1. Coat the prawns in the salt, pepper, cumin powder, and lemon juice.
2. In a bowl, combine together the whisked egg, beer, a quarter-cup of the flour, baking powder, curry, and ginger.
3. In a second bowl, put the remaining quarter-cup of flour, and in a third bowl, the flaked coconut.

4. Dredge the prawns in the flour, before coating them in the beer mixture. Finally, coat your prawns in the flaked coconut.
5. Air-fry at 360°F for 5 minutes. Flip them and allow to cook on the other side for another 2 to 3 minutes before serving.

195. GRILLED SALMON-MEDITERRANEAN WAY

Servings: 4
Preparation time: 10 minutes
Cookingtime: 8 minutes

Ingredients:

- 4 salmon fillets, each about 5 ounces
- 4 green olives, thinly
- 1 tablespoon finely chopped garlic
- ½ teaspoon ground black pepper
- 4 tablespoons freshly chopped basil
- 1 tablespoon freshly chopped parsley
- extra virgin olive oil, as needed
- 4 thin slices of lemon
- 2 tablespoons of lemon juice

Directions:

1. Switch on the broiler, arrange cooking rack 4-inch away from heat source and let it preheat over high heat.
2. Meanwhile, combine together garlic, basil, parsley and lemon juice until well mixed.
3. Brush salmon fillets with olive oil on each side, sprinkle with black pepper, then top evenly with prepared herb and garlic mixture and place under the broiler.
4. Cook for 3 to 4 minutes, then flip each fillets and place them on an aluminum foil and continue with cooking at medium-low heat for about 4 minutes or until meat thermometer inserted into thickest part of fish reaches 145 degrees F.
5. When cooked, transfer salmon to a serving plate and garnish with sliced olives and fresh lemon slices.

196. FRESH TUNA SALAD – MEDITERRANEAN STYLE

Servings: 1
Preparation time: 10 minutes
Cookingtime: 15 minutes

Ingredients:

- 12 ounce cooked tuna, cut into medium chunks
- 1 pound baby potatoes
- ½ cup pimiento-stuffed green olives
- 1 pound green beans, stem ends removed

- 1 teaspoon sugar
- ½ teaspoon ground black pepper
- 1 tablespoon brown mustard
- 1 tablespoon fresh lemon juice
- 3 tablespoons olive oil
- Lemon wedges for garnishing
- Freshly chopped parsley for serving

Directions:
1. In a large pot place in potatoes and cover them with water. Bring to a boil over medium-high heat.
2. Then switch heat from medium to lower level and simmer for another 5 minutes, covering the pot.
3. Add green beans to the pot and simmer for another 5 minutes or until beans and potatoes are quite tender. Optionally you can cover the pot.
4. While that's cooking, place stuffed olives in a blender and add in sugar, pepper, mustard and fresh lemon juice and pulse for 1 to 2 minutes or until smooth mixture forms.
5. Drain potatoes and beans and divide them evenly among four serving dishes.
6. Add in chunks of tuna and top with prepared olives blend.
7. Garnish with parsley and lemon wedges.

Nutrition Values: Calories: 328; Total Fat: 15g; Protein: 20g; Carbs: 3 1g; Fiber: 8g; Sugar: 7g

197. SALMON WITH LEMON AND LIMA BEANS

Servings: 4
Preparation time: 15 minutes
Cookingtime: 20 minutes

Ingredients:
- 4 skinless salmon fillet, each about 5-ounce
- 1 pound frozen lima beans
- 1 ½ teaspoon thinly chopped garlic
- 1 teaspoon salt
- 1/2 teaspoon ground black pepper
- 1/8 teaspoon red pepper flakes
- 3/4 teaspoon dried oregano
- 3/4 teaspoon paprika
- 2 teaspoons olive oil
- 1 lemon, halved
- 1/2 cup of Greek yogurt
- 2 tablespoons chopped parsley
- 1 1/2cups water

Directions:

1. Switch on and preheat the broiler.
2. Cut 1 lemon half into four thinly pieces and set aside.
3. Zest the other half of lemon and set aside, then squeeze its juice in a bowl, add yogurt and 1/4teaspoon paprika and whisk until well incorporated.
4. Place a saucepan over medium heat, and add in 1 teaspoon oil, heat well and add in garlic, red pepper flakes and oregano.
5. Cook for about 2 minutes or until garlic is nicely golden brown and softened, then add lima beans, lemon zest and water.
6. Simmer for 20 minutes, whisking and covering the pan occasionally.
7. Meanwhile, stir together remaining paprika, 1/2 teaspoon salt, black pepper in a bowl and apply this mixture all over salmon fillet.
8. Place well seasoned salmon on a baking sheet, lined with aluminum foil or baking paper, and top each fillet with a lemon slices.
9. Place the baking sheet near the broiler and cook for about 8 minutes or until cooked.
10. 1Season beans with 1 teaspoon salt and ½ teaspoon ground black pepper and then remove the pan from heat and stir in parsley, remaining oil and 1 teaspoon of yogurt mixture.
11. 1Serve cooked salmon in serving plates and garnish each with lime beans and prepared yogurt mixture.

1Nutrition Values: Calories: 340; Total Fat: 8g; Protein: 40g; Carbs: 25g; Fiber: 7g; Sugar: 2g

198. BAKED SALMON WITH WARM TOMATO SALAD

Servings: 4
Preparation time: 10 minutes
Cookingtime: 6 minutes

Ingredients:
- 4 salmon fillets, each about 4 ounces and 1 1/4 inches thick
- 2 medium tomatoes, cut into 1-inch chinks
- 1 cup sliced celery
- 1/2 cup roughly diced pitted kalamata olives
- 1/4 cup diced fresh mint
- ½ teaspoon minced garlic
- 1 teaspoon salt
- 1/4 teaspoon red pepper flakes
- 1 tablespoon honey
- 5 tablespoons olive oil and more for brushing
- 1 tablespoon and 1 teaspoon apple cider

vinegar

Directions:

1. Preheat the broiler.
2. In a bowl combine together: salt, red pepper flakes, honey, 1 teaspoon vinegar and 2 tablespoons olive oil. Mix all the Ingredients: until well blended and combined.
3. Brush this mixture on all sides of fish fillets.
4. Take a baking pan, line with aluminum foil, brush with olive oil and place fillets on it with skin - side down.
5. Place the pan under the preheated broiler and cook for 4 to 6 minutes or until golden brown and cooked through.
6. Meanwhile, in a bowl mix well garlic and ½ teaspoon salt.
7. Put a small saucepan over medium-high heat, and add in remaining olive oil , alongside with olives, garlic mixture, and 1 tablespoon of apple cider vinegar and cook for 3 minutes or until bubbles come in .
8. To make the salad, transfer the mixture to a bowl, and add in celery, tomato and mint, season with remaining salt and mix well until combine.
9. When salmon is ready, serve it with tomato salad.

199. MUSSELS WITH POTATOES AND OLIVES

Servings: 4
Preparation time: 5 minutes
Cookingtime: 25 minutes

Ingredients:

- 2 1/4 pounds mussels, scrubbed
- 2 large potatoes, peeled
- 14.5-ounce roughly diced tomatoes
- 2/3 cup halved pitted green olives
- 1 medium white onion, thinly sliced
- 2 teaspoons minced garlic
- 1 ½ teaspoon salt
- 1/8 teaspoon cayenne pepper
- 1/2 teaspoon paprika
- 1/8 teaspoon allspice
- 1/2 cup chopped fresh parsley
- 2 tablespoons olive oil
- 1 cup water

Directions:

1. In a heatproof bowl cut already cut peeled potatoes into 1 –inch cubes and cover them with water by lA inch and cover the bowl with plastic wrap.

2. Place this bowl into the microwave oven and microwave at high heat for 6 minutes
3. Meanwhile, place a large pot over medium-high heat, and preheat the oil, when hot, add in thinly sliced onion and minced garlic and cook for 6 minutes or until golden brown and soften.
4. Drain potatoes, add to the pot with onion and garlic mixture, season with salt, cayenne pepper, paprika, allspice, and stir until potatoes are well coated with spices and oil.
5. Cook for additional 2 to 3 minutes, then add in water, tomato and stir well to remove browned spots from the bottom of the pot.
6. Bring the whole mixture to simmer and cook for 10 minutes more, covering the pot.
7. Add in scrubbed mussels, halved olives, and parsley and continue cooking for the final 5 minutes, covering the pot.
8. Serve immediately in a nice plate.

200. SALMON WITH HERB AND MUSTARD GLAZE

Servings: 6
Preparation time: 10 minutes
Cookingtime: 7 minutes

Ingredients:

- 6 salmon fillets, each about 8 ounce
- 1 teaspoon minced garlic
- 1 ½ teaspoon salt
- 3/4 teaspoon ground black pepper
- 3/4 teaspoon chopped rosemary leaves 3/4 teaspoon chopped thyme leaves
- 1 tablespoon olive oil
- 1 tablespoon dry white wine
- 2tablespoons Dijon mustard
- 2 tablespoons whole-grain mustard
- 6 wedges of lemon

Directions:

1. Preheat the broiler.
2. 2.In a food processor place in garlic, rosemary, thyme, oil, wine, Dijon mustard and 1 tablespoon whole-grain mustard and pulse for 30 seconds until well incorporated.
3. Transfer the mixture in a bowl and add remaining 1 tablespoon of whole-grain mustard and mix until combined, set aside until required.
4. Place salmon fillets on a baking sheet skin-side down and season with salt and black pepper and broil for about 2 minutes.
5. Then top fillets with prepared mustard glaze and broil for additional 5 minutes or until

completely cooked through and golden brown.

6. When they will be done, transfer fillets to serving plates and garnish with lemon wedges.

201. GREEK FARRO AND SHRIMP DISH

Servings: 2
Preparation time: 10 minutes
Cookingtime: 15 minutes

Ingredients:

- 16 shrimps, peeled and deveined
- 4-ounce farro, uncooked
- 1 medium Persian cucumber, sliced
- 1 medium shallot, peeled and quartered
- 1 Roma tomato, diced into small chunks
- 2 tablespoons fresh parsley leaves
- 2 ¼teaspoons salt
- 1 teaspoon ground black pepper
- 1 teaspoon chopped fresh oregano leaves
- 2 teaspoons red wine vinegar
- 3 tablespoons olive oil and more for cooking
- ½of lemon, juiced
- 3.5-ounce crumbled feta cheese
- 2 cups water

Directions:

1. In a small saucepan, pour in water, add ¾teaspoon of salt and bring to boil over high heat .
2. Add in farro and cook for about 15 minutes or until completely cooked, covering the pan.
3. Meanwhile, place sliced cucumber in a bowl, add in shallots, tomato, mint, crumbled cheese, oil, vinegar, remaining ½ teaspoon salt and ½ teaspoon black pepper, combine until well mixed and set aside.
4. Drain cooked farro and set aside.
5. In a large bowl combine together: 1 teaspoon salt, ½teaspoon black pepper and lemon juice, add in oregano and shrimps and toss until evenly coated on all sides.
6. Preheat a large skillet with oil over medium-high heat and add shrimps in a single layer and cook for 2 minutes each side.
7. To assemble, divide cooked faro between two serving bowls, add prepared cucumber salad and then top each bowl with shrimps.
8. Serve immediately, when warm.

202. MEDITERRANEAN PENNE PASTA WITH HERB SHRIMP

Servings: 6
Preparation time: 10 minutes
Cookingtime: 10 minutes

Ingredients:

- 1 cup half-and-half
- 4 ounces cream cheese, cubed
- ¼teaspoon salt
- 1 teaspoon Italian seasoning
- 2 teaspoons roasted garlic & bell pepper seasoning
- 1 pound large shrimp, peeled and deveined
- 2 cups frozen small broccoli florets
- 8 ounces penne pasta, cooked 1/4 cup freshly grated parmesan cheese

Directions:

1. In a large saucepan place in half-and-half and place it over medium to high heat and bring it to simmer.
2. When it comes to simmer, reduce the heat to medium-low level and add in cream cheese, salts, and all seasonings. Stir well until all cream cheese melts completely in the mixture.
3. Add in shrimps, broccoli florets and penne pasta to the sauce and combine until well coated with sauce and sprinkle with parmesan cheese.
4. Serve warm and immediately.

203. ROASTED SALMON FILLETS WITH HERBS

Servings: 4
Preparation time: 10 minutes
Cookingtime: 18 minutes

Ingredients:

- 4 salmon fillets, each about 6-ounce
- 2 teaspoons minced garlic
- ¾teaspoon salt
- ½teaspoon ground black pepper
- 1 teaspoon dried rosemary
- ½teaspoon dried thyme
- 1 tablespoon olive oil

Directions:

1. Preheat the oven at 425 degrees F.
2. Take a 15x10x1-inch baking pan, grease well with olive oil and place in salmon fillets, skin-side down.
3. Stir together remaining Ingredients: and rub this mixture over the salmon fillets.
4. Place the fillets into the oven and cook for 15 to 18 minutes or until baked.
5. Serve immediately in a serving plate.

204. GREEK STYLED TACOS WITH FISH

Servings: 8

Preparation time: 10 minutes
Cookingtime: 12 minutes

Ingredients:

- 1 pound cod
- 2 cups shredded green cabbage
- 1 cup grape tomatoes, sliced into small pieces
- 1 cup kalamata olives, halved
- 1 medium cucumber, seeded and diced in small chunks
- 1 teaspoon salt
- ½ teaspoon ground black pepper
- ½cup crumbled feta cheese
- 1 tablespoon olive oil
- 8 small corn tortillas
- Tzatziki sauce for topping
- Lemon wedges for serving

Directions:

1. Season cod fish with salt and black pepper on all sides.
2. Preheat a large skillet pan with oil over medium-high heat, and add in seasoned cod.
3. Cook it for 3 to 4 minutes per each side or until completely cooked through.
4. When cooking process is done, transfer cod to a plate and flake it with a help of two forks.
5. To assemble Greek styled tacos, layer tortillas with cabbage, flaked cod, olives, tomatoes, and cucumbers,
6. 6.Top each tortilla with feta cheese and drizzle with Tzatziki sauce.
7. Serve each taco with lemon wedges.

205. SALSA VERDE CHICKEN

Preparation Time: 5 minutes
Cooking Time: minutes
Servings: 6

Ingredients:

- 6 chicken breasts, skin and bones removed
- 2 cups salsa Verde
- 1 bottle of beer
- 2 teaspoons cumin
- 1 jalapeno, chopped
- Salt and pepper to taste
- 1 tsp oil

Directions:

1. Place a heavy bottomed pot on medium high fire and heat for 2 minutes. Add oil and swirl to coat bottom and sides of pot and heat for a minute.
2. Brown chicken breasts for 4 minutes per side. Transfer to a chopping board and chop into bite-sized pieces.
3. In same pot, add remaining ingredients and chicken. Cover and simmer for 30 minutes. Stirring bottom of pot every now and then. Adjust seasoning to taste.
4. Serve and enjoy.

Nutrition Values:

Calories: 557; Fat: 27.6g; Carbs: 7.5g; Protein: 61.1g

206. ROSEMARY GRILLED CHICKEN

Preparation Time: minutes
Cooking Time: 12 minutes
Servings: 4

Ingredients:

- 1 tablespoon fresh parsley, finely chopped
- 1 tablespoon fresh rosemary, finely chopped
- 1 tablespoon olive oil
- 4 pieces of 4-oz chicken breast, boneless and skinless
- 5 cloves garlic, minced
- Pepper and salt to taste

Directions:

1. In a shallow and large bowl mix salt, parsley, rosemary, olive oil and garlic. Place chicken breast and marinate in bowl of herbs for at least an hour or more before grilling.
2. Grease grill grate and preheat grill to medium high. Once hot, grill chicken for 4 to 5 minutes per side or until juices run clear and internal temperature of chicken is 168oF.

Nutrition Values:

Calories: 218; Fat: 8.0g; Carbs: 1.0g; Protein: 34.0g

207. TURKEY WITH BLUEBERRY PAN SAUCE

Preparation Time: 15 minutes
Cooking Time: 35 minutes
Servings: 4

Ingredients:

- 3 tbsp balsamic vinegar
- 2 cups blueberries
- 1 tbsp fresh thyme, chopped
- ¼ cup shallots, chopped
- 1 lb. turkey tenderloin
- ½ tsp ground pepper
- ¾ tsp salt, divided
- ¼ cup all-purpose flour
- 1 tbsp extra virgin olive oil

Directions:

1. In a shallow dish, mix ½ tsp salt, flour and pepper. Dredge the turkey in this mixture and discard the leftover flour.
2. In an ovenproof skillet, heat oil and add the turkey. Cook for three to five minutes on each side or until golden brown.
3. Turn off the heat and transfer the skillet with the turkey in the oven. Roast it in 450 o Fahrenheit preheated oven for 15 minutes or until the turkey is cooked through. Remove the turkey.
4. In the same skillet, sauté the shallots and thyme for thirty seconds.
5. Add the blueberries, ¼ tsp salt and vinegar and cook for 4 to 5 minutes.
6. Plate the turkey slices with the blueberry sauce.
7. Serve warm.

Nutrition Values:

Calories: 230; Fat: 4.0g; Carbs: 20.0g; Protein: 29.0g

208. CHICKEN, CHARRED TOMATO AND BROCCOLI SALAD

Preparation Time: 15 minutes
Cooking Time: 30 minutes
Servings: 6

Ingredients:

- ¼ cup lemon juice
- ½ tsp chili powder
- 1 ½ lbs. boneless chicken breast

- 1 ½ lbs. medium tomato
- 4 cups broccoli florets
- 5 tbsp extra virgin olive oil, divided to 2 and 3 tablespoons
- 1 tsp freshly ground pepper
- 1 tsp salt

Directions:

1. Place the chicken in a skillet and add just enough water to cover the chicken. Bring to a simmer over high heat. Reduce the heat once the liquid boils and cook the chicken thoroughly for 12 minutes. Once cooked, shred the chicken into bite-sized pieces.
2. On a large pot, bring water to a boil and add the broccoli. Cook for 5 minutes until slightly tender. Drain and rinse the broccoli with cold water. Set aside.
3. Core the tomatoes and cut them crosswise. Discard the seeds and set the tomatoes cut side down on paper towels. Pat them dry.
4. In a heavy skillet, heat the pan over high heat until very hot. Brush the cut sides of the tomatoes with olive oil and place them on the pan. Cook the tomatoes until the sides are charred. Set aside.
5. In the same pan, heat the remaining 3 tablespoon olive oil over medium heat. Stir the salt, chili powder and pepper and stir for 45 seconds. Pour over the lemon juice and remove the pan from the heat.
6. Plate the broccoli, shredded chicken and chili powder mixture dressing.

Nutrition Values:
Calories: 277; Fat: 9.0g; Carbs: 6.0g; Protein: 28.0g

209. CHICKEN JAMBALAYA
Preparation Time: 20 minutes
Cooking Time: 30 minutes
Servings: 6

Ingredients:

- ½ cup celery
- 3 chicken breast halves, skinless and boneless, chopped to bite sized pieces
- 3 tbsp garlic, minced
- 3 whole tomatoes, chopped
- 1 tbsp Cajun seasoning
- 3 cups water
- 1 tbsp olive oil
- 1 tsp salt
- 1 tsp pepper or to taste

Directions:

1. Place a pot on high fire and heat oil for 2 minutes.
2. Add chicken and garlic. Sauté for 5 minutes.
3. Add tomatoes, Cajun seasoning, salt, and pepper. Sauté for another 5 minutes.
4. Add water and simmer chicken for 10 minutes.
5. Stir in celery and continue cooking for another 5 minutes.
6. Adjust seasoning if needed.
7. Serve and enjoy.

Nutrition Values:
Calories: 419; Fat: 10.0g; Carbs: 47.0g; Protein: 35.0g

210. HERBS AND LEMONY ROASTED CHICKEN
Preparation Time: 20 minutes
Cooking Time: 90 minutes
Servings: 8

Ingredients:

- 1 3-lb whole chicken
- 1 tbsp garlic powder
- 2 lemons
- 2 tsp Italian seasoning
- 1 tsp ground black pepper
- 1 tsp salt

Directions:

1. In small bowl, mix well black pepper, garlic powder, mustard powder, and salt.
2. Rinse chicken well and slice off giblets.
3. In a greased 9 x 13 baking dish, place chicken and add 1 ½ tsp of seasoning made earlier inside the chicken and rub the remaining seasoning around chicken.
4. Drizzle lemon juice all over chicken.
5. Bake chicken in a preheated 350oF oven until juices run clear, around 1 ½ hours. Occasionally, baste chicken with its juices.

Nutrition Values:
Calories: 190; Fat: 9.0g; Carbs: 2.0g; Protein: 35.0g

211. BAKED CHICKEN PESTO
Preparation Time: minutes
Cooking Time: minutes
Servings: 4

Ingredients:

- 2 tsp grated parmesan cheese
- 6 tbsp shredded reduced fat mozzarella cheese
- 1 medium tomato (thinly sliced
- 4 tsp basil pesto
- 2 boneless, skinless chicken breasts around 1-lb
- Salt and pepper to taste

Directions:

1. In cool water, wash chicken and dry using a paper towel. Create 4 thin slices of chicken breasts by slicing horizontally.
2. Preheat oven to 400 o Fahrenheit and then line a baking sheet with parchment or foil.
3. Put into the baking sheet the slices of chicken. Season with pepper and salt. And spread at least 1 teaspoon of pesto on each chicken slice.
4. For 15 minutes, bake the chicken and ensure that the center is no longer pink. After which remove baking sheet and top chicken with parmesan cheese, mozzarella, and tomatoes.
5. Put into oven once again and heat for another 3 to 5 minutes to melt the cheese, then ready to serve.

Nutrition Values:
Calories: 238; Fat: 8.0g; Carbs: 2.0g; Protein: 40.0g

212. CHICKEN PENNE PESTO

Preparation Time: 15 minutes
Cooking Time: 35 minutes
Servings: 8

Ingredients:

- 3 tbsp grated Parmesan cheese
- ¼ cup pesto
- 1 ¼ cups heavy cream
- 4 skinless, boneless chicken breast halves, cut into thin strips
- 1 16-oz package penne pasta
- Pepper to taste
- 1/8 tsp salt
- 2 tbsp olive oil

Directions:

1. Cook penne according to manufacturer's instructions.
2. While penne is cooking, on medium fire place a large saucepan and melt butter.
3. Add garlic and chicken, sauté for 7 minutes or until chicken strips are nearly cooked.
4. Lower fire and add Parmesan cheese, pesto, cream, pepper and salt.
5. Continue cooking for 5-10 minutes more or until chicken is fully cooked. Stir frequently.
6. Once penne is cooked, drain well and pour into large saucepan, toss to coat and serve.

Nutrition Values:
Calories: 214; Fat: 22.0g; Carbs: 18.0g; Protein: 30.0g

213. HEART HEALTHY CHICKEN SALAD

Preparation Time: 30 minutes
Cooking Time: 45 minutes
Servings: 4

Ingredients:

- 3 tbsp mayonnaise, low-fat
- ½ tsp onion powder
- 1 tbsp lemon juice
- ¼ cup celery (chopped
- 3 ¼ cups chicken breast (cooked, cubed, and skinless
- Salt and pepper to taste

Directions:

1. Bake chicken breasts for 45 minutes at 350oF. Let it cool and cut them into cubes and place them in the refrigerator.
2. Combine all other ingredients in a large bowl then add the chilled chicken.
3. Mix well and ready to serve.
4. Enjoy!

Nutrition Values:
Calories: 408; Fat: 22.0g; Carbs: 1.0g; Protein: 50.0g

214. GINGER, CHICKEN, AND SPINACH STIR FRY

Preparation Time: 5 minutes
Cooking Time: 10 minutes
Servings: 4

Ingredients:

- 2 cloves of garlic, minced
- 1 tablespoon fresh ginger, grated
- 1 ¼ pounds boneless chicken breasts, cut into strips
- 2 tablespoons yellow miso, diluted in water
- 2 cups baby spinach
- 2 tablespoons olive oil
- Pepper and salt to taste

Directions:

1. Heat oil in a skillet over medium-high heat and sauté the garlic for 30 seconds until fragrant.
2. Stir in the ginger and chicken breasts. Season lightly with pepper and salt.
3. Cook for 5 minutes while stirring constantly.
4. Stir in the diluted miso paste.
5. Continue cooking for 3 more minutes before adding spinach.
6. Cook for another minute or until the spinach leaves have wilted.

Nutrition Values:
Calories: 237; Fat: 10.5g; Carbs: 1.3g; Protein: 32.5g

215. CHICKEN AND MUSHROOMS

Preparation Time: 5 minutes
Cooking Time: 15 minutes
Servings: 8

Ingredients:

- 1 large shallot, diced
- 8 chicken breasts, cubed
- 4 large cremini mushrooms, sliced
- ¼ cup yogurt
- 1 tablespoons olive oil
- ½ cup water
- Salt and pepper to taste

Directions:

1. Heat oil in a skillet over medium flame and sauté the shallot until fragrant.
2. Stir in the chicken breasts and continue cooking for 3 minutes while stirring constantly.
3. Add the mushrooms, water, and yogurt.
4. Season with salt and pepper to taste.
5. Close the lid and bring to a boil.
6. Reduce the heat to medium-low and allow simmering for 10 minutes.

Nutrition Values:
Calories: 312; Fat: 7.7g; Carbs: 1.5g; Protein: 55.8g

216. OVEN-BAKED SKILLET LEMON CHICKEN

Preparation Time: 10 minutes
Cooking Time: 60 minutes
Servings: 4

Ingredients:

- 6 small chicken thighs
- 1 medium onion
- 1 lemon
- ¼ cup lemon juice, freshly squeezed
- Salt and pepper to taste

Directions:

1. Place all ingredients in a Ziploc bag and allow to marinate for at least 6 hours in the fridge.
2. Preheat the oven to 3500F.
3. Place the chicken–sauce and all–into a skillet.
4. Put the skillet in the oven and bake for 1 hour or until the chicken is tender.

Nutrition Values:
Calories: 661; Fat: 42.4g; Carbs: 6.2g; Protein: 48.2g

217. CHICKEN BARLEY SOUP

Preparation Time: 15 minutes
Cooking Time: 95 minutes
Servings: 8

Ingredients:

- 2 pounds chicken breasts, boneless
- 1 ½ cups chopped carrots
- 1 onion, chopped
- ¾ cup pearl barley

- 3 bay leaves
- 8 cups water
- 1 teaspoon salt
- ¼ teaspoon ground black pepper
- 2 tablespoons lemon juice (optional

Directions:

1. Put water and chicken thighs in a pot and bring to a boil for 15 minutes to make the chicken stock.
2. Take the chicken out and shred. Set aside.
3. To the pot, Add the carrots, onions, pearl barley, and bay leaves.
4. Season with salt and pepper to taste.
5. Close the lid and allow to boil for another 15 minutes.
6. Turn the heat to low and cook for 60 minutes or until the barley is soft.
7. Add the shredded chicken and cook for 5 more minutes.
8. Stir in lemon juice before serving, if using.

Nutrition Values:
Calories: 352; Fat: 15.4g; Carbs: 25.0g; Protein: 27.5g

218. BARBECUED CHIPOTLE CHICKEN

Preparation Time: 10 minutes
Cooking Time: 15 minutes
Servings: 4

Ingredients:

- 2 tablespoons minced garlic
- 1-pound boneless chicken breasts
- 1/3 cup apple cider vinegar
- 2 tablespoons chipotle sauce
- 2 tablespoons mustard
- Salt and pepper to taste

Directions:

1. Place all ingredients in a bowl and allow to marinate for at least overnight inside the fridge.
2. Heat the grill to medium and cook the chicken for at least 7 minutes on each side.
3. Serve and enjoy.

Nutrition Values:
Calories: 341; Fat: 24.5g; Carbs: 8.4g; Protein: 21.7g

219. TENDER TURKEY BREAST

Preparation Time: 10 minutes
Cooking Time: 25 minutes
Servings: 12

Ingredients:

- 4 peeled garlic cloves
- 4 fresh rosemary sprigs
- 1 bone-in turkey breast (7-pounds

- ¼ teaspoon salt
- ½ cup water
- ½ teaspoon coarsely ground pepper

Directions:
1. Add all ingredients in a pot on high fire and bring to a boil.
2. Once boiling, lower fire to a simmer and cook for 20 minutes.
3. Adjust seasoning to taste.
4. Serve and enjoy.

Nutrition Values:
Calories: 179; Fat: 2.7g; Carbs: 0.8g; Protein: 35.8g

220. CHICKEN CHIPOTLE
Preparation Time: 10 minutes
Cooking Time: 25 minutes
Servings: 8

Ingredients:
- 4 tablespoons McCormick grill mates' chipotle
- Roasted garlic seasoning
- 8 garlic cloves peeled and crushed
- 5-pounds whole chicken
- ½ cup water

Directions:
1. Add all ingredients in a pot on high fire and bring to a boil.
2. Once boiling, lower fire to a simmer and cook for 25 minutes.
3. Adjust seasoning to taste.
4. Serve and enjoy.

Nutrition Values:
Calories: 613; Fat: 42.5g; Carbs: 5.7g; Protein: 52.0g

221. BROCCOLI CHICKEN STEW
Preparation Time: 5 minutes
Cooking Time: 30 minutes
Servings: 4

Ingredients:
- 1 package frozen chopped broccoli (10-ounces
- 1 cup shredded sharp cheddar cheese
- ½ cup sour cream
- 1 can Campbell's broccoli cheese soup
- 4 boneless skinless chicken breasts, thawed
- ½ cup water
- 1 cup water

Directions:
1. Add all ingredients, except for broccoli in a pot on high fire and bring to a boil.
2. Once boiling, lower fire to a simmer and cook for 20 minutes, stirring frequently.

3. Adjust seasoning to taste. Add broccoli and continue cooking and stirring for another 5 minutes.
4. Serve and enjoy.

Nutrition Values:
Calories: 511; Fat: 22.1g; Carbs: 11.7g; Protein: 63.9g

222. CHICKEN COUNTRY STYLE
Preparation Time: 5 minutes
Cooking Time: minutes
Servings: 4

Ingredients:
- 1 packet dry Lipton's onion soup mix
- 1 can (14.5-ounceCampbell's chicken gravy
- 4 skinless and boneless chicken breasts
- 1/3 teaspoon pepper
- 1 cup water

Directions:
1. Add all ingredients in a pot on high fire and bring to a boil.
2. Once boiling, lower fire to a simmer and cook for 25 minutes.
3. Adjust seasoning to taste.
4. Serve and enjoy.

Nutrition Values:
Calories: 366; Fat: 11.9g; Carbs: 6.8g; Protein: 53.7g

223. STEWED CHICKEN SALSA
Preparation Time: 10 minutes
Cooking Time: 25 minutes
Servings: 4

Ingredients:
- 1 cup shredded cheddar cheese
- 8-ounces cream cheese
- 16-ounces salsa
- 4 skinless and boneless thawed chicken breasts
- 1 can corn
- 1 cup water

Directions:
1. Add all ingredients in a pot, except for sour cream, on high fire and bring to a boil.
2. Once boiling, lower fire to a simmer and cook for 20 minutes.
3. Adjust seasoning to taste and stir in sour cream.
4. Serve and enjoy.

Nutrition Values:
Calories: 658; Fat: 32.6g; Carbs: 31.8g; Protein: 67.8g

224. GREEK CHICKEN STEW
Preparation Time: 5 minutes
Cooking Time: 30 minutes

Servings: 4

Ingredients:

- ¼ cup feta cheese
- Sliced and pitted Kalamata olives
- 1 bottle (16-ounceken's steak house Greek dressing with Feta cheese, olive oil, and black olives
- 4 boneless and skinless thawed chicken breasts
- 1 cup water

Directions:

1. Add all ingredients in a pot, except for feta, on high fire and bring to a boil.
2. Once boiling, lower fire to a simmer and cook for 25 minutes.
3. Adjust seasoning to taste and stir in feta.
4. Serve and enjoy.

Nutrition Values:

Calories: 818; Fat: 65.1g; Carbs: 3.2g; Protein: 54.4g

225. YUMMY CHICKEN QUESO

Preparation Time: 5 minutes
Cooking Time: 25 minutes
Servings: 4

Ingredients:

- ½ teaspoon garlic salt
- 4-ounce can diced drained green chiles
- 10-ounce can mild rotel drained
- ¾ cup medium queso dip
- 4 boneless skinless boneless fresh or thawed chicken breasts
- 1 cup water

Directions:

1. Add all ingredients in a pot on high fire and bring to a boil.
2. Once boiling, lower fire to a simmer and cook for 20 minutes. Stir frequently.
3. Adjust seasoning to taste.
4. Serve and enjoy.

Nutrition Values:

Calories: 407; Fat: 11.7g; Carbs: 17.2g; Protein: 56.6g

226. STEWED ITALIAN CHICKEN

Preparation Time: 5 minutes
Cooking Time: 25 minutes
Servings: 4

Ingredients:

- 1 (16-ouncebottle wish-bone Italian dressing
- 4 boneless skinless chicken breasts thawed
- ½ cup water
- Salt and pepper to taste

Directions:

1. Add all ingredients in a pot on high fire and bring to a boil.
2. Once boiling, lower fire to a simmer and cook for 20 minutes.
3. Adjust seasoning to taste.
4. Serve and enjoy.

Nutrition Values:

Calories: 565; Fat: 31.0g; Carbs: 14.2g; Protein: 53.6g

227. BACON CHICKEN ALFREDO

Preparation Time: 20 minutes
Cooking Time: 35 minutes
Servings: 4

Ingredients:

- 4-ounces mushrooms drained and sliced
- 1 cup shredded mozzarella cheese
- 1 jar (15-ouncesClassico creamy alfredo sauce
- 6 slices chopped hickory bacon
- 4 boneless skinless chicken breasts thawed or fresh
- Pepper and salt to taste
- ½ cup water

Directions:

1. Add all ingredients in a pot on high fire and bring to a boil.
2. Once boiling, lower fire to a simmer and cook for 30 minutes, stir every now and then.
3. Adjust seasoning to taste.
4. Serve and enjoy.

Nutrition Values:

Calories: 976; Fat: 70.8g; Carbs: 7.7g; Protein: 75.8g

228. CREAMY STEWED CHICKEN

Preparation Time: 5 minutes
Cooking Time: 30 minutes
Servings: 6

Ingredients:

- 10.5-ounce can cream of chicken soup
- 12-ounce package frozen broccoli
- 0.6-ounce package Italian dry mix dressing
- 8-ounces cream cheese
- 1 ½-pounds skinless, boneless chicken breasts
- ½ cup water
- Pepper and salt to taste

Directions:

1. Add all ingredients in a pot on high fire and bring to a boil.
2. Once boiling, lower fire to a simmer and cook for 25 minutes, stir every now and then.
3. Adjust seasoning to taste.
4. Serve and enjoy.

Nutrition Values:
Calories: 250; Fat: 10.5g; Carbs: 7.0g; Protein: 31.0g

229. COCONUT-CRUSTED LIME CHICKEN

Preparation Time: 10 mins
Servings: 4

Ingredients:

- 50g desiccated coconut
- Mango chutney and rice
- 2 limes zest and juice
- 1 tsp. chilli powder
- 2 tsps. Medium curry powder
- 8 skinless, de-boned chicken thighs
- 1 tbsp. vegetable oil

Directions:

1. Heat oven to 200C/180C fan.
2. Put the chicken in a large bowl with the lime zest and juice, curry powder, chilli powder, if using, and seasoning.
3. Mix well, then toss in the coconut. Place chicken on a rack sitting in a roasting tin, drizzle with the oil, then bake for 25 mins until cooked through and tender.
4. Serve with mango chutney, lime wedges for squeezing over and rice, if you like.

Nutrition Values:
Calories: 316, Fat:16 g, Carbs:2 g, Protein:41 g, Sugars:1 g, Sodium:600 mg

230. BALSAMIC TURKEY AND PEACH MIX

Preparation Time: 10 mins
Servings: 4

Ingredients:

- 4 sliced peaches
- ¼ tsp. black pepper
- 1 tbsp. avocado oil
- 1 skinless, boneless and sliced turkey breast
- 1 chopped yellow onion
- 2 tbsps.chopped chives
- ¼ c. balsamic vinegar

Directions:

1. Heat up a pan with the oil over medium-high heat, add the meat and the onion, toss and brown for 5 minutes.
2. Add the rest of the ingredients except the chives, toss gently and bake at390 0F for 20 minutes.
3. Divide everything between plates and serve with the chives sprinkled on top.

Nutrition Values:

Calories: 123, Fat:1.6 g, Carbs:18.8 g, Protein:9.1 g, Sugars:6.6 g, Sodium:998 mg

231. CHICKEN AND ASPARAGUS MIX

Preparation Time: 10 mins
Servings: 4

Ingredients:

- ½ tsp. sweet paprika
- 2 chopped spring onions
- 2 tbsps.avocado oil
- 1 bunch trimmed and halved asparagus
- 14 oz. no-salt-added, drained and chopped canned tomatoes
- 2 skinless, boneless and cubed chicken breasts
- ¼ tsp. black pepper

Directions:

1. Heat up a pan with the oil over medium-high heat, add the meat and the spring onions, stir and cook for 5 minutes.
2. Add the asparagus and the other ingredients, toss, cover the pan and cook over medium heat for 20 minutes.
3. Divide everything between plates and serve.

Nutrition Values:
Calories: 171, Fat:6.4 g, Carbs:6.4 g, Protein:22.2 g, Sugars:0 g, Sodium:430 mg

232. CHICKEN AND DILL GREEN BEANS MIX

Preparation Time: 10 mins
Servings: 4

Ingredients:

- 10 oz. trimmed and halved green beans
- 1 chopped yellow onion
- ½ tsp. crushed red pepper flakes
- 2 tbsps.olive oil
- 1 tbsp. chopped dill
- 2 c. no-salt-added tomato sauce
- 2 skinless, boneless and halved chicken breasts

Directions:

1. Heat up a pan with the oil over medium-high heat, add the onion and the meat and brown it for 2 minutes on each side.
2. Add the green beans and the other ingredients, toss, introduce in the oven and bake at 380 0F for 20 minutes.
3. Divide between plates and serve right away.

Nutrition Values:
Calories: 391, Fat:17.8 g, Carbs:14.8 g, Protein:43.9 g, Sugars:1.7 g, Sodium:149 mg

233. TURKEY WITH BEANS AND

OLIVES

Preparation Time: 10 mins
Servings: 4

Ingredients:

- 1 lb. skinless, boneless and sliced turkey breast
- 1 c. pitted and halved green olives
- 1 c. no-salt-added tomato sauce
- 1 c. no-salt-added and drained black beans
- 1 tbsp. olive oil
- 1 tbsp. chopped cilantro

Directions:

1. Grease a baking dish with the oil, arrange the turkey slices inside, add the other ingredients as well, introduce in the oven and bake at 380 0F for 35 minutes.
2. Divide between plates and serve.

Nutrition Values:

Calories: 331, Fat:6.4 g, Carbs:38.5 g, Protein:30.7 g, Sugars:4.8 g, Sodium:616 mg

234. PARMESAN TURKEY

Preparation Time: 10 mins
Servings: 4

Ingredients:

- ½ c. grated low-fat parmesan
- 1 c. coconut milk
- 1 tbsp. olive oil
- 2 chopped shallots
- Black pepper
- 1 lb. skinless, boneless and cubed turkey breast

Directions:

1. Heat up a pan with the oil over medium-high heat, add the shallots, toss and cook for 5 minutes.
2. Add the meat, coconut milk, and black pepper, toss and cook over medium heat for 15 minutes more.
3. Add the parmesan, cook for 2-3 minutes, divide everything between plates and serve.

Nutrition Values:

Calories: 320, Fat:11.4 g, Carbs:14.3 g, Protein:11.3 g, Sugars:5 g, Sodium:990 mg

235. CHICKEN AND BEETS MIX

Preparation Time: 10 mins
Servings: 4

Ingredients:

- 2 peeled and shredded beets
- 1 c. skinless, deboned, cooked and shredded smoked chicken breast
- 1 shredded carrot
- 1 tsp. chopped chives
- ½ c. avocado mayonnaise

Directions:

1. In a bowl, combine the chicken with the beets and the other ingredients, toss and serve right away.

Nutrition Values:

Calories: 288, Fat:24.6 g, Carbs:6.5 g, Protein:14 g, Sugars:13 g, Sodium:504 mg

236. TURKEY AND BOK CHOY

Preparation Time: 10 mins
Servings: 4

Ingredients:

- ½ c. low-sodium veggie stock
- 2 tbsps.olive oil
- 1 lb. torn bokchoy
- 1 boneless, skinless and roughly cubed turkey breast
- 2 chopped scallions
- ¼ tsp. black pepper
- ½ tsp. grated ginger

Directions:

1. Heat up a pot with the oil over medium-high heat, add the scallions and the ginger and sauté for 2 minutes.
2. Add the meat and brown for 5 minutes more.
3. Add the rest of the ingredients, toss, simmer for 13 minutes more, divide between plates and serve.

Nutrition Values:

Calories: 125, Fat:8 g, Carbs:5.5 g, Protein:9.3 g, Sugars:2 g, Sodium:540 mg

237. CREAMY CHICKEN AND SHRIMP MIX

Preparation Time: 10 mins
Servings: 4

Ingredients:

- 1 lb. skinless, boneless and cubed chicken breast
- 1 lb. peeled and deveined shrimp
- 1 tbsp. olive oil
- ¼ c. low-sodium chicken stock
- 1 tbsp. chopped cilantro
- ½ c. coconut cream

Directions:

1. Heat up a pan with the oil over medium heat, add the chicken, toss and cook for 8 minutes.
2. Add the shrimp and the other ingredients,

toss, cook everything for 6 minutes more, divide into bowls and serve.

Nutrition Values:
Calories: 370, Fat:12.3 g, Carbs:12.6 g, Protein:8 g, Sugars:0.1 g, Sodium:274 mg

238. ALLSPICE CHICKEN WINGS

Preparation Time: 10 mins | Servings: 4

Ingredients:

- 2 tsps. ground allspice
- 2 tbsps.chopped chives
- Black pepper
- 2 lbs. chicken wings
- 2 tbsps.avocado oil
- 5 minced garlic cloves

Directions:

1. In a bowl, combine the chicken wings with the allspice and the other ingredients and toss well.
2. Arrange the chicken wings in a roasting pan and bake at 400 0F for 20 minutes.
3. Divide the chicken wings between plates and serve.

Nutrition Values:
Calories: 449, Fat:17 g, Carbs:1 g, Protein:6 g, Sugars:9 g, Sodium:113 mg

239. CHEDDAR TURKEY MIX

Preparation Time: 10 mins
Servings: 4

Ingredients:

- 1 c. shredded fat-free cheddar cheese
- 1 lb. skinless, boneless and sliced turkey breast
- Black pepper
- 2 tbsps.chopped parsley
- 2 tbsps.olive oil
- 1 c. no-salt-added and chopped canned tomatoes

Directions:

1. Grease a baking dish with the oil, arrange the turkey slices into the pan, spread the tomatoes over them, season with black pepper, sprinkle the cheese and parsley on top, introduce in the oven at 400 0F and bake for 1 hour.
2. Divide everything between plates and serve.

Nutrition Values:
Calories: 350, Fat:13.1 g, Carbs:32.4 g, Protein:14 g, Sugars:12 g, Sodium:460 mg

240. TURKEY WITH CELERY SALAD

Preparation Time: 4 mins
Servings: 4

Ingredients:

- 1 c. chopped celery stalks
- 1 c. pitted and halved black olives
- 2 c. skinless, boneless, cooked and shredded turkey breast
- 1 tbsp. olive oil
- 1 c. fat-free yogurt
- 2 chopped spring onions
- 1 tsps.lime juice

Directions:

1. In a bowl, combine the turkey with the celery and the other ingredients, toss and serve cold.

Nutrition Values:
Calories: 157, Fat:8 g, Carbs:10.8 g, Protein:11.5 g, Sugars:230 g, Sodium:0 mg

241. LEMONY LEEK AND CHICKEN

Preparation Time: 10 mins
Servings: 4

Ingredients:

- 1 c. low-sodium veggie stock
- 4 roughly chopped leek
- ¼ tsp. black pepper
- 1 lb. skinless, boneless and cubed chicken breast
- 1 tbsp. no-salt-added tomato sauce
- ½ c. lemon juice
- 2 tbsps.avocado oil

Directions:

2. Heat up a pan with the oil over medium heat, add the leeks, toss and sauté for 10 minutes.
3. Add the chicken and the other ingredients, toss, cook over medium heat for 20 minutes more, divide between plates and serve.

Nutrition Values:
Calories: 1199, Fat:18.3 g, Carbs:16.6 g, Protein:26.5 g, Sugars:1 g, Sodium:50 mg

242. CHICKEN AND CORN

Preparation Time: 10 mins
Servings: 4

Ingredients:

- 2 c. corn
- 1 c. low-sodium chicken stock
- 1 bunch chopped green onions
- 1 tsp. smoked paprika
- 2 tbsps.avocado oil
- ¼ tsp. black pepper
- 2 lbs. skinless, boneless and halved chicken breast

Directions:

1. Heat up a pan with the oil over medium-high heat, add the green onions, stir and sauté them for 5 minutes.
2. Add the chicken and brown it for 5 minutes more.
3. Add the corn and the other ingredients, toss, introduce the pan in the oven and cook at 390 0F for 25 minutes.
4. Divide the mix between plates and serve.

Nutrition Values:
Calories: 270, Fat:12.4 g, Carbs:12 g, Protein:9 g, Sugars:17 g, Sodium:586 mg

243. CHICKEN AND SNOW PEAS

Preparation Time: 10 mins
Servings: 4

Ingredients:
- 1 chopped red onion
- 2 c. snow peas
- 2 tbsps.chopped parsley
- 2 lbs. skinless, boneless and cubed chicken breasts
- 2 tbsps.olive oil
- ¼ tsp. black pepper
- 1 c. no-salt-added canned tomato sauce

Directions:
1. Heat up a pan with the oil over medium heat, add the onion and the meat and brown for 5 minutes.
2. Add the peas and the rest of the ingredients, bring to a simmer and cook over medium heat for 25 minutes.
3. Divide the mix between plates and serve.

Nutrition Values:
Calories: 551, Fat:24.2 g, Carbs:11.7 g, Protein:69 g, Sugars:2 g, Sodium:681 mg

244. TURKEY AND BERRIES

Preparation Time: 10 mins
Servings: 4

Ingredients:
- 1 chopped red onion
- 1 c. low-sodium chicken stock
- ¼ c. chopped cilantro
- 2 lbs. skinless, boneless and cubed turkey breasts
- 1 c. cranberries
- Black pepper
- 1 tbsp. olive oil

Directions:
1. Heat up a pot with the oil over medium-high heat, add the onion, stir and sauté for 5

minutes.
2. Add the meat, berries and the other ingredients, bring to a simmer and cook over medium heat for 30 minutes more.
3. Divide the mix between plates and serve.

Nutrition Values:
Calories: 293, Fat:7.3 g, Carbs:14.7 g, Protein:39.3 g, Sugars:4 g, Sodium:595 mg

245. BALSAMIC BAKED TURKEY

Preparation Time: 10 mins
Servings: 4

Ingredients:
- 2 tbsps.balsamic vinegar
- 2 minced garlic cloves
- 1 skinless, boneless and sliced big turkey breast
- 1 tbsp. olive oil
- 1 tbsp. chopped cilantro
- Black pepper
- 1 tbsp. Italian seasoning

Directions:
1. In a baking dish, mix the turkey with the vinegar, the oil and the other ingredients, toss, introduce in the oven at 400 0F and bake for 40 minutes.
2. Divide everything between plates and serve with a side salad.

Nutrition Values:
Calories: 280, Fat:12.7 g, Carbs:22.1 g, Protein:14 g, Sugars:3 g, Sodium:760 mg

246. TURKEY WITH SPICED GREENS

Preparation Time: 10 mins
Servings: 4

Ingredients:
- Black pepper
- 1 c. mustard greens
- 1 tsp. ground allspice
- 1 lb. boneless, skinless and cubed turkey breast
- 1 tsp. ground nutmeg
- 1 tbsp. olive oil
- 1 chopped yellow onion

Directions:
1. Heat up a pan with the oil over medium-high heat, add the onion and the meat and brown for 5 minutes.
2. Add the rest of the ingredients, toss, cook over medium heat for 12 minutes more, divide between plates and serve.

Nutrition Values:

Calories: 270, Fat: 8.4g, Carbs:33.3 g, Protein:9 g, Sugars:0 g, Sodium:533 mg

247. CHICKEN WITH GINGER ARTICHOKES

Preparation Time: 10 mins
Servings: 4

Ingredients:

- 1 tbsp. grated ginger
- 2 tbsps.lemon juice
- ¼ tsp. black pepper
- 2 skinless, boneless and halved chicken breasts
- 1 c. no-salt-added and chopped canned tomatoes
- 2 tbsps.olive oil
- 10 oz. no-salt-added, drained and quartered canned artichokes

Directions:

1. Heat up a pan with the oil over medium heat, add the ginger and the artichokes, toss and cook for 5 minutes.
2. Add the chicken and cook for 5 minutes more.
3. Add the rest of the ingredients, bring to a simmer and cook for 20 minutes more.
4. Divide everything between plates and serve.

Nutrition Values:

Calories: 300, Fat:14.5 g, Carbs:16.4 g, Protein:15.1 g, Sugars:0 g, Sodium:377 mg

248. HAMBURGER PATTIES

Servings: 6
Preparation Time: 30 mins

Ingredients

- 1 egg
- 25 oz. ground beef
- 3 oz. feta cheese, crumbled
- 2 oz. butter, for frying
- Salt and black pepper, to taste

Directions

1. Mix together egg, ground beef, feta cheese, salt and black pepper in a bowl.
2. Combine well and form equal sized patties.
3. Heat butter in a pan and add patties.
4. Cook on medium low heat for about 3 minutes per side.
5. Dish out and serve warm.

Nutrition Values:

Calories335
Total Fat 18.8g
Saturated Fat 10g
Cholesterol 166mg
Sodium 301mg
Total Carbohydrate 0.7g
Dietary Fiber 0g
Total Sugars 0.7g
Protein 38.8g

249. BUTTERY BEEF CURRY

Servings: 2
Preparation Time: 30 mins

Ingredients

- ½ cup butter
- ½ pound grass fed beef
- ½ pound onions
- Salt and red chili powder, to taste
- ½ pound celery, chopped

Directions

1. Put some water in a pressure cooker and add all the ingredients.
2. Lock the lid and cook on High Pressure for about 15 minutes.
3. Naturally release the pressure and dish out the curry to a bowl to serve.

Nutrition Values:

Calories450
Total Fat 38.4g
Saturated Fat 22.5g1
Cholesterol 132mg

Sodium 340mg
Total Carbohydrate 9.8g
Dietary Fiber 3.1g
Total Sugars 4.3g
Protein 17.2g

250. CHEESY BEEF

Servings: 6
Preparation Time: 40 mins

Ingredients

- 1 teaspoon garlic salt
- 2 pounds beef
- 1 cup cream cheese
- 1 cup mozzarella cheese, shredded
- 1 cup low carb Don Pablo's sauce

Directions

1. Season the meat with garlic salt and add to the instant pot.
2. Put the remaining ingredients in the pot and set the instant pot on low.
3. Cook for about 2 hours and dish out.

Nutrition Values:

Calories471
Total Fat 27.7g
Saturated Fat 14.6g
Cholesterol 187mg
Sodium 375mg
Total Carbohydrate 2.9g
Dietary Fiber 0.1g
Total Sugars 1.5g
Protein 50.9g

251. BEEF QUICHE

Servings: 3
Preparation Time: 30 mins

Ingredients

- ¼ cup grass fed beef, minced
- 2 slices bacon, cooked and crumbled
- ¼ cup goat cheddar cheese, shredded
- ¼ cup coconut milk
- 3 large pastured eggs

Directions

1. Preheat the oven to 3650F and grease 3 quiche molds.
2. Whisk together eggs and coconut milk in a large bowl.
3. Put beef in quiche molds and stir in the egg mixture.
4. Top with the crumbled bacon and cheddar cheese.

5. Transfer quiche molds to the oven and bake for about 20 minutes.
6. Remove from the oven and serve warm.

Nutrition Values:
Calories293
Total Fat 21.4g
Saturated Fat 10.4g
Cholesterol 232mg
Sodium 436mg
Total Carbohydrate 2.7g
Dietary Fiber 0.4g
Total Sugars 1.1g
Protein 21.8g

252. CHILI BEEF

Servings: 8
Preparation Time: 50 mins

Ingredients

- 3 celery ribs, finely diced
- 2 pounds grass fed beef, ground
- 2 tablespoons chili powder
- 2 tablespoons avocado oil, divided
- 2 cups grass fed beef broth

Directions

1. Heat avocado oil in a skillet on medium heat and add beef.
2. Sauté for about 3 minutes on each side and stir in broth and chili powder.
3. Cover the lid and cook for about 30 minutes on medium low heat.
4. Add celery and dish out in a bowl to serve.

Nutrition Values:
Calories223
Total Fat 11.8g
Saturated Fat 4.7g
Cholesterol 75mg
Sodium 198mg
Total Carbohydrate 2.4g
Dietary Fiber 1.2g
Total Sugars 0.5g
Protein 24.8g

253. SMOKED BRISKET WITH MAPLE SYRUP

Servings: 8
Preparation Time: 40 mins

Ingredients

- 1 tablespoon sugar free maple syrup
- 3 pounds grass fed beef briskets
- 3 tablespoons almond oil
- 2 cups bone broth
- 4 tablespoons liquid smoke

Directions

1. Heat almond oil in a skillet on medium heat and add beef briskets.
2. Sauté for about 4 minutes per side and stir in the bone broth and liquid smoke.
3. Cover the lid and cook for about 30 minutes on medium low heat.
4. Dish out in a platter and drizzle with sugar free maple syrup to serve.

Nutrition Values:
Calories422
Total Fat 17g
Saturated Fat 4.9g
Cholesterol 117mg
Sodium 130mg
Total Carbohydrate 1.7g
Dietary Fiber 0g
Total Sugars 1.5g
Protein 61.6g

254. KETO BEEF SIRLOIN STEAK

Servings: 3
Preparation Time: 45 mins

Ingredients

- 3 tablespoons butter
- ½ teaspoon garlic powder
- 1 pound beef top sirloin steaks
- Salt and black pepper, to taste
- 1 garlic clove, minced

Directions

1. Heat butter in a large grill pan and add beef top sirloin steaks.
2. Brown the steaks on both sides by cooking for about 3 minutes per side.
3. Season the steaks with garlic powder, salt and black pepper and cook for about 30 minutes, flipping once.
4. Dish out the steaks to a serving platter and serve hot.

Nutrition Values:
Calories386
Total Fat 21g
Saturated Fat 10.9g
Cholesterol 166mg
Sodium 182mg
Total Carbohydrate 0.7g
Dietary Fiber 0.1g
Total Sugars 0.1g
Protein 46.1g

255. BACON SWISS BEEF STEAKS

Servings: 4
Preparation Time: 25 mins

Ingredients

- ½ cup Swiss cheese, shredded
- 4 beef top sirloin steaks
- 6 bacon strips, cut in half
- Salt and black pepper, to taste
- 1 tablespoon butter

Directions

1. Season the beef steaks generously with salt and black pepper.
2. Put butter in the skillet and heat on medium low heat.
3. Add beef top sirloin steaks and cook for about 5 minutes per side.
4. Add bacon strips and cook for about 15 minutes.
5. Top with Swiss cheese and cook for about 5 minutes on low heat.
6. Remove from heat and dish out on a platter to serve.

Nutrition Values:

Calories385
Total Fat 25.4g
Saturated Fat 10.7g
Cholesterol 96mg
Sodium 552mg
Total Carbohydrate 0.8g
Dietary Fiber 0g
Total Sugars 0.2g
Protein 35.5g

256. MEXICAN TACO CASSEROLE

Servings: 3
Preparation Time: 35 mins

Ingredients

- ½ cup cheddar cheese, shredded
- ½ cup low carb salsa
- ½ cup cottage cheese
- 1 pound ground beef
- 1 tablespoon taco seasoning

Directions

1. Preheat the oven to 4250F and lightly grease a baking dish.
2. Mix together the taco seasoning and ground beef in a bowl.
3. Stir in the cottage cheese, salsa and cheddar cheese.
4. Transfer the ground beef mixture to the baking dish and top with cheese mixture.
5. Bake for about 25 minutes and remove from the oven to serve warm.

Nutrition Values:

Calories432
Total Fat 20.4g

Saturated Fat 10g
Cholesterol 165mg
Sodium 526mg
Total Carbohydrate 3.2g
Dietary Fiber 0g
Total Sugars 1.6g
Protein 56.4g

257. MUSTARD BEEF STEAKS

Servings: 4
Preparation Time: 40 mins

Ingredients

- 2 tablespoons butter
- 2 tablespoons Dijon mustard
- 4 beef steaks
- Salt and black pepper, to taste
- 1 tablespoon fresh rosemary, coarsely chopped

Directions

1. Marinate the beef steaks with Dijon mustard, fresh rosemary, salt and black pepper for about 2 hours.
2. Put the butter and marinated beef steaks in a nonstick skillet.
3. Cover the lid and cook for about 30 minutes on medium low heat.
4. Dish out when completely cooked and serve hot.

Nutrition Values:

Calories217
Total Fat 11.5g
Saturated Fat 5.7g
Cholesterol 91mg
Sodium 186mg
Total Carbohydrate 1g
Dietary Fiber 0.6g
Total Sugars 0.1g
Protein 26.3g

258. BEEF ROAST

Servings: 6
Preparation Time: 55 mins

Ingredients

- 2 pounds beef
- Salt and black pepper, to taste
- 1 cup onion soup
- 2 teaspoons lemon juice
- 1 cups beef broth

Directions

1. Put the beef in a pressure cooker and stir in the beef broth, lemon juice, onion soup, salt and black pepper.
2. Lock the lid and cook at High Pressure for about 40 minutes.

3. Naturally release the pressure and dish out on a platter to serve.

Nutrition Values:
Calories307
Total Fat 10.2g
Saturated Fat 3.7g
Cholesterol 135mg
Sodium 580mg
Total Carbohydrate 2.9g
Dietary Fiber 0.3g
Total Sugars 1.3g
Protein 47.9g

259. KETO MINCED MEAT

Servings: 4
Preparation Time: 30 mins

Ingredients

- 1 pound ground lamb meat
- 1 cup onions, chopped
- 2 tablespoons ginger garlic paste
- 3 tablespoons butter
- Salt and cayenne pepper, to taste

Directions

1. Put the butter in a pot and add garlic, ginger and onions.
2. Sauté for about 3 minutes and add ground meat and all the spices.
3. Cover the lid and cook for about 20 minutes on medium high heat.
4. Dish out to a large serving bowl and serve hot.

Nutrition Values:
Calories459
Total Fat 35.3g
Saturated Fat 14.7g
Cholesterol 133mg
Sodium 154mg
Total Carbohydrate 4.8g
Dietary Fiber 0.6g
Total Sugars 1.2g
Protein 28.9g

260. KETO TACO CASSEROLE

Servings: 8
Preparation Time: 55 mins

Ingredients

- 2 pounds ground beef
- 1 tablespoon extra-virgin olive oil
- Taco seasoning mix, kosher salt and black pepper
- 2 cups Mexican cheese, shredded
- 6 large eggs, lightly beaten

Directions

1. Preheat the oven to 3600F and grease a 2 quart baking dish.
2. Heat oil over medium heat in a large skillet and add ground beef.
3. Season with taco seasoning mix, kosher salt and black pepper.
4. Cook for about 5 minutes on each side and dish out to let cool slightly.
5. Whisk together eggs in the beef mixture and transfer the mixture to the baking dish.
6. Top with Mexican cheese and bake for about 25 minutes until set.
7. Remove from the oven and serve warm.

Nutrition Values:
Calories382
Total Fat 21.6g
Saturated Fat 9.1g
Cholesterol 266mg
Sodium 363mg
Total Carbohydrate 1.7g
Dietary Fiber 0g
Total Sugars 0.4g
Protein 45.3g

261. KETO BURGER FAT BOMBS

Servings: 10
Preparation Time: 30 mins

Ingredients

- ½ teaspoon garlic powder
- 1 pound ground beef
- Kosher salt and black pepper, to taste
- ¼ (8 oz.block cheddar cheese, cut into 20 pieces
- 2 tablespoons cold butter, cut into 20 pieces

Directions

1. Preheat the oven to 3750F and grease mini muffin tins with cooking spray.
2. Season the beef with garlic powder, kosher salt and black pepper in a medium bowl.
3. Press about 1 tablespoon of beef into each muffin tin, covering the bottom completely.
4. Layer with small piece of butter and add 1 more tablespoon of beef.
5. Top with a piece of cheese in each cup and press the remaining beef.
6. Transfer to the oven and bake for about 20 minutes.
7. Allow to slightly cool and dish out to serve hot.

Nutrition Values:
Calories128
Total Fat 7g
Saturated Fat 3.7g
Cholesterol 53mg
Sodium 81mg

Total Carbohydrate 0.2g
Dietary Fiber 0g
Total Sugars 0.1g
Protein 15.2g

262. ICE-BURGERS

Servings: 4
Preparation Time: 30 mins

Ingredients

- 4 slices bacon, cooked and crisped
- 1 large head iceberg lettuce, sliced into 8 rounds
- 1 pound ground beef
- 4 slices cheddar cheese
- Kosher salt and black pepper, to taste

Directions

1. Make 4 large patties out of ground beef and season both sides with salt and black pepper.
2. Grill for about 10 minutes per side and top with cheddar cheese slices.
3. Place one iceberg round on a plate and layer with grilled beef.
4. Place a slice of bacon and close with second iceberg round.
5. Repeat with the remaining ingredients and serve warm.

Nutrition Values:

Calories452
Total Fat 24.6g
Saturated Fat 11.2g
Cholesterol 152mg
Sodium 698mg
Total Carbohydrate 6.3g
Dietary Fiber 1.2g
Total Sugars 2g
Protein 49.3g

263. BEEF IN CHEESE TACO SHELLS

Servings: 4
Preparation Time: 30 mins

Ingredients

- 2 cups cheddar cheese, shredded
- 1 tablespoon olive oil
- 1 tablespoon taco seasoning
- Freshly ground black pepper, to taste
- 1 pound ground beef

Directions

1. Preheat the oven to 3750F and grease a baking dish.
2. Arrange cheddar cheese on the baking sheet and season with black pepper.
3. Bake for about 7 minutes until cheese melts and becomes slightly crispy.

4. Form shells with the help of a wooden spoon and allow them to cool.
5. Meanwhile, heat oil in a large skillet over medium heat and add ground beef.
6. Cook for about 10 minutes and season with taco seasoning.
7. Place beef in the shells and serve.

Nutrition Values:

Calories478
Total Fat 29.3g
Saturated Fat 15.1g
Cholesterol 161mg
Sodium 636mg
Total Carbohydrate 2.7g
Dietary Fiber 0g
Total Sugars 0.8g
Protein 48.5g

264. MEXICAN GROUND BEEF

Servings: 3
Preparation Time: 30 mins

Ingredients

- 1 pound ground beef
- ½ cup cheddar cheese, shredded
- ¼ cup water
- Salt and black pepper, to taste
- 2 tablespoons organic Mexican seasoning

Directions

1. Put beef in a nonstick pan and season with salt and black pepper.
2. Cook for about 8 minutes until brown and pour in the water and Mexican seasoning.
3. Cook for about 5 minutes and dish out in a bowl to serve.

Nutrition Values:

Calories372
Total Fat 15.7g
Saturated Fat 7.5g
Cholesterol 155mg
Sodium 527mg
Total Carbohydrate 3.2g
Dietary Fiber 0g
Total Sugars 0.1g
Protein 51.1g

265. CHEESESTEAK STUFFED PEPPERS

Servings: 4
Preparation Time: 55 mins

Ingredients

- 16 oz. cremini mushrooms, sliced
- 4 bell peppers, halved
- Italian seasoning, kosher salt and black pepper
- 16 provolone cheese slices

- 1½ pounds sirloin steak, thinly sliced

Directions

1. Preheat the oven to 3250F and grease a large baking dish.
2. Arrange bell peppers in the baking dish and transfer to the oven.
3. Bake for about 30 minutes until tender and dish out.
4. Grease a nonstick pan and add mushrooms, Italian seasoning, kosher salt and black pepper.
5. Cook for about 6 minutes and add sirloin steak.
6. Cook for about 3 minutes, stirring occasionally and dish out.
7. Put provolone cheese to the bottom of baked bell peppers and top with steak mixture.
8. Top with the rest of provolone cheese and broil for about 3 minutes until golden.
9. Serve and enjoy.

Nutrition Values:

Calories521
Total Fat 27.5g
Saturated Fat 15.5g
Cholesterol 153mg
Sodium 736mg
Total Carbohydrate 10.8g
Dietary Fiber 1.5g
Total Sugars 5.8g
Protein 56.2g

266. BEEF WITH GREEN OLIVES AND PRUNES

Servings: 4
Preparation Time: 40 mins

Ingredients

- 2 tablespoons salted butter
- 1¼ pounds beef
- 1 cup reduced sodium chicken broth
- ¼ cup prunes, pitted and chopped
- ¼ cup green olives, pitted and chopped

Directions

1. Heat butter in a large nonstick skillet over medium high heat and add beef.
2. Cook for about 2 minutes per side until browned and add broth.
3. Bring to a simmer, stirring occasionally and add olives and prunes.
4. Reduce heat to low and cover with lid.
5. Cook until the beef is tender and no longer pink in the center, 12 to 15 minutes.
6. Transfer beef to a plate and serve hot.

Nutrition Values:

Calories350
Total Fat 15g

Saturated Fat 7.1g
Cholesterol 142mg
Sodium 328mg
Total Carbohydrate 7g
Dietary Fiber 0.8g
Total Sugars 4.2g
Protein 44.5g

267. STIR FRIED SPICY BEEF STEAKS

Servings: 7
Preparation Time: 30 mins

Ingredients

- Cayenne pepper, paprika, salt and black pepper
- 3 tablespoons olive oil
- 1 scoop Stevia
- 1½ pounds top round steaks
- 1 (16 ouncepackage frozen bell pepper and onion mix

Directions

1. Mix together Stevia, cayenne pepper, paprika, salt and black pepper in a bowl.
2. Add top round steaks and toss to coat well.
3. Cover and refrigerate overnight.
4. Heat olive oil in a large nonstick skillet over high heat and add bell pepper and onion mix.
5. Cook for about 7 minutes, stirring occasionally and add the spice rubbed steaks.
6. Cook for about 15 minutes and dish out to serve hot.

Nutrition Values:

Calories311
Total Fat 14.8g
Saturated Fat 3.9g
Cholesterol 82mg
Sodium 60mg
Total Carbohydrate 11.6g
Dietary Fiber 2.9g
Total Sugars 6.2g
Protein 32.5g

268. KETO SAUSAGE BALLS

Servings: 6
Preparation Time: 35 mins

Ingredients

- 1 cup blanched almond flour
- 1 pound bulk Italian sausage
- 1¼ cups sharp cheddar cheese, shredded
- 2 teaspoons baking powder
- 1 large egg

Directions

1. Preheat the oven to 3500F and place a wire rack on the baking sheet.
2. Mix together all the ingredients in a large bowl

until well incorporated.
3. Form small meatballs out of the meat mixture and arrange them on the wire rack.
4. Bake for about 20 minutes until golden brown and remove from the oven to serve hot.

Nutrition Values:
Calories477
Total Fat 39g
Saturated Fat 12.8g
Cholesterol 119mg
Sodium 732mg
Total Carbohydrate 5.1g
Dietary Fiber 2g
Total Sugars 0.2g
Protein 25.6g

269. CUMIN SPICED BEEF WRAPS

Servings: 6
Preparation Time: 25 mins

Ingredients

- 2 pounds ground beef
- Salt and black pepper, to taste
- 3 tablespoons coconut oil
- 2 teaspoons cumin
- 8 large cabbage leaves, boiled for 20 seconds and plunged in cold water

Directions

1. Heat coconut oil in a pan on medium heat and add the ground beef.
2. Sauté for about 5 minutes and add cumin, salt and black pepper.
3. Place the cabbage leaves on a plate and spoon the ground beef mixture on it.
4. Fold into a roll and serve warm.

Nutrition Values:
Calories353
Total Fat 16.4g
Saturated Fat 9.5g
Cholesterol 135mg
Sodium 109mg
Total Carbohydrate 2.9g
Dietary Fiber 1.2g
Total Sugars 1.4g
Protein 46.6g

270. PORK FILLED EGG MUFFINS

Servings: 6
Preparation Time: 25 mins

Ingredients

- 4 eggs
- 4 slices pork, precooked
- ½ teaspoon lemon pepper seasoning
- 4 tablespoons goat cheddar cheese, shredded
- 1 green onion, diced

Directions

1. Preheat the oven to 3750F and grease 6 muffin molds lightly.
2. Mix together eggs, onion, pork, lemon pepper seasoning and cheddar cheese in a bowl.
3. Pour the batter into the muffin molds and transfer to the oven.
4. Bake for about 15 minutes and take the muffins from oven to serve.

Nutrition Values:
Calories136
Total Fat 9.6g
Saturated Fat 3.4g
Cholesterol 161mg
Sodium 359mg
Total Carbohydrate 1.7g
Dietary Fiber 0.1g
Total Sugars 0.1g
Protein 10.1g

271. PORK BREAD

Servings: 6
Preparation Time: 35 mins

Ingredients

- ½ cup almond milk
- ½ cup almond oil
- 2 pastured eggs
- ½ pound pork, precooked and shredded
- ¼ teaspoon baking soda

Directions

1. Preheat the oven to 3750F and grease a baking dish with almond oil.
2. Mix eggs, almond milk, baking soda and pork in a bowl.
3. Pour the batter into the baking dish and transfer the oven.
4. Bake for about 20 minutes and remove from the oven.
5. Slice and serve hot.

Nutrition Values:
Calories284
Total Fat 25.8g
Saturated Fat 6.7g
Cholesterol 99mg
Sodium 98mg
Total Carbohydrate 1.5g
Dietary Fiber 0.4g
Total Sugars 0.7g
Protein 12.4g

272. GARLIC CREAMY PORK CHOPS

Servings: 8
Preparation Time: 45 mins

Ingredients

- ½ cup butter
- Salt and black pepper, to taste
- 4 garlic cloves, minced
- 2 pounds pork chops
- 1½ cups heavy cream

Directions

1. Rub the pork chops with garlic, salt and black pepper.
2. Marinate the chops with butter and cream and set aside for 1 hour.
3. Preheat the grill to medium high heat and transfer the steaks to it.
4. Grill for about 15 minutes on each side and transfer to a plate and serve hot.

Nutrition Values:

Calories545
Total Fat 48g
Saturated Fat 23g1
Cholesterol 159mg
Sodium 170mg
Total Carbohydrate 1.2g
Dietary Fiber 0g
Total Sugars 0.1g
Protein 26.2g

273. PORK FAJITAS

Servings: 4
Preparation Time: 40 minutes

Ingredients

- 1 tablespoon butter
- 1 bell pepper, sliced
- 1 pound pork tenderloins, sliced
- 1 tablespoon fajita seasoning
- 1 onion, sliced

Directions

1. Put the butter in the bottom of a skillet and add onions.
2. Sauté for about 3 minutes and add bell pepper.
3. Cook for about 2 minutes and stir in pork tenderloins and fajita seasoning.
4. Cover with lid and cook for about 25 minutes on medium low heat.
5. Dish out the delicious pork fajitas and serve hot.

Nutrition Values:

Calories265
Total Fat 10.1g
Saturated Fat 4.5g
Cholesterol 109mg
Sodium 228mg
Total Carbohydrate 6.4g

Dietary Fiber 1g
Total Sugars 2.7g
Protein 35g

274. AMAICAN JERK PORK ROAST

Servings: 3
Preparation Time: 35 mins

Ingredients

- 1 tablespoon butter
- 1/8 cup beef broth
- 1 pound pork shoulder
- 1/8 cup Jamaican jerk spice blend
- Salt, to taste

Directions

1. Season the pork with Jamaican jerk spice blend.
2. Heat the butter in the pot and add seasoned pork.
3. Cook for about 5 minutes and add beef broth.
4. Cover with lid and cook for about 20 minutes on low heat.
5. Dish out on a serving platter and serve hot.

Nutrition Values:

Calories477
Total Fat 36.2g
Saturated Fat 14.3g
Cholesterol 146mg
Sodium 212mg
Total Carbohydrate 0g
Dietary Fiber 0g
Total Sugars 0g
Protein 35.4g

275. PORK CARNITAS

Servings: 3
Preparation Time: 40 mins

Ingredients

- 1 pound pork shoulder, bone-in
- Salt and black pepper, to taste
- 1 tablespoon butter
- 1 orange, juiced
- ½ teaspoon garlic powder

Directions

1. Season the pork with salt and black pepper.
2. Put butter in the pressure cooker and add garlic powder.
3. Sauté for 1 minute and add seasoned pork.
4. Sauté for 3 minutes and pour orange juice.
5. Lock the lid and cook on high pressure for about 20 minutes.
6. Naturally release the pressure and dish out.
7. Shred the pork with a fork and transfer back to the cooker.
8. Sauté for about 3 minutes and serve warm.

Nutrition Values:
Calories506
Total Fat 36.3g
Saturated Fat 14.3g
Cholesterol 146mg
Sodium 130mg
Total Carbohydrate 7.6g
Dietary Fiber 1.5g
Total Sugars 5.8g
Protein 35.9g

276. ZESTY PORK CHOPS

Servings: 4
Preparation Time: 50 mins

Ingredients

- 4 tablespoons butter
- 3 tablespoons lemon juice
- 4 pork chops, bone-in
- 2 tablespoons low carb flour mix
- 1 cup picante sauce

Directions

1. Coat the pork chops with low carb flour mix.
2. Mix picante sauce and lemon juice in a bowl.
3. Heat oil in a skillet on medium heat and add the chops and picante mixture.
4. Cook covered for about 35 minutes and dish out to serve hot.

Nutrition Values:
Calories398
Total Fat 33.4g
Saturated Fat 15g
Cholesterol 99mg
Sodium 441mg
Total Carbohydrate 4g
Dietary Fiber 0.7g
Total Sugars 2.1g
Protein 19.7g

277. GREEK PORK GYROS

Servings: 4
Preparation Time: 40 mins

Ingredients

- 4 garlic cloves
- 3 teaspoons ground marjoram
- 1 pound pork meat, ground
- Salt and black pepper, to taste
- ½ small onion, chopped

Directions

1. Preheat the oven to 4000F and grease a loaf pan lightly.
2. Put onions, garlic, marjoram, salt and black pepper in a food processor and process until well combined.

3. Add ground pork meat and process again.
4. Press meat mixture into the loaf pan until compact and very tight.
5. Tightly cover with tin foil and poke some holes in the foil.
6. Bake in the oven for about 25 minutes and dish out to serve warm.

Nutrition Values:
Calories310
Total Fat 24.2g
Saturated Fat 9g
Cholesterol 80mg
Sodium 66mg
Total Carbohydrate 2.1g
Dietary Fiber 0.4g
Total Sugars 0.4g
Protein 19.4g

278. GARLIC ROSEMARY PORK CHOPS

Servings: 4
Preparation Time: 30 mins

Ingredients

- 1 tablespoon rosemary, freshly minced
- 2 garlic cloves, minced
- 4 pork loin chops
- ½ cup butter, melted
- Salt and black pepper, to taste

Directions

1. Preheat the oven to 3750F and season pork chops with salt and black pepper.
2. Mix together ¼ cup butter, rosemary and garlic in a small bowl.
3. Heat the rest of the butter in an oven safe skillet and add pork chops.
4. Sear for about 4 minutes per side until golden and brush pork chops generously with garlic butter.
5. Place skillet in the oven and bake for about 15 minutes until cooked through.
6. Dish out and serve hot.

Nutrition Values:
Calories465
Total Fat 43g
Saturated Fat 22.1g1
Cholesterol 130mg
Sodium 220mg
Total Carbohydrate 1.1g
Dietary Fiber 0.4g
Total Sugars 0g
Protein 18.4g

279. LEMONY GRILLED PORK CHOPS

Servings: 4
Preparation Time: 20 mins

Ingredients
- 2 tablespoons extra-virgin olive oil
- 4 pork chops
- 2 tablespoons butter
- Kosher salt and black pepper, to taste
- 2 lemons, sliced

Directions
1. Preheat the grill to high heat.
2. Brush pork chops with olive oil and season with salt and black pepper.
3. Put the pork chops on grill and top with lemon slices.
4. Grill for about 10 minutes per side until lemons are charred and chops are cooked through.
5. Dish out on a platter and serve hot.

Nutrition Values:
Calories375
Total Fat 32.7g
Saturated Fat 12.1g
Cholesterol 84mg
Sodium 97mg
Total Carbohydrate 2.7g
Dietary Fiber 0.8g
Total Sugars 0.7g
Protein 18.4g

280. CHEDDAR MAPLE SQUASH
Servings: 4
Preparation Time: 30 mins

Ingredients
- 1½ pounds summer squash, peeled, halved, seeded, and cut into 1½ inch cubes
- 1 cup aged white cheddar cheese, coarsely grated
- 1 tablespoon sugar free maple syrup
- 1 tablespoon fresh sage, chopped and crushed
- 2 slices pork bacon, cooked and chopped

Directions
1. Boil the summer squash for about 15 minutes and mash with a potato masher.
2. Stir in cheddar cheese, sage and maple syrup and top with cooked pork bacon to serve.

Nutrition Values:
Calories196
Total Fat 13.7g
Saturated Fat 7.4g
Cholesterol 40mg
Sodium 414mg
Total Carbohydrate 7.1g
Dietary Fiber 2.1g
Total Sugars 3.1g
Protein 12.7g

281. SPINACH PORK ROLL UPS
Servings: 8
Preparation Time: 15 mins

Ingredients
- 2 teaspoons honey mustard
- 8 thin slices bacon, smoked
- 1 cup Monterey Jack cheese, cut lengthwise into quarters
- 1 cup fresh baby spinach leaves
- ½ medium red bell pepper, seeded and cut into thin strips

Directions
1. Spread the honey mustard over bacon slices.
2. Divide spinach leaves among 8 plates and place bacon slices on it.
3. Top with red bell pepper and cheese to serve.

Nutrition Values:
Calories161
Total Fat 12.3g
Saturated Fat 5.3g
Cholesterol 33mg
Sodium 524mg
Total Carbohydrate 1.6g
Dietary Fiber 0.2g
Total Sugars 0.7g
Protein 10.7g

282. STUFFED PORK CHOPS
Servings: 6
Preparation Time: 40 mins

Ingredients
- 4 garlic cloves, minced
- 2 pounds cut boneless pork chops
- 1½ teaspoons salt
- 8 oz. provolone cheese
- 2 cups baby spinach

Directions
1. Preheat the oven to 3500F and grease a baking sheet.
2. Mix garlic with salt and rub on one side of the pork chops.
3. Place half of the pork chops garlic side down on a baking sheet and top with spinach and provolone cheese.
4. Top with rest of the pork chops garlic side up and place in the oven.
5. Bake for about 30 minutes and dish out to serve hot.

Nutrition Values:
Calories430
Total Fat 20.2g
Saturated Fat 9.8g

Cholesterol 165mg
Sodium 1005mg
Total Carbohydrate 1.8g
Dietary Fiber 0.3g
Total Sugars 0.3g
Protein 57.2g

283. PORK WITH BUTTERNUT SQUASH STEW

Servings: 4
Preparation Time: 40 mins

Ingredients

- ½ pound butternut squash, peeled and cubed
- 1 pound lean pork
- 2 tablespoons butter
- Salt and black pepper, to taste
- 1 cup beef stock

Directions

1. Put the butter and lean pork in a skillet and cook for about 5 minutes.
2. Add butternut squash, beef stock and season with salt and black pepper.
3. Cover with lid and cook for about 25 minutes on medium low heat.
4. Dish out to a bowl and serve hot.

Nutrition Values:

Calories319
Total Fat 17.1g
Saturated Fat 7.9g
Cholesterol 105mg
Sodium 311mg
Total Carbohydrate 6.7g
Dietary Fiber 1.1g
Total Sugars 1.3g
Protein 33.7g

284. KETO SWEET MUSTARD PORK

Servings: 4
Preparation Time: 40 mins

Ingredients

- ¼ cup Dijon mustard
- 4 pork chops
- 1 tablespoon granular Erythritol
- 2 tablespoons olive oil
- ½ cup sour cream

Directions

1. Preheat the oven to 3500F.
2. Mix together Dijon mustard, Erythritol and sour cream in a bowl.
3. Combine the pork chops and half of the mustard dressing in a bowl.
4. Marinate the pork chops overnight in the refrigerator.

5. Heat olive oil over medium high heat in a large oven proof skillet and add pork.
6. Cook for about 4 minutes on both sides until brown and pour in the remaining mustard dressing.
7. Place the skillet into the oven and bake for about 20 minutes.
8. Dish out and serve hot.

Nutrition Values:

Calories388
Total Fat 33.5g
Saturated Fat 12.2g
Cholesterol 81mg
Sodium 249mg
Total Carbohydrate 5.8g
Dietary Fiber 0.5g
Total Sugars 3.9g
Protein 19.6g

285. BARBECUE DRY RUB RIBS

Servings: 8
Preparation Time: 2 hours 50 mins

Ingredients

- 2 tablespoons olive oil
- 2 pounds pork baby back ribs
- 1½ tablespoons smoked paprika
- 1 tablespoon Erythritol
- Garlic powder, onion powder, chili powder and sea salt

Directions

1. Preheat the oven to 3000F and line a baking sheet with aluminum foil.
2. Mix together garlic powder, onion powder, chili powder, sea salt, Erythritol and smoked paprika in a bowl.
3. Place the pork baby back ribs on the baking sheet and brush with olive oil.
4. Sprinkle the dry rub over both sides of the ribs and place in the oven.
5. Bake for about 2 hours until the ribs are juicy and tender.
6. Dish out onto a platter and serve hot.

Nutrition Values:

Calories451
Total Fat 37.5g
Saturated Fat 14.2g
Cholesterol 96mg
Sodium 77mg
Total Carbohydrate 3.3g
Dietary Fiber 0.6g
Total Sugars 2.2g
Protein 26g

286. PORK ENCHILADA CASSEROLE

Servings: 5

Preparation Time: 1 hour
Ingredients
- 1 pound boneless pork
- 1½ cups enchilada sauce
- 3 cups cheddar cheese, shredded
- Salt and black pepper, to taste
- ½ cup fresh cilantro, minced

Directions
1. Preheat the oven to 4500F and grease a casserole dish with olive oil.
2. Season pork with salt and black pepper.
3. Put the pork and 1 cup enchilada sauce in a saucepan and cook on medium low heat for about 30 minutes.
4. Dish out the pork and shred with a fork.
5. Combine shredded pork, ½ cup enchilada sauce and cilantro in the casserole dish and top with cheddar cheese.
6. Transfer to the oven and bake for about 15 minutes.
7. Dish out and serve hot.

Nutrition Values:
Calories433
Total Fat 26g
Saturated Fat 15.5g
Cholesterol 137mg
Sodium 479mg
Total Carbohydrate 8.4g
Dietary Fiber 3.1g
Total Sugars 0.4g
Protein 41.9g

287. CHEESY BACON PORK CHOPS
Servings: 6
Preparation Time: 50 mins
Ingredients
- ½ pound bacon, cut strips in half
- 6 pork chops
- 1 cup cheddar cheese, shredded
- Salt and black pepper, to taste
- 2 tablespoons paprika, smoked

Directions
1. Preheat the oven to 3600F and grease a baking dish.
2. Season the pork chops with paprika, salt and black pepper.
3. Put the pork chops in the baking dish and top with bacon.
4. Sprinkle the cheese over the pork chops and bacon and transfer to the oven.
5. Bake for about 35 minutes and dish out to serve hot.

Nutrition Values:
Calories543

Total Fat 42.2g
Saturated Fat 16.7g
Cholesterol 130mg
Sodium 1047mg
Total Carbohydrate 2.1g
Dietary Fiber 0.9g
Total Sugars 0.3g
Protein 37g

288. KETOGENIC EASY PORK BRISKETS
Servings: 6
Preparation Time: 7 hours 10 mins
Ingredients
- 1 tablespoon butter
- 2 pounds pork briskets
- 2 garlic cloves, minced
- Salt and black pepper, to taste
- 1 small onion, sliced

Directions
1. Put all the ingredients in a large slow cooker and cover the lid.
2. Cook on low for about 7 hours and dish out the pork briskets onto a cutting board.
3. Slice with a knife into desired slices to serve.

Nutrition Values:
Calories304
Total Fat 11.4g
Saturated Fat 4.8g
Cholesterol 140mg
Sodium 114mg
Total Carbohydrate 1.4g
Dietary Fiber 0.3g
Total Sugars 0.5g
Protein 46.1g

289. GROUND PORK WITH ZUCCHINI
Servings: 6
Preparation Time: 35 mins
Ingredients
- 2 large zucchinis, chopped
- 2 pounds lean ground pork
- 3 tablespoons butter
- Salt and black pepper, to taste
- ½ cup homemade bone broth

Directions
1. Put the butter and pork in a skillet and cook for about 5 minutes.
2. Add the bone broth, zucchini, salt and black pepper.
3. Cook for about 20 minutes and dish out to serve hot.

Nutrition Values:
Calories164
Total Fat 12g

Saturated Fat 5.5g
Cholesterol 50mg
Sodium 90mg
Total Carbohydrate 3.6g
Dietary Fiber 1.2g
Total Sugars 1.9g
Protein 10.9g

290. CREAMY BBQ PORK

Servings: 6
Preparation Time: 55 mins

Ingredients

- ½ cup BBQ sauce
- 2 pounds pork, boneless
- 4 tablespoons butter
- Salt, to taste
- 1 cup cream

Directions

1. Heat butter in a skillet and add pork and salt.
2. Cook for about 5 minutes and stir in the BBQ sauce and cream.
3. Cover and cook for about 35 minutes.
4. Dish out in a bowl and serve hot.

Nutrition Values:

Calories406
Total Fat 19.4g
Saturated Fat 9.8g
Cholesterol 163mg
Sodium 427mg
Total Carbohydrate 8.8g
Dietary Fiber 0.1g
Total Sugars 6.2g
Protein 46.3g

291. KETOGENIC LIME CHILI PORK BRISKETS

Servings: 4
Preparation Time: 8 hours 10 mins

Ingredients

- 4 green chilies, chopped
- Salt, to taste
- 1 pound pork briskets
- 1 tablespoon lime juice
- 1 cup bone broth

Directions

1. Season the pork briskets with salt and lime juice.
2. Add the seasoned beef, green chilies and broth to the slow cooker.
3. Set the slow cooker on low and cook for about 8 hours.
4. Dish out onto a platter and serve hot.

Nutrition Values:

Calories124

Total Fat 1.9g
Saturated Fat 0.1g
Cholesterol 30mg
Sodium 666mg
Total Carbohydrate 3g
Dietary Fiber 0.2g
Total Sugars 1.5g
Protein 25.6g

292. KETO BROCCOLI PORK

Servings: 4
Preparation Time: 45 mins

Ingredients

- 3 cups broccoli florets
- 1 pound pork, thinly sliced and chopped into 2 inch pieces
- 2 tablespoons butter
- 2 tablespoons cornstarch + 4 tablespoons cold water
- 1 cup bone broth

Directions

1. Heat butter on medium heat in a skillet and add pork.
2. Sauté for about 3 minutes on each side and add broccoli and bone broth.
3. Cook for about 30 minutes and stir in the cornstarch with water.
4. Cover the skillet and cook for about 4 minutes.
5. Dish out and serve hot.

Nutrition Values:

Calories261
Total Fat 10.3g
Saturated Fat 5.1g
Cholesterol 98mg
Sodium 319mg
Total Carbohydrate 8.4g
Dietary Fiber 1.8g
Total Sugars 1.3g
Protein 32.9g

293. BUTTERNUT SQUASH AND CHICKPEA PASTA

Preparation Time: minutes
Cooking Time: minutes; Serves

Ingredients:

- 1 can chickpeas, rinsed
- 3 cups butternut squash, cubed
- 2 ½ cups vegetable broth
- 12-ounce pasta noodles, uncooked
- 1 cup heavy cream
- Pepper and salt to taste
- 1 tsp oil

Directions:

1. Place a heavy bottomed pot on medium high fire. Add broth and pasta. Bring to a boil and boil for 4 minutes.
2. Stir in chickpeas and squash. Lower fire to a simmer.
3. Season with pepper and salt. Cook for 8 minutes.
4. Once pasta is nearly done to your liking, stir in heavy cream and mix well.
5. Adjust seasoning if needed.
6. Turn off fire and let pasta rest for 5 minutes.
7. Serve and enjoy.

Nutrition Values:
Calories: 235; Fat: 5.5g; Carbs: 35.3g; Protein: 9.2g

294. CHEESY PESTO PASTA

Preparation Time: 15 minutes
Cooking Time: 15 minutes
Servings: 9

Ingredients:

- 1 jar commercial pesto sauce
- 1 package elbow macaroni, cooked according to package Directions:
- 1 cup cottage cheese
- 1 cup parmesan cheese
- 1 cup mozzarella cheese
- Pepper and salt to taste

Directions:

1. Place a heavy bottomed pot on medium high fire and add pesto sauce.
2. Sauté for 3 minutes, season with pepper and salt.
3. Stir in cottage cheese, parmesan, and mozzarella. Mix well and cook for 5 minutes until melted.
4. Stir pasta and mix well.
5. Cook and mix until heated through, around 5 minutes.
6. Serve and enjoy.

Nutrition Values:
Calories: 406; Fat: 34.8g; Carbs: 9.7g; Protein: 16.1g

295. STIR FRIED BRUSSELS SPROUTS AND CARROTS

Preparation Time: 20 minutes
Cooking Time: 15 minutes
Servings: 6

Ingredients:

- 1 tbsp cider vinegar
- 1 lb. Brussels sprouts, halved lengthwise
- 1 lb. carrots cut diagonally into ½-inch thick lengths
- 3 tbsp unsalted butter, divided
- 2 tbsp chopped shallot
- ½ tsp pepper
- ¾ tsp salt
- 1/3 cup water

Directions:

1. On medium high fire, place a nonstick medium fry pan and heat 2 tbsp butter.
2. Add shallots and cook until softened, around one to two minutes while occasionally stirring.
3. Add pepper salt, Brussels sprouts and carrots. Stir fry until vegetables starts to brown on the edges, around 3 to 4 minutes.
4. Add water, cook and cover.
5. After 5 to 8 minutes, or when veggies are already soft, add remaining butter.
6. If needed season with more pepper and salt to taste.
7. Turn off fire, transfer to a platter, serve and enjoy.

Nutrition Values:
Calories: 98; Fat: 4.2g; Carbs: 13.9g; Protein: 3.5g

296. PROVOLONE OVER HERBED PORTOBELLO MUSHROOMS

Preparation Time: 10 minutes
Cooking Time: 10 minutes
Servings: 2

Ingredients:

- ¼ cup grated provolone cheese
- 1 tsp minced garlic

- ¼ tsp dried rosemary
- ½ cup balsamic vinegar
- 2 Portobello mushrooms, stemmed and wiped clean
- 1 tbsp brown sugar

Directions:

1. In oven, position rack 4-inches away from the top and preheat broiler.
2. Prepare a baking dish by spraying with cooking spray lightly.
3. Stemless, place mushroom gill side up.
4. Mix well garlic, rosemary, brown sugar and vinegar in a small bowl.
5. Drizzle over mushrooms equally.
6. Marinate for at least 5 minutes before popping into the oven and broiling for 4 minutes per side or until tender.
7. Once cooked, remove from oven, sprinkle cheese, return to broiler and broil for a minute or two or until cheese melts.
8. Remove from oven and serve right away.

Nutrition Values:
Calories: 168; Fat: 5.1g; Carbs: 21.5g; Protein: 8.6g

297. ASPARAGUS WITH RASPBERRY VINAIGRETTE

Preparation Time: minutes
Cooking Time: 15 minutes
Servings: 4

Ingredients:

- 1 tbsp flat-leaf parsley, chopped
- 1/3 cup grapeseed oil
- 2 small shallots, chopped
- ½ cup raspberry vinegar
- 2 bunches of asparagus, woody portion trimmed
- Salt to taste
- 1 tbsp olive oil
- A dash of ground pepper

Directions:

1. In a large skillet, bring water to a boil. Add a pinch of salt and cook the asparagus spears for two minutes. Submerge in cold water and drain. Set aside.
2. In a saucepan, mix the shallots and vinegar. Bring to a simmer and remove. Let it cool and set aside.
3. Add the grapeseed oil to the vinegar mixture and whisk. Add the parsley and season the vinaigrette with salt and pepper to taste.
4. Arrange the cooked asparagus spears on a plate and pour the vinaigrette.

Nutrition Values:
Calories: 93; Fat: 8.9g; Carbs: 2.2g; Protein: 0.4g

298. GREEK STYLED VEGGIE-RICE

Preparation Time: 15 minutes
Cooking Time: 20 minutes; Serves

Ingredients:

- 3 tbsp chopped fresh mint
- ½ cup grape tomatoes, halved
- 1 head cauliflower, cut into large florets
- ¼ cup fresh lemon juice
- ½ yellow onion, minced
- pepper and salt to taste
- ¼ cup extra virgin olive oil

Directions:

1. In a bowl mix lemon juice and onion and leave for 30 minutes. Then drain onion and reserve the juice and onion bits.
2. In a blender, shred cauliflower until the size of a grain of rice.
3. On medium fire, place a medium nonstick skillet and for 8-10 minutes cook cauliflower while covered.
4. Add grape tomatoes and cook for 3 minutes while stirring occasionally.
5. Add mint and onion bits. Cook for another three minutes.
6. Meanwhile, in a small bowl whisk pepper, salt, 3 tbsp reserved lemon juice and olive oil until well blended.
7. Remove cooked cauliflower, transfer to a serving bowl, pour lemon juice mixture and toss to mix.
8. Before serving, if needed season with pepper and salt to taste.

Nutrition Values:
Calories: 120; Fat: 9.5g; Carbs: 8.0g; Protein: 2.3g

299. BLUE CHEESE, FIG AND ARUGULA SALAD

Preparation Time: 10 minutes
Cooking Time: 0 minutes
Servings: 4

Ingredients:

- 1 tsp Dijon mustard
- 3 tbsp Balsamic Vinegar
- ¼ cup crumbled blue cheese
- 2 bags arugula
- 1-pint fresh figs, quartered
- Pepper and salt to taste
- 3 tbsp olive oil

Directions:

1. Whisk thoroughly together pepper, salt, olive oil, Dijon mustard, and balsamic vinegar to make the dressing. Set aside in the ref for at least 30 minutes to marinate and allow the spices to combine.
2. On four serving plates, evenly arrange arugula and top with blue cheese and figs.
3. Drizzle each plate of salad with 1 ½ tbsp of prepared dressing.
4. Serve and enjoy.

Nutrition Values:
Calories: 162; Fat: 10.0g; Carbs: 15.5g; Protein: 2.5g

300. CRUNCHY KALE CHIPS

Preparation Time: 15 minutes
Cooking Time: 2 hours
Servings: 8

Ingredients:
- 2 tbsp nutritional yeast
- 1 lemon, juiced
- 1 cup sweet potato, grated
- 1 cup fresh cashews, soaked 2 hours
- 2 bunches green curly kale, washed, ribs and stems removed, leaves torn into bite sized pieces
- 2 tbsp filtered water
- ½ tsp sea salt
- 1 tbsp sugar

Directions:
1. Prepare a baking sheet by covering with an unbleached parchment paper. Preheat oven to 150oF.
2. In a large mixing bowl, place kale.
3. In a food processor, process remaining ingredients until smooth. Pour over kale.
4. With your hands, coat kale with marinade.
5. Evenly spread kale onto parchment paper and pop in the oven. Dehydrate for 2 hours and turn leaves after the first hour of baking.
6. Remove from oven; let it cool completely before serving.

Nutrition Values:
Calories: 209; Fat: 15.9g; Carbs: 13.0g; Protein: 7.0g

301. CHEESE AND BROCCOLI BALLS

Preparation Time: 15 minutes
Cooking Time: 5 minutes
Servings: 4

Ingredients:
- ¾ cup almond flour
- 2 large eggs
- 4 ounces fresh broccoli
- 4 ounces mozzarella cheese
- 7 tablespoons flaxseed meal
- Salt and Pepper to taste
- 2 teaspoons baking powder
- Pepper and salt to taste

Directions:
1. To make the cheese and broccoli balls: Place broccoli in food processor and pulse into small pieces. Transfer to a bowl.
2. Add baking powder, ¼ cup flaxseed meal, almond flour, and cheese. Season with pepper and salt if the desired. Mix well. Place remaining flaxseed meal in a small bowl.
3. Add eggs and combine thoroughly. Roll the batter into 1-inch balls. And then roll in flaxseed meal to coat the balls.
4. Cook balls in a 375oF deep fryer until golden brown, about 5 minutes. Transfer cooked balls on to a paper towel lined plate.

Nutrition Values:
Calories: 212; Fat: 18.2g; Carbs: 4.6g; Protein: 9.7g

302. GARLIC 'N SOUR CREAM ZUCCHINI BAKE

Preparation Time: minutes
Cooking Time: 20 minutes
Servings: 3

Ingredients:
- 1/4 cup grated Parmesan cheese
- 1 tablespoon minced garlic
- 1 large zucchini, cut lengthwise then in half
- 1 cup sour cream
- 1 (8 ouncepackage cream cheese, softened
- Salt and pepper to taste

Directions:
1. Lightly grease a casserole dish with cooking spray.
2. Place zucchini slices in a single layer in dish.
3. In a bowl whisk well, remaining ingredients. Spread on top of zucchini slices. Sprinkle pepper and salt to taste.
4. Cover dish with foil.
5. For 10 minutes, cook in preheated 390oF oven.
6. Remove foil and cook for 10 minutes.
7. Serve and enjoy.

Nutrition Values:
Calories: 385; Fat: 32.4g; Carbs: 13.5g; Protein: 11.9g

303. PAPRIKA 'N CAJUN SEASONED ONION RINGS

Preparation Time: 15 minutes
Cooking Time: 25 minutes

Servings: 6

Ingredients:

- ½ teaspoon Cajun seasoning
- ¾ cup almond flour
- 1 ½ teaspoon paprika
- 1 large white onion
- 2 large eggs, beaten
- Salt and pepper to taste
- ¼ cup water

Directions:

1. Preheat a pot with oil for 8 minutes.
2. Peel the onion, cut off the top and slice into circles.
3. In a mixing bowl, combine the water and the eggs. Season with pepper and salt.
4. Soak the onion in the egg mixture.
5. In another bowl, combine the almond flour, paprika powder, Cajun seasoning, salt and pepper.
6. Dredge the onion in the almond flour mixture.
7. Place in the pot and cook in batches until golden brown, around 8 minutes per batch.

Nutrition Values:
Calories: 62; Fat: 4.1g; Carbs: 3.9g; Protein: 2.8g

304. CREAMY KALE AND MUSHROOMS

Preparation Time: 10 minutes
Cooking Time: 15 minutes
Servings: 3

Ingredients:

- 3 cloves of garlic, minced
- 1 onion, chopped
- 1 bunch kale, stems removed and leaves chopped
- 5 white button mushrooms, chopped
- 1 cup coconut milk
- 3 tablespoons oil
- Salt and pepper to taste

Directions:

1. Heat oil in a pot.
2. Sauté the garlic and onion until fragrant for 2 minutes.
3. Stir in mushrooms. Season with pepper and salt. Cook for 8 minutes.
4. Stir in kale and coconut milk. Simmer for 5 minutes.
5. Adjust seasoning to taste.

Nutrition Values:
Calories: 365; Fat: 35.5g; Carbs: 17.9g; Protein: 6.0g

305. STIR-FRIED BUTTERY MUSHROOMS

Preparation Time: 15 minutes
Cooking Time: 15 minutes
Servings: 4

Ingredients:

- 2 tablespoons butter
- 3 cloves of garlic, minced
- 16 ounces fresh brown mushrooms, sliced
- 7 ounces fresh shiitake mushrooms, sliced
- A dash of thyme
- 2 tablespoons olive oil
- Salt and pepper to taste

Directions:

1. Heat the butter and oil in a pot.
2. Sauté the garlic until fragrant, around 2 minutes.
3. Stir in the rest of the ingredients and cook until soft, around 13 minutes.

Nutrition Values:
Calories: 192; Fat: 15.5g; Carbs: 12.7g; Protein: 3.8g

306. STIR FRIED BOK CHOY

Preparation Time: minutes
Cooking Time: 15 minutes
Servings: 4

Ingredients:

- 4 cloves of garlic, minced
- 1 onion, chopped
- 2 heads bokchoy, rinsed and chopped
- 2 tablespoons sesame oil
- 2 tablespoons sesame seeds, toasted
- 3 tablespoons oil
- Salt and pepper to taste

1. **Directions:**
2. Heat the oil in a pot for 2 minutes.
3. Sauté the garlic and onions until fragrant, around 3 minutes.
4. Stir in the bokchoy, salt and pepper.
5. Cover pan and cook for 5 minutes.
6. Stir and continue cooking for another 3 minutes.
7. Drizzle with sesame oil and sesame seeds on top before serving.

Nutrition Values:
Calories: 358; Fat: 28.4g; Carbs: 5.2g; Protein: 21.5g

307. CAULIFLOWER FRITTERS

Preparation Time: 20 minutes
Cooking Time: 15 minutes
Servings: 6

Ingredients:

- 1 large cauliflower head, cut into florets
- 2 eggs, beaten
- ½ teaspoon turmeric
- 1 large onion, peeled and chopped
- ½ teaspoon salt
- ¼ teaspoon black pepper
- 6 tablespoons oil

Directions:

1. Place the cauliflower florets in a pot with water.
2. Bring to a boil and drain once cooked.
3. Place the cauliflower, eggs, onion, turmeric, salt, and pepper into the food processor.
4. Pulse until the mixture becomes coarse.
5. Transfer into a bowl. Using your hands, form six small flattened balls and place in the fridge for at least 1 hour until the mixture hardens.
6. Heat the oil in a skillet and fry the cauliflower patties for 3 minutes on each side.
7. Serve and enjoy.

Nutrition Values:

Calories: 157; Fat: 15.3g; Carbs: 2.28g; Protein: 3.9g

308. BLACK BEANS AND QUINOA

Preparation Time: 10 minutes
Cooking Time: 30 minutes
Servings: 6

Ingredients:

- ½ cup chopped cilantro
- 2 15-oz cans black beans, rinsed and drained
- 1 cup frozen corn kernels
- 2 tsp ground cumin
- ¾ cup quinoa
- Pepper and salt to taste
- 1 tsp vegetable oil
- 1 ½ cups water

Directions:

1. On medium fire, place a saucepan and heat oil.
2. Add quinoa. Pour water and bring to a boil while increasing fire.
3. As you wait for broth to boil, season quinoa mixture with pepper, salt, and cumin.
4. Once boiling, reduce fire to a simmer, cover and simmer around 20 minutes or until liquid is fully absorbed.
5. Once liquid is fully absorbed, stir in black beans and frozen corn. Continue cooking until heated through, around 5 minutes.
6. To serve, add cilantro, toss well to mix, and enjoy.

Nutrition Values:

Calories: 262; Fat: 2.9g; Carbs: 47.1g; Protein: 13.0g

309. SCRAMBLED EGGS WITH MUSHROOMS AND SPINACH

Preparation Time: 3 minutes
Cooking Time: 15 minutes
Servings: 2

Ingredients:

- 2 large eggs
- 1 teaspoon butter
- 1/2 cup thinly sliced fresh mushrooms
- 1/2 cup fresh baby spinach, chopped
- 2 tablespoons shredded provolone cheese
- 1/8 teaspoon salt
- 1/8 teaspoon pepper

Directions:

1. In a small bowl, whisk eggs, salt and pepper until blended. In a small nonstick skillet, heat butter over medium-high heat. Add mushrooms; cook and stir 3-4 minutes or until tender. Add spinach; cook and stir until wilted. Reduce heat to medium.

Add egg mixture; cook and stir just until eggs are thickened and no liquid egg remains. Stir in cheese.

Nutrition Values:

Calories: 162; Fat: 11g; Carbs: 2g; Protein: 14g

310. ENDIVES MIX WITH LEMON DRESSING

Preparation Time: 15 minutes
Cooking Time: 0 minutes
Servings: 8

Ingredients:

- 1 bunch watercress (4 ounces
- 2 heads endive, halved lengthwise and thinly sliced
- 1 cup pomegranate seeds (about 1 pomegranate
- 1 shallot, thinly sliced
- 2 lemons, juiced and zested
- 1/4 teaspoon salt
- 1/8 teaspoon pepper
- 1/3 cup olive oil

Directions:

1. In a large bowl, combine watercress, endive, pomegranate seeds and shallot.
2. In a small bowl, whisk the lemon juice, zest, salt, pepper, and olive oil. Drizzle over salad; toss to coat.

Nutrition Values:

Calories: 121; Fat: 9g; Carbs: 9g; Protein: 2g

311. GREEN BEANS AND RADISH

Preparation Time: 5 minutes
Cooking Time: 0 minutes
Servings: 4

Ingredients:

- 1 tablespoon butter
- 1/2-pound fresh green or wax beans, trimmed
- 1 cup thinly sliced radishes
- 1/2 teaspoon sugar
- 2 tablespoons pine nuts, toasted
- 1/4 teaspoon salt

Directions:

1. In a large skillet, heat butter over medium-high heat. Add beans; cook and stir 3-4 minutes or until crisp-tender.
2. Add radishes; cook 2-3 minutes longer or until vegetables are tender, stirring occasionally. Stir in sugar and salt; sprinkle with nuts.

Nutrition Values:

Calories: 75; Fat: 6g; Carbs: 5g; Protein: 2g

312. GRILLED PARMESAN EGGPLANT

Preparation Time: 5 minutes
Cooking Time: 15 minutes
Servings: 4

Ingredients:

- 1 large eggplant (about 2 pounds
- 1 log (1 poundfresh mozzarella cheese, cut into sixteen slices
- 1 large tomato, cut into eight slices
- 1/2 cup shredded Parmesan cheese
- Chopped fresh basil or parsley
- 1/2 teaspoon salt
- 1 tablespoon olive oil
- 1/2 teaspoon pepper

Directions:

1. Trim ends of eggplant; cut eggplant crosswise into eight slices. Sprinkle with salt; let stand 5 minutes.
2. Blot eggplant dry with paper towels; brush both sides with oil and sprinkle with pepper. Grill, covered, over medium heat 4-6 minutes on each side or until tender. Remove from grill.
3. Top eggplant with mozzarella cheese, tomato and Parmesan cheese.Grill, covered, 1-2 minutes longer or until cheese begins to melt. Top with basil.

Nutrition Values:

Calories: 449; Fat: 31g; Carbs: 15g; Protein: 26g

313. ARTICHOKE AND SPINACH RIGATONI

Preparation Time: 5 minutes
Cooking Time: 0 minutes
Servings: 4

Ingredients:

- 3 cups uncooked rigatoni or large tube pasta
- 1 package (10 ouncesfrozen creamed spinach
- 1 can (14 ounceswater-packed artichoke hearts quartered
- 2 cups shredded part-skim mozzarella cheese, divided
- 1/4 cup grated Parmesan cheese
- 1/2 teaspoon salt
- 1/4 teaspoon pepper

Directions:

1. Preheat broiler. Prepare rigatoni and spinach according to package directions.
2. Drain pasta, reserving 1/2 cup pasta water; return to pan. Add artichoke hearts, 1/2 cup mozzarella cheese, Parmesan cheese, salt, pepper and creamed spinach; toss to combine, adding some of the reserved pasta water to thin, if desired.
3. Transfer to a greased 2-qt. broiler-safe baking dish; sprinkle with remaining mozzarella cheese. Broil 4-6 in. from heat 2-3 minutes or until cheese is melted.

Nutrition Values:

Calories: 448; Fat: 14g; Carbs: 54g; Protein: 28g

314. EGG AND TOMATO SALAD

Preparation Time: 20 minutes
Cooking Time: 1 minutes
Servings: 2

Ingredients:

- 4 hard-boiled eggs, peeled and sliced
- 2 red tomatoes, chopped
- 1 small red onion, chopped
- 2 tablespoons lemon juice, freshly squeezed
- Salt and pepper to taste

Directions:

1. Place all ingredients in a mixing bowl.
2. Toss to coat all ingredients.
3. Garnish with parsley if desired.
4. Serve over toasted whole wheat bread.

Nutrition Values:

Calories: 189; Fat: 10.9g; Carbs: 9.1g; Protein: 14.7g

315. CUCUMBER AND TOMATO

SANDWICH

Preparation Time: 5 minutes
Cooking Time: 2 minutes
Servings: 1

Ingredients:

- 2 slices of keto bread, toasted
- 2 slices of tomatoes
- 2 slices of cucumber
- Pepper and salt to taste

Directions:

1. Season tomatoes and cucumber slices with pepper and salt.
2. Put slices of tomatoes and cucumber in between two slices of toasted bread.
3. Slice diagonally before serving.

Nutrition Values:

Calories: 168; Fat: 11.1g; Carbs: 8.8g; Protein: 8.3g

316. BLACK BEAN AND COUSCOUS SALAD

Preparation Time: 10 minutes
Cooking Time: 15 minutes
Servings: 4

Ingredients:

- 1 cup couscous, uncooked
- 1 teaspoon lemon juice
- ¼ cup fresh cilantro, chopped
- 1 cup corn kernels, fresh
- 2 cans black beans, rinsed and drained

Salt and pepper to taste

- 1 ¼ cups water
- 2 tablespoons extra virgin olive oil
- ½ teaspoon ground cumin

Directions:

1. Put the couscous and water in a pot and bring to a boil. Once the water has boiled, reduce the heat to medium-low. Cook for 15 minutes. Once cooked, drain the excess liquid and allow to cool.
2. Meanwhile, mix the olive oil, lemon juice, and cumin in a small bowl. Set aside.
3. Assemble the salad by putting the couscous and the rest of the ingredients into a bowl. Mix gently and pour over the sauce.
4. Season with more salt and pepper to taste.

Nutrition Values:

Calories: 224; Fat: 4.2g; Carbs: 37.9g; Protein: 10.6g

317. CURRIED TOFU

Preparation Time: 5 minutes
Cooking Time: 15 minutes
Servings: 6

Ingredients:

- 2 cloves of garlic, minced
- 1 onion, cubed
- 12-ounce firm tofu, drained and cubed
- 1 teaspoon curry powder
- 1 tablespoon soy sauce
- ¼ teaspoon pepper
- 1 tablespoon olive oil

Directions:

1. Heat the oil in a skillet over medium flame.
2. Sauté the garlic and onion until fragrant.
3. Stir in the tofu and stir for 3 minutes.
4. Add the rest of the ingredients and adjust the water.
5. Close the lid and allow simmering for 10 minutes.
6. Serve and enjoy.

Nutrition Values:

Calories: 90; Fat: 6.1g; Carbs: 4.4g; Protein: 6.2g

318. BEAN BURRITO

Preparation Time: 5 minutes
Cooking Time: 5 minutes
Servings: 1

Ingredients:

- 1 large whole wheat tortilla
- ½ cup red kidney beans, rinsed and drained
- 2 romaine lettuce leaves
- ½ avocado, peeled and sliced
- A sprig of cilantro, chopped

Salt to taste

- 1 tablespoon lime juice (optional

Directions:

1. Lay the tortilla wrap on a flat surface.
2. Place the beans, lettuce leaves, and avocado in the middle of the wrap.
3. Sprinkle with salt and drizzle with lime juice if using.
4. Put the chopped cilantro last before rolling the burrito.

Nutrition Values:

Calories: 400; Fat: 19.3g; Carbs: 48.6g; Protein: 13.1g

319. DATES AND CABBAGE SAUTÉ

Preparation Time: 5 mins
Servings: 4

Ingredients:

- 2 tbsps.olive oil
- 2 tbsps.lemon juice
- 1 lb. shredded red cabbage
- Black pepper
- 8 pitted and sliced dates

- 2 tbsps.chopped chives
- ¼ c. low-sodium veggie stock

Directions:

1. Heat up a pan with the oil over medium heat, add the cabbage and the dates, toss and cook for 4 minutes.
2. Add the stock and the other ingredients, toss, cook over medium heat for 11 minutes more, divide between plates and serve.

Nutrition Values:

Calories: 280, Fat:8.1 g, Carbs:8.7 g, Protein:6.3 g, Sugars:4.7 g, Sodium:430 mg

320. BAKED SQUASH MIX

Preparation Time: 10 mins
Servings: 4

Ingredients:

- 2 tsps. chopped cilantro
- 2 lbs. peeled and sliced butternut squash
- ¼ tsp. black pepper
- 1 tsp. garlic powder
- 2 tbsps.olive oil
- 1 tsp. chili powder
- 1 tbsp. lemon juice

Directions:

1. In a roasting pan, combine the squash with the oil and the other ingredients, toss gently, bake in the oven at 400 0F for 45 minutes, divide between plates and serve.

Nutrition Values:

Calories: 167, Fat:7.4 g, Carbs:27.5 g, Protein:2.5 g, Sugars:4.4 g, Sodium:10 mg

321. LEMONY ENDIVES

Preparation Time: 10 mins
Servings: 4

Ingredients:

- 1 tbsps.grated lemon zest
- 4 halved endives
- 2 tbsps.olive oil
- 1 tbsp. lemon juice
- ¼ tsp. black pepper
- 2 tbsps.grated fat-free parmesan

Directions:

1. In a baking dish, combine the endives with the lemon juice and the other ingredients except the parmesan and toss.
2. Sprinkle the parmesan on top, bake the endives at 400 0F for 20 minutes, divide between plates and serve as a side dish.

Nutrition Values:

Calories: 71, Fat:7.1 g, Carbs:2.3 g, Protein:0.9 g, Sugars:2 g, Sodium:58 mg

322. GARLIC MUSHROOMS AND CORN

Preparation Time: 10 mins
Servings: 4

Ingredients:

- 2 c. corn
- 1 lb. halved white mushrooms
- ¼ tsp. black pepper
- ½ tsp. chili powder
- 2 tbsps.olive oil
- 1 c. no-salt-added, chopped and canned tomatoes
- 4 minced garlic cloves

Directions:

1. Heat up a pan with the oil over medium heat, add the mushrooms, garlic and the corn, stir and sauté for 10 minutes.
2. Add the rest of the ingredients, toss, cook over medium heat for 10 minutes more, divide between plates and serve.

Nutrition Values:

Calories: 285, Fat:13 g, Carbs:14.6 g, Protein:6.7 g, Sugars:2 g, Sodium:260 mg

323. CILANTRO BROCCOLI

Preparation Time: 10 mins
Servings: 4

Ingredients:

- 2 tbsps.chili sauce
- 2 tbsps.olive oil
- 2 minced garlic cloves
- ¼ tsp. black pepper
- 1 lb. broccoli florets
- 2 tbsps.chopped cilantro
- 1 tbsp. lemon juice

Directions:

1. In a baking pan, combine the broccoli with the oil, garlic and the other ingredients, toss a bit, introduce in the oven and bake at 400 0F for 30 minutes.
2. Divide the mix between plates and serve.

Nutrition Values:

Calories: 103, Fat:7.4 g, Carbs:8.3 g, Protein:3.4 g, Sugars:33 g, Sodium:1.7 mg

324. PAPRIKA CARROTS

Preparation Time: 10 mins
Servings: 4

Ingredients:

- 1 tbsp. sweet paprika
- 1 tsp. lime juice
- 1 lb. trimmed baby carrots
- ¼ tsp. black pepper
- 3 tbsps.olive oil
- 1 tsp. sesame seeds

Directions:

1. Arrange the carrots on a lined baking sheet, add the paprika and the other ingredients except the sesame seeds, toss, introduce in the oven and bake at 400 0F for 30 minutes.
2. Divide the carrots between plates, sprinkle sesame seeds on top and serve.

Nutrition Values:
Calories: 142, Fat:11.3 g, Carbs:11.4 g, Protein:1.2 g, Sugars:7 g, Sodium:200 mg

325. MASHED CAULIFLOWER

Preparation Time: 10 mins
Servings: 4

Ingredients:

- ½ c. coconut milk
- 1 tbsp. chopped chives
- 2 lbs. cauliflower florets
- ¼ tsp. black pepper
- 1 tbsp. chopped cilantro
- ½ c. low-fat sour cream

Directions:

1. Put the cauliflower in a pot, add water to cover, bring to a boil over medium heat, and cook for 25 minutes and drain.
2. Mash the cauliflower, add the milk, black pepper and the cream, whisk well, divide between plates, sprinkle the rest of the ingredients on top and serve.

Nutrition Values:
Calories: 188, Fat:13.4 g, Carbs:15 g, Protein:6.1 g, Sugars:5 g, Sodium:339 mg

326. SPINACH SPREAD

Preparation Time: 10 mins
Servings: 4

Ingredients:

1. 1 c. coconut cream
2. 1 tbsp. chopped dill
3. 1 lb. chopped spinach
4. ¼ tsp. black pepper
5. 1 c. shredded low-fat mozzarella
6. Directions:
7. In a baking pan, combine the spinach with the cream and the other ingredients, stir well, introduce in the oven and bake at 400 0F for 20 minutes.

8. Divide into bowls and serve.

Nutrition Values:
Calories: 340, Fat:33 g, Carbs:4 g, Protein:5 g, Sugars:3 g, Sodium:640 mg

327. MUSTARD GREENS SAUTÉ

Preparation Time: 10 mins
Servings: 4

Ingredients:

- 2 tbsps.olive oil
- 2 chopped spring onions
- 6 c. mustard greens
- 2 tbsps.sweet paprika
- Black pepper
- ½ c. coconut cream

Directions:

1. Heat up a pan with the oil over medium-high heat, add the onions, paprika and black pepper, stir and sauté for 3 minutes.
2. Add the mustard greens and the other ingredients, toss, cook for 9 minutes more, divide between plates and serve.

Nutrition Values:
Calories: 163, Fat:14.8 g, Carbs:8.3 g, Protein:3.6 g, Sugars:7 g, Sodium:390 mg

328. BASIL TURNIPS MIX

Preparation Time: 10 mins
Servings: 4

Ingredients:

- ¼ c. low-sodium veggie stock
- 4 sliced turnips
- ¼ c. chopped basil
- 2 minced garlic cloves
- 1 tbsp. avocado oil
- ½ c. chopped walnuts
- Black pepper

Directions:

1. Heat up a pan with the oil over medium-high heat, add the garlic and the turnips and brown for 5 minutes.
2. Add the rest of the ingredients, toss, cook for 10 minutes more, divide between plates and serve.

Nutrition Values:
Calories: 140, Fat:9.7 g, Carbs:10.5 g, Protein:5 g, Sugars:3 g, Sodium:357 mg

329. BAKED MUSHROOMS

Preparation Time: 10 mins
Servings: 4

Ingredients:

- Black pepper
- 1 tbsp. chopped chives
- 1 lb. small mushroom caps
- 1 tbsp. chopped rosemary
- 2 tbsps.olive oil

Directions:

1. Put the mushrooms in a roasting pan, add the oil and the rest of the ingredients, toss, bake at 400 0F for 25 minutes, divide into bowls and serve

Nutrition Values:

Calories: 215, Fat:12.3 g, Carbs:15.3 g, Protein:3.5 g, Sugars:4.5 g, Sodium:309 mg

330. CELERY AND KALE MIX

Preparation Time: 10 mins
Servings: 4

Ingredients:

- 5 c. torn kale
- 2 chopped celery stalks
- 1 tbsp. extra-virgin olive oil
- 3 tbsps.water

Directions:

1. Heat up a pan while using the oil over medium-high heat, add celery, stir and cook for 10 minutes.
2. Add kale and water, toss, cook for ten minutes more, divide between plates and serve.
3. Enjoy!

Nutrition Values:

Calories: 140, Fat:1 g, Carbs:6 g, Protein:6 g, Sugars:20 g, Sodium:169 mg

331. SPICY AVOCADO

Preparation Time: 10 mins
Servings: 1

Ingredients:

- 2 tbsps.hot sauce
- Sea salt
- 1 c. halved ripe avocado
- ½ Juiced lemon

Directions:

1. Slice the avocado in half a few times, spin and slice a few more times perpendicular to the first slices. You should end up with several cubes that are still attached to the peel.
2. Drizzle the lemon juice and hot sauce onto the avocado. Eat with a fork.

Nutrition Values:

Calories: 124, Fat:10.8 g, Carbs:9.5 g, Protein:1.9 g, Sugars:0.4 g, Sodium:95 mg

332. CAULIFLOWER RISOTTO

Preparation Time: 10 mins
Servings: 4

Ingredients:

- 2 minced garlic cloves
- 1 tbsp. fresh lemon juice
- 2 tbsps.essential organic olive oil
- 2 tbsps.chopped thyme
- ¼ tsp. black pepper
- 12 oz. cauliflower rice
- Zest of ½ grated lemon

Directions:

1. Heat up a pan with the oil over medium-high heat, add cauliflower rice and garlic, stir and cook for 5 minutes.
2. Add freshly squeezed fresh lemon juice, lemon zest, thyme, salt and pepper, stir, cook for two main minutes more, divide between plates and serve.
3. Enjoy!

Nutrition Values:

Calories: 130, Fat:2 g, Carbs:6 g, Protein:8 g, Sugars:0.3 g, Sodium: 160 mg

333. KALE DIP

Preparation Time: 10 mins
Servings: 4

Ingredients:

- 1 c. coconut cream
- 1 tsp. chili powder
- 1 bunch kale leaves
- 1 chopped shallot
- ¼ tsp. black pepper
- 1 tbsp. olive oil

Directions:

1. Heat up a pan with the oil over medium heat, add the shallots, stir and sauté for 4 minutes.
2. Add the kale and the other ingredients, bring to a simmer and cook over medium heat for 16 minutes.
3. Blend using an immersion blender, divide into bowls and serve.

Nutrition Values:

Calories: 188, Fat:17.9 g, Carbs:7.6 g, Protein:2.5 g, Sugars:0.8 g, Sodium:23 mg

334. DILL CABBAGE

Preparation Time: 10 mins
Servings: 4

Ingredients:

- 1 chopped yellow onion

- ¼ tsp. black pepper
- 1 lb. shredded green cabbage
- 1 tbsp. chopped dill
- 1 tbsp. olive oil
- 1 cubed tomato

Directions:

1. Heat up a pan with the oil over medium heat, add the onion and sauté for 5 minutes.
2. Add the cabbage and the rest of the ingredients, toss, cook over medium heat for 10 minutes, divide between plates and serve.

Nutrition Values:

Calories: 74, Fat:3.7 g, Carbs:10.2 g, Protein:2.1 g, Sugars:2 g, Sodium:115 mg

335. CURRIED CAULIFLOWER STEAKS WITH RED RICE

Preparation Time: 6 mins
Servings: 4

Ingredients:

- 1/3 c. extra-virgin olive oil
- 2 tsps. curry powder
- ½ tsps. kosher salt
- 2 cauliflower heads
- 1 tbsp. lemon juice
- 2 tbsps.chopped fresh cilantro
- 1 c. brown rice

Directions:

1. Preheat oven to 450 0F. Line a large baking sheet with tin foil.
2. Follow directions to prepare rice.
3. Whisk together oil, curry powder, and salt in a bowl.
4. Prepare cauliflower, making sure to keep stems intact. Place stem-side down on a cutting board and cut into thick slices to create "steaks." Get 4 steaks. Then slice the remaining cauliflower into smaller slices to get 4 cups.
5. Place steaks and florets onto a baking sheet. Brush both sides of the steaks with the curry mixture.
6. Place steaks in oven, turning after 15 minutes. Finish baking until steaks are tender and brown.
7. Divide rice evenly onto 4 plates and top each plate with a cauliflower steak. Sprinkle with cilantro.

Nutrition Values:

Calories: 410, Fat:21 g, Carbs:49 g, Protein:10 g, Sugars:5 g, Sodium:317 mg

336. FETA, EGGPLANT AND SAUSAGE PENNE

Servings: 6
Cooking time: 20 minutes

Ingredients:
- ¼ cup chopped fresh parsley
- ½ cup crumbled feta cheese
- 6 cups hot cooked penne
- 1 14.5-oz can dice tomatoes
- ¼ tsp ground black pepper
- 1 tsp dried oregano
- 2 tbsp tomato paste
- 4 garlic cloves, minced
- ½ lb. bulk pork breakfast sausage
- 4 ½ cups cubed peeled eggplant

Directions:
1. On medium high fire, place a nonstick, big fry pan and cook for seven minutes garlic, sausage and eggplant or until eggplants are soft and sausage are lightly browned.
2. Stir in diced tomatoes, black pepper, oregano and tomato paste. Cover and simmer for five minutes while occasionally stirring.
3. Remove pan from fire, stir in pasta and mix well.
4. Transfer to a serving dish, garnish with parsley and cheese before serving.

Nutrition Values:
Calories: 368; Carbs: 48.3g; Protein: 14.1g; Fats: 14.3g; Saturated Fat: 5.4g; Sodium: 436mg

337. PASTITSIO WILD MUSHROOM

Servings: 5
Cooking time: 60 minutes

Ingredients:
- 4 cups fusilli pasta, cooked and drained
- 1 ½ cups shredded low fat mozzarella cheese, divided
- 2 cups skim milk
- 1 ½ tbsp All-purpose flour
- 3 tbsp chopped fresh parsley
- 2 large eggs, lightly beaten
- 1 8oz can tomato sauce
- 1/8 tsp ground nutmeg
- ¼ tsp black pepper
- 1 tbsp chopped fresh oregano
- 2 8oz packages pre-sliced exotic mushroom blend, chopped
- 2 garlic cloves, minced
- 1 cup chopped onion
- 4 tsp olive oil, divided

Directions:
1. On medium high fire, place Dutch oven with 1 tbsp oil and for three minutes fry garlic and onion. Stir in mushroom and cook until liquid has evaporated around eight minutes. Add tomato sauce, nutmeg, pepper, and oregano. Stir constantly and cook for another two minutes before removing from fire and put aside.
2. In a large bowl mix parsley and eggs. In same pan, heat 1 tsp oil and cook for a minute the flour. While constantly mixing, pour in milk gradually and boil for two minutes and let it thicken. Remove from fire and allow to stand for four minutes before whisking in 1 cup cheese. While stirring vigorously, slowly pour in the egg mixture. Then toss in pasta and mix.
3. In a greased rectangular glass dish, evenly spread 2 cups pasta mixture, top with mushroom mixture and pour remaining pasta. With foil, cover the dish and bake in a preheated 350oF oven for 30 minutes.
4. Remove dish from oven and set oven to broiler. Remove foil and sprinkle ½ cup of cheese. Return to oven and broil for five minutes. Remove from oven and allow to stand for fifteen minutes before serving.

Nutrition Values:
Calories: 399; Carbs: 47.5g; Protein: 23.7g; Fats: 13.8g; Saturated Fat: 5.7g; Sodium: 98mg

338. PENNE ANTI-PASTO

Servings: 5
Cooking time: 15 minutes

Ingredients:
- ¼ cup pine nuts, toasted
- ½ cup grated low fat Parmigiana-Reggiano cheese, divided
- 8-oz penne pasta, cooked and drained
- 1 6oz jar drained, sliced, marinated and quartered artichoke hearts
- 1 7 oz jar drained and chopped sun-dried tomato halves packed in oil
- 3 oz chopped prosciutto
- 1/3 cup pesto
- 1/4 cup pitted and chopped Kalamata olives

- 1 medium red bell pepper

Directions:
1. Slice bell pepper, discard membranes, seeds and stem. On a foiled lined baking sheet, place bell pepper halves, press down by hand and broil in oven for eight minutes. Remove from oven, put in a sealed bag for 5 minutes before peeling and chopping.
2. Place chopped bell pepper in a bowl and mix in artichokes, tomatoes, prosciutto, pesto and olives.
3. Toss in ¼ cup cheese and pasta. Transfer to a serving dish and garnish with ¼ cup cheese and pine nuts. Serve and enjoy!

Nutrition Values:
Calories: 493.6; Carbs: 53.0g; Protein: 17.7g; Fats: 25.9g; Saturated Fat: 5.4g; Sodium: 340.8mg

339. FILLING MUSHROOM BOLOGNESE

Servings: 6
Cooking time: 60 minutes

Ingredients:
- ¼ cup chopped fresh parsley
- ¼ cup low fat Parmigiano-Reggiano cheese, grated
- 10-oz whole wheat spaghetti, cooked and drained
- ¼ cup skim milk
- 1 14oz can whole peeled tomatoes
- ½ cup white wine
- 2 tbsp tomato paste
- 1 tbsp minced garlic
- 8 cups finely chopped cremini mushrooms
- ½ lb. ground pork
- ½ tsp freshly ground black pepper, divided
- 2 ½ cups chopped onion
- 1 tbsp olive oil
- 1 cup boiling water
- ½-oz dried porcini mushrooms

Directions:
1. Let porcini stand in a boiling bowl of water for twenty minutes, drain (reserve liquid), rinse and chop. Set aside.
2. On medium high fire, place a Dutch oven with olive oil and cook for ten minutes pork, ¼ tsp pepper, and onions. Constantly mix to break ground pork pieces.
3. Stir in ¼ tsp pepper, garlic and cremini mushrooms. Continue cooking until liquid has evaporated, around fifteen minutes.
4. Stirring constantly, add porcini and sauté for a

minute.
5. Stir in wine, porcini liquid, tomatoes and tomato paste. Let it simmer for forty minutes. Stir occasionally. Pour milk and cook for another two minutes before removing from fire.
6. Stir in pasta and transfer to a serving dish. Garnish with parsley and cheese before serving.

Nutrition Values:
Calories: 353; Carbs: 55.4g; Protein: 23.6g; Fats: 7.0g; Saturated Fat: 2.0g; Sodium: 78mg

340. FRESH HERBS AND CLAMS LINGUINE

Servings: 4
Cooking time: 15 minutes

Ingredients:
- ½ tsp freshly ground black pepper
- 1.5-lbs. littleneck clams
- ½ cup white wine
- 4 garlic cloves, sliced
- ¼ tsp crushed red pepper
- 2 cups vertically sliced red onion
- 2 tbsp olive oil
- 2 tsp grated lemon zest
- 1 tbsp chopped fresh oregano
- 1/3 cup parsley leaves
- 8-oz linguine, cooked and drained

Directions:
1. Chop finely lemon rind, oregano and parsley. Set aside.
2. On medium high fire, place a nonstick fry pan with olive oil and fry for four minutes garlic, red pepper and onion.
3. Add clams and wine and cook until shells have opened, around five minutes. Throw any unopened clam.
4. Transfer mixture into a large serving bowl. Add pepper and pasta. Toss to mix well. Serve with parsley garnish.

Nutrition Values:
Calories: 335; Carbs: 54.2g; Protein: 12.3g; Fats: 8.5g; Saturated Fat: 1.2g; Sodium: 41mg

341. PASTA SHELLS STUFFED WITH FETA, SPINACH AND ARTICHOKE

Servings: 10
Cooking time: 40 minutes

Ingredients:
- Cooking spray
- 20 jumbo pasta shells, cooked and drained

- 2 garlic cloves, minced
- 5 oz frozen chopped spinach, thawed, drained and squeezed dry
- 1 9oz package frozen artichoke hearts, thawed and chopped
- ¼ tsp freshly ground black pepper
- ½ cup fat free cream cheese softened
- 1 cup crumbled feta cheese
- 1 cup shredded provolone cheese, divided
- 1 8oz can no salt added tomato sauce
- 1 28oz can fire roasted crushed tomatoes with added puree
- ¼ cup chopped pepperoncini peppers
- 1 tsp dried oregano

Directions:

1. On medium fire, place a medium fry pan and for 12 minutes cook tomato sauce, crushed tomatoes, peppers and oregano. Put aside.
2. In a medium bowl, mix garlic, spinach, artichoke, black pepper, cream cheese, feta cheese and ½ cup provolone. Evenly stuff these to the cooked pasta shells.
3. Grease a rectangular glass dish and arrange all the pasta shells within. Cover with tomato mixture and top with provolone.
4. Bake for 25 minutes in a preheated 375oF oven.

Nutrition Values:
Calories: 224; Carbs: 31.8g; Protein: 12.3g; Fats: 6.5g; Saturated Fat: 4.0g; Sodium: 383mg

342. CREAMY ALFREDO FETTUCCINE
Servings: 4
Cooking time: 5 minutes

Ingredients:
- 1 cup grated low fat, low sodium parmesan cheese
- 1/8 tsp freshly ground black pepper
- ½ tsp salt
- 1/4 cup whipping cream
- 1 tbsp olive oil
- 8 oz dried fettuccine, cooked and drained

Directions:
1. On medium high fire, place a big fry pan and heat oil.
2. Add pepper, ¾ cup parmesan, and cream gently boil for three to five minutes.
3. Once thickened, turn off fire and quickly stir in 1/4 cup of parmesan cheese. Toss in pasta, mix well.
4. Serve and enjoy.

Nutrition Values:

Calories: 355; Carbs: 46.4g; Protein: 14.8g; Fats: 12.9g; Saturated Fat: 5.9g; Sodium: 309mg

343. LIP SMACKING CHICKEN TETRAZZINI
Servings: 10
Cooking time: 3 hours

Ingredients:
- ¾ cup thinly sliced green onion
- 2/3 cup grated parmesan cheese
- 10 oz dried spaghetti or linguine, cooked and drained
- ¼ tsp ground nutmeg
- ¼ tsp ground black pepper
- ¼ cup chicken broth
- 1 16oz jar of Alfredo pasta sauce
- 2 4.5oz jars of sliced mushrooms, drained
- 1-lb skinless chicken breasts cut into ½ inch slices

Directions:
1. In a slow cooker, mix mushrooms and chicken.
2. In a bowl, mix well nutmeg, pepper, broth and alfredo sauce before pouring over chicken and mushrooms.
3. Set on high heat, cover and cook for two to three hours.
4. Once chicken is cooked, pour over pasta, garnish with green onion and serve.

Nutrition Values:
Calories: 318; Carbs: 23.5g; Protein: 22.5g; Fats: 14.7g; Saturated Fat: 8.3g; Sodium: 403mg

344. PASTA SHELLS STUFFED WITH SCAMPI
Servings:10
Cooking time: 40 minutes

Ingredients:
- 1/3 cup grated fresh Parmigiano-Reggiano cheese
- 3 cups lower-sodium marinara sauce, divided
- Cooking spray
- 1 tbsp potato starch
- 1 lb. medium shrimp, peeled, deveined and chopped coarsely
- 1/3 cup chopped fresh basil
- ¼ tsp ground red pepper
- ¼ cup reduced fat milk
- ½ cup 1/3-less fat cream cheese
- 2 tbsp minced garlic
- ½ cup chopped shallots

- 1 ½ tbsp olive oil
- 20 jumbo pasta shells, cooked and drained

Directions:

1. On medium fire, place a nonstick fry pan with oil and fry for four minutes the shallots while occasionally mixing. Stir in garlic and cook for another minute.
2. In a bowl, place shrimp and sprinkle with potato starch and set aside.
3. Add pepper, milk and cream cheese while stirring constantly and cooking until cheese is melted and well mixed. Remove from fire and quickly stir in shrimp and basil.
4. In a greased rectangular glass dish, pour a cup of marinara sauce and spread evenly. Then equally stuff the pasta shells with the shrimp mixture and arrange the shells in the glass dish. Pour remaining marinara sauce on top of shells and garnish with cheese.
5. Place the dish in a preheated 400oF oven and cook for 20 minutes.

Nutrition Values:
Calories: 165; Carbs: 16.1g; Protein: 10.3g; Fats: 6.5g; Saturated Fat: 2.2g; Sodium: 388mg

345. VEGGIES AND SUN-DRIED TOMATO ALFREDO

Servings: 6
Cooking time: 40 minutes

Ingredients:

- 2 tsp finely shredded lemon peel
- ½ cup finely shredded Parmesan cheese
- 1 ¼ cups skim milk
- 2 tbsp all-purpose flour
- 8 fresh mushrooms, sliced
- 1 ½ cups fresh broccoli florets
- 4 oz fresh trimmed and quartered Brussels sprouts
- 4 oz trimmed fresh asparagus spears
- 1 tbsp olive oil
- 4 tbsp low fat butter
- ½ cup chopped dried tomatoes
- 8 oz dried fettuccine

Directions:

1. In a boiling pot of water, add fettuccine and cook following manufacturer's instructions. Two minutes before the pasta is cooked, add the dried tomatoes. Drain pasta and tomatoes and return to pot to keep warm. Set aside.
2. On medium high fire, in a big fry pan with 1 tbsp butter, fry mushrooms, broccoli, Brussels sprouts and asparagus. Cook for

eight minutes while covered, transfer to a plate and put aside.

3. Using same fry pan, add remaining butter and flour. Stirring vigorously, cook for a minute or until thickened. Add Parmesan cheese, milk and mix until cheese is melted around five minutes.
4. Toss in the pasta and mix. Transfer to serving dish. Garnish with Parmesan cheese and lemon peel before serving.

Nutrition Values:
Calories: 223; Carbs: 44.4g; Protein: 8.5g; Fats: 3.3g; Saturated Fat: 0.6g; Sodium: 142mg

346. CREAMY ARTICHOKE LASAGNA

Servings: 9
Cooking time: 1 hour 30 minutes

Ingredients:

- 1 cup shredded mozzarella cheese
- 2 cups light cream
- ¼ cup all-purpose flour
- 1 cup vegetable broth
- 1 egg
- 1 cup snipped fresh basil
- 1 cup finely shredded Parmesan cheese
- 1 15oz carton ricotta cheese
- 4 cloves garlic, minced
- ½ cup pine nuts
- 3 tbsp olive oil
- 9 dried lasagna noodles, cooked, rinsed in cold water and drained
- 15 fresh baby artichokes
- ¼ cup lemon juice
- 3 cups water

Directions:

1. Prepare in a medium bowl lemon juice and water. Put aside. Slice off artichoke base and remove yellowed outer leaves and cut into quarters. Immediately soak sliced artichokes in prepared liquid and drain after a minute.
2. Over medium fire, place a big saucepan with 2 tbsp oil and fry half of garlic, pine nuts and artichokes. Stir frequently and cook until artichokes are soft around ten minutes. Turn off fire and transfer mixture to a big bowl and quickly stir in egg, ½ cup of basil, ½ cup of parmesan cheese and ricotta cheese. Mix thoroughly.
3. In a small bowl mix flour and broth. In same pan, add 1 tbsp oil and fry remaining garlic for half a minute. Add light cream and flour mixture. Stir constantly and cook until thickened. Remove from fire and stir in ½

cup of basil.

4. In a separate bowl mix ½ cup parmesan and mozzarella cheese.
5. Assemble the lasagna by layering the following in a greased rectangular glass dish: lasagna, 1/3 of artichoke mixture, 1/3 of sauce, sprinkle with the dried cheeses and repeat layering procedure until all ingredients are used up.
6. For forty minutes, bake lasagna in a pre-heated oven of 350oF. Remove lasagna from oven and before serving, let it stand for fifteen minutes.

Nutrition Values:
Calories: 388; Carbs: 23.7g; Protein: 23.6g; Fats: 22.1g; Saturated Fat: 5.0g; Sodium: 202mg

347. GORGONZOLA AND CHICKEN PASTA

Servings: 6
Cooking time: 30 minutes

Ingredients:

- 12 oz pasta, cooked and drained
- ¼ cup snipped fresh Italian parsley
- 2/3 cup Parmesan cheese
- 1 cup crumbled Gorgonzola cheese
- 2 cups whipping cream
- 8 oz stemmed fresh cremini or shiitake mushrooms
- 1 tbsp olive oil
- ½ tsp ground pepper
- 1-lb skinless chicken breast, cut into ½-inch slices

Directions:

1. Season chicken breasts with ¼ tsp pepper.
2. On medium high fire, place a nonstick pan with 1 tbsp oil and stir fry half of the chicken until cooked and lightly browned. Transfer chicken to a clean dish and repeat procedure to remaining batch of uncooked chicken.
3. In same pan, stir fry mushroom until liquid is evaporated and mushrooms are soft, around eight minutes. Stir occasionally.
4. Add chicken back to the mushrooms along with cream and simmer for three minutes. Then add the remaining pepper, parmesan cheese and ½ cup of Gorgonzola cheese. Cook until mixture is uniform. Turn off fire.
5. Add pasta into the mixture, tossing to combine. Transfer to serving dish and garnish with remaining Gorgonzola cheese and serve.

Nutrition Values:
Calories: 337; Carbs: 25.2g; Protein: 29.3g; Fats: 13.2g;

Saturated Fat: 4.2g; Sodium: 304mg

348. PASTITSIO AN ITALIAN PASTA DISH

Servings: 4
Cooking time: 30 minutes

Ingredients:

- 2 tbsp chopped fresh flat leaf parsley
- ¾ cup shredded low fat mozzarella cheese
- 1 3oz package of fat free cream cheese
- ½ cup less fat cream cheese
- 1 can 14.5oz of diced tomatoes, drained
- 2 cups fat free milk
- 1 tbsp all-purpose flour
- 5 garlic cloves, minced
- 1 ½ cups chopped onion
- 1 tbsp olive oil
- 1/2 lb. ground sirloin
- Cooking spray
- 8 oz uncooked penne, cooked and drained

Directions:

1. On medium high fire, place a big nonstick saucepan and for five minutes sauté beef.Keep on stirring to break up the pieces of ground meat. Once cooked, remove from pan and drain fat.
2. Using same pan, heat oil and fry onions until soft around four minutes while occasionally stirring.
3. Add garlic and continue cooking for another minute while constantly stirring.
4. Stir in beef and flour, cook for another minute. Mix constantly.
5. Add the fat free cream cheese, less fat cream cheese, tomatoes and milk. Cook until mixture is smooth and heated. Toss in pasta and mix well.
6. Transfer pasta into a greased rectangular glass dish and top with mozzarella. Cook in a preheated broiler for four minutes. Remove from broiler and garnish with parsley before serving.

Nutrition Values:
Calories: 376; Carbs: 49.6g; Protein: 28.5g; Fats: 7.1g; Saturated Fat: 4.6g; Sodium: 365mg

349. PORCINI-RICOTTA FILLED BOLOGNESE LASAGNA

Servings: 12
Cooking time: 1 hour 30-minutes

Ingredients:

- Snipped fresh Italian parsley

- 1 cup finely shredded parmesan cheese
- 15 dried lasagna noodles, cooked, rinsed in cold water and drained
- ½ cup skim milk
- ¼ tsp ground black pepper
- 2 tsp dried oregano
- 1 tbsp dried basil
- 1 can of 6oz tomato paste
- 1 can of 28oz crushed tomatoes
- 4 cloves garlic, minced
- 3 oz bacon, chopped
- ¼ cup chopped celery
- ½ cup chopped green sweet pepper
- ½ cup finely chopped carrot
- 1 cup chopped onion
- ½-lb. ground beef

Directions:

1. Meat Sauce: In a medium pot placed on medium high fire, cook garlic, bacon, celery, sweet pepper, carrot, onion, and ground beef until ground meat is cooked. Ensure to break up the ground meat while sautéing. Remove from fire and drain fat.
2. Return the meat to pot and stir in black pepper, oregano, dried basil, tomato paste and tomatoes. For thirty minutes, let the mixture simmer while covered as you stir occasionally. After thirty minutes add oregano, basil and milk.
3. Assemble lasagna in a greased rectangular glass dish (as long as the lasagna). On the bottom of dish, add 1 cup of meat sauce and spread, top with 3 lasagna noodles, top again with meat sauce, noodles, noodles, meat sauce, noodles and the last of the sauce and cheese.
4. Cover the lasagna with tin foil and for thirty minutes bake in a pre-heated 350oF oven. After that, remove foil, add more parmesan cheese and continue baking for another twenty minutes. Turn off the oven and allow lasagna to stand inside oven for another half hour. Remove from oven and serve.

Nutrition Values:
Calories: 230; Carbs: 26.6g; Protein: 13.5g; Fats: 7.6g; Saturated Fat: 1.7g; Sodium: 374mg

350. ROASTED RED PEPPERS AND SHRIMP PASTA
Servings: 6
Cooking time: 20 minutes

Ingredients:

- 12 oz pasta, cooked and drained
- 1 cup finely shredded Parmesan Cheese
- ¼ cup snipped fresh basil
- ½ cup whipping cream
- 1 12oz jar roasted red sweet peppers, drained and chopped
- ¼ tsp crushed red pepper
- 6 cloves garlic, minced
- 1/3 cup finely chopped onion
- 1 tbsp olive oil
- 1 ½ lbs. fresh, peeled, deveined, rinsed and drained medium shrimps

Directions:

1. On medium high fire, heat oil in a big fry pan and add garlic and onions. Stir fry until onions are soft, around two minutes. Add crushed red pepper and shrimps, sauté for another two minutes before adding roasted peppers.
2. Allow mixture to boil before lowering heat to low fire and for two minutes, let the mixture simmer uncovered. Stirring occasionally, add cream once shrimps are cooked and simmer for a minute.
3. Add basil and remove from fire. Toss in the pasta and mix gently. Transfer to serving plates and top with cheese.

Nutrition Values:
Calories: 501; Carbs: 77.0g; Protein: 18.6g; Fats: 14.7g; Saturated Fat: 6.0g; Sodium: 383mg

351. PROSCIUTTO E FAGIOLI
Servings: 6
Cooking time: 20 minutes

Ingredients:

- 12 oz pasta, cooked and drained
- Pepper to taste
- 3 tbsp snipped fresh chives
- 3 cups arugula or watercress leaves, loosely packed
- ½ cup chicken broth, warm
- ½ cup shredded pecorino toscano
- 4 oz prosciutto, cut into bite sizes
- 2 cups cherry tomatoes, halved
- 16-oz white kidney beans, rinsed and drained
- 1 tsp olive oil

Directions:

1. Heat over medium low fire olive oil, cheese, prosciutto, tomatoes and beans in a big saucepan. Once mixture is simmering, stir constantly to melt cheese while gradually stirring in the broth. Once cheese is fully

melted and incorporated, add chives, arugula, pepper and salt.

2. Turn off the fire and toss in the cooked pasta. Serve and enjoy.

Nutrition Values:
Calories: 404; Carbs: 64.1g; Protein: 22.1g; Fats: 7.4g; Saturated Fat: 2.5g; Sodium: 370mg

352. 3-KIND MUSHROOM LASAGNA

Servings: 12
Cooking time: 1 hour 30 minutes

Ingredients:

- ½ cup grated Parmigiano-Reggiano cheese
- No boil lasagna noodles
- Cooking spray
- ¼ cup all-purpose flour
- 3 cups reduced fat milk, divided
- 2 tbsp chopped fresh chives, divided
- 1/3 cup less fat cream cheese
- 6 garlic cloves, minced and divided
- 1 ½ tbsp chopped fresh thyme
- ½ tsp freshly ground black pepper, divided
- 1 package 4 oz pre-sliced exotic mushroom blend
- 1 package 8oz pre-sliced cremini mushrooms
- 1 ¼ cups chopped shallots
- 2 tbsp olive oil, divided
- 1 oz dried porcini mushrooms
- 1 cup boiling water

Directions:

1. For 30 minutes, submerge porcini in 1 cup boiling hot water. With a sieve, strain mushroom and reserve liquid.
2. Over medium high fire, heat 1 tbsp oil and for three minutes fry shallots. Add ¼ tsp pepper, exotic mushrooms and cremini, cook for six minutes. Stir in 3 garlic cloves and thyme, cook for a minute. Bring to a boil as your pour wine by increasing fire to high and cook until liquid evaporates around a minute. Turn off fire and stir in porcini mushrooms, 1 tbsp chives and cream cheese. Mix well.
3. On medium high fire, place a separate medium sized pan with 1 tbsp oil. Sauté for half a minute 3 garlic cloves. Then bring to a boil as you pour 2 ¾ cups milk and reserved porcini liquid. Season with remaining pepper and salt. In a separate bowl whisk together flour and ¼ cup milk and pour into pan. Stir constantly and cook until mixture thickens.
4. In a greased rectangular glass dish, pour and spread ½ cup of sauce, top with lasagna, top

with half of mushroom mixture and another layer of lasagna. Repeat the layering process and instead of lasagna layer, end with the mushroom mixture and cover with cheese.

5. For 45 minutes, bake the lasagna in a preheated 350oF oven. Garnish with chives before serving.

Nutrition Values:
Calories: 243; Carbs: 39.2g; Protein: 7.8g; Fats: 6.7g; Saturated Fat: 2.1g; Sodium: 328mg

353. LIGHT AND CREAMY MAC 'N CHEESE

Servings: 12
Cooking time: 75 minutes

Ingredients:

- 2 tbsp chopped fresh parsley
- 1/4 cup panko
- 1 tsp olive oil
- Cooking spray
- 1 lb. uncooked cavatappi
- ¼ cup finely grated fresh Parmigiano-Reggiano cheese, divided
- 1 cup grated pecorino Romano cheese
- 1 ¼ cups shredded Gruyere cheese
- ½ tsp freshly ground black pepper
- 2 tbsp plain fat free Greek yogurt
- 2 garlic cloves, peeled
- 1 ½ cups fat free milk
- 1 ¼ cups fat free chicken broth
- 3 cups butternut squash, cubed and peeled

Directions:

1. In a boiling pot of water, cook pasta according to manufacturer's instructions, drain and set aside.
2. On medium high fire, boil milk, broth and squash in a medium sized pan. Once boiling, reduce fire and allow mixture to simmer for 25 minutes or until squash is soft. Remove from fire and transfer to a blender and puree. Add Greek yogurt, pepper and salt. Continue to puree mixture until smooth.
3. Transfer squash mixture into a bowl and mix in 2 tbsp Parmigiano-Reggiano, pecorino Romano and Gruyere. Thoroughly mix.
4. Then add the pasta to the squash and cheese mixture. Mix well. Transfer into a greased 13x9 inch glass dish.
5. On medium fire, place a medium fry pan with oil and for two minutes fry panko. Turn off the fire and stir in the remaining Parmigiano-Reggiano. Quickly pour on top of pasta and

6. Place dish in a preheated 375oF oven and bake for 25 minutes.
7. Garnish with parsley before serving.

Nutrition Values:
Calories: 273; Carbs: 36.8g; Protein: 11.7g; Fats: 9.4g; Saturated Fat: 5.2g; Sodium: 128mg

354. CHARD AND RICOTTA ORECCHIETTE

Servings: 8
Cooking time: 35 minutes

Ingredients:
- Freshly grated pecorino cheese or ricotta salata
- Pepper
- ¼ cup fresh, low fat ricotta cheese
- ground nutmeg
- 2 oz ricotta salata, grated
- Crushed red pepper – optional
- 2 tbsp olive oil
- ¾ lb. dried orecchiette
- 1 large bunch rainbow swiss chard

Directions:
1. In a boiling pot of water, boil Orecchiette for ten minutes.
2. Meanwhile, remove the stems from the chard leaves. After ten minutes of boiling the pasta, add the chard leaves and continue to boil for another two minutes before draining (ensure that you reserve ¼ cup of the liquid). Set Aside.
3. On medium high fire and a big fry pan with olive oil, sauté chard stems until tender and crisp around three to five minutes.
4. Then return pasta and chard leaves to the pot and cook on low fire. Add sautéed chard stem with oil and all, reserved cooking liquid, and crushed red pepper. Mix well.
5. Add nutmeg, pepper and grated ricotta salata and toss.
6. Remove from fire, transfer to serving bowls and top with more ricotta salata or pecorino cheese.

Nutrition Values:
Calories: 138; Carbs: 15.2g; Protein: 5.1g; Fats: 6.7g; Saturated Fat: 2.3g; Sodium: 225mg

355. ROCKET AND SMOKE SALMON SPAGHETTI

Servings: 8
Cooking time: minutes

Ingredients:

- o oz black olives, pitted and chopped
- 1 lemon juice
- 2 garlic cloves, crushed
- 2 tbsp olive oil
- 10 oz Smoked Salmon
- 1 bunch rocket
- 2 tbsp pine nuts
- 1 leek, sliced thinly
- 1-lb Whole wheat spaghetti

Directions:
1. In a boiling pot of water. Once water is in a rolling boil, add pasta and cook following manufacturer's instructions. Drain and put aside.
2. Meanwhile on a fry pan, toast pine nuts until lightly browned. Remove from pan and put aside.
3. In same pan, heat oil and sauté for five minutes the leeks. Mix in garlic and continue sautéing for another two minutes. Turn off fire and stir in the smoked salmon, pine nuts, olives, rocket, lemon juice and pasta. Mix until well combined and serve.

Nutrition Values:
Calories: 291; Carbs: 45.5g; Protein: 15.1g; Fats: 7.0g; Saturated Fat: 1.1g; Sodium: 336mg

MODERN PASTA AND BEANS

Servings: 8
Cooking time: 40 minutes

Ingredients:
- 1 can Borlotti Bean, drained and rinsed
- 1 onion diced
- 2 tbsp olive oil
- 1 ½ cup vegetable stock
- ½ cup tomato sauce
- 2 cups collard greens chopped
- ¼ cup fresh parsley chopped
- 6 cloves garlic peeled, thinly sliced
- 1 box Barilla medium shells, 12-oz

Directions:
1. Bring a big pot of water to a boil. Once boiling add the medium shells and cook for two minutes less than manufacturer's cooking instructions. Drain and set aside.
2. Meanwhile, in a separate pot, sauté onions and garlic in olive oil for seven to eight minutes or until onions are soft over medium fire.
3. Add collard greens and parsley and continue cooking for ten more minutes while pot is covered.

4. Add vegetable stock, tomato sauce and beans. Increase fire to high until mixture is boiling then put back to medium low and for 15 minutes allow to simmer while covered.
5. Add pepper to taste before pouring in the cooked pasta shells and simmering for ten minutes.
6. Remove from fire and serve.

Nutrition Values:
Calories: 262; Carbs: 48.8g; Protein: 7.4g; Fats: 5.3g; Saturated Fat: 0.7g; Sodium: 96mg

357. RICOTTA AND SPINACH RAVIOLI

Servings: 6
Cooking time: 30 minutes

Ingredients:
- 1 cup chicken stock
- 1 cup frozen spinach, thawed
- 1 batch pasta dough
- 3 tbsp heavy cream
- 1 cup ricotta
- 1 ¾ cups baby spinach
- 1 small onion, finely chopped
- 2 tbsp low fat butter

Directions:
1. Create the filling: In a fry pan, sauté onion and butter around five minutes. Add the baby spinach leaves and continue simmering for another four minutes. Remove from fire, drain liquid and mince the onion and leaves. Then combine with 2 tbsp cream and the ricotta ensuring that it is well combined. Add pepper and salt to taste.
2. With your pasta dough, divide it into four balls. Roll out one ball to ¼ inch thick rectangular spread. Cut a 1 ½ inch by 3-inch rectangles. Place filling on the middle of the rectangles, around 1 tablespoonful and brush filling with cold water. Fold the rectangles in half, ensuring that no air is trapped within and seal using a cookie cutter. Use up all the filling.
3. Create Pasta Sauce: Until smooth, puree chicken stock and spinach. Pour into heated fry pan and for two minutes cook it. Add 1 tbsp cream and season with pepper and salt. Continue cooking for a minute and turn of fire.
4. Cook the raviolis by submerging in a boiling pot of water with salt. Cook until al dente then drain. Then quickly transfer the cooked ravioli into the fry pan of pasta sauce, toss to mix and serve.

Nutrition Values:
Calories: 192; Carbs: 17.9g; Protein: 10.0g; Fats: 9.4g; Saturated Fat: 5.4g; Sodium: 157mg

358. SPAGHETTI IN LEMON AVOCADO WHITE SAUCE

Servings: 6
Cooking time: 30 minutes

Ingredients:
- Freshly ground black pepper
- Zest and juice of 1 lemon
- 1 avocado, pitted and peeled
- 12-oz whole wheat spaghetti
- Pepper to taste
- 2 tbsp Olive oil
- 8 oz small shrimp, shelled and deveined
- 1 large onion, finely sliced
- 2 tbsp water

Directions:
1. Let a big pot of water boil. Once boiling add the spaghetti or pasta and cook following manufacturer's Directions:until al dente. Drain and set aside.
2. In a large fry pan, over medium fire sauté wine and onions for ten minutes or until onions are translucent and soft.
3. Add the shrimps into the fry pan and increase fire to high while constantly sautéing until shrimps are cooked around five minutes. Turn the fire off. Season with pepper and add the oil right away. Then quickly toss in the cooked pasta, mix well.
4. In a blender, until smooth, puree the lemon juice, water, and avocado. Pour into the fry pan of pasta, combine well. Garnish with pepper and lemon zest then serve.

Nutrition Values:
Calories: 340; Carbs: 49.0g; Protein: 17.0g; Fats: 10.7g; Saturated Fat: 1.6g; Sodium: 54mg

SOUPS AND STEWS

359. PORTUGUESE KALE AND SAUSAGE SOUP

Servings:4
Preparation Time: 10 minutes
Cooking Time: 35 minutes

Ingredients:

- 1 yellow onion, chopped
- 16 ounces sausage, chopped
- 3 sweet potatoes, chopped
- 4 cups chicken stock
- 1 pound kale, chopped
- pepper as needed

Directions:

1. Take a pot and place it over medium heat.
2. Add sausage and brown both sides.
3. Transfer to bowl.
4. Heat pot again over medium heat.
5. Add onion and stir for 5 minutes.
6. Add stock, sweet potatoes, stir and bring to a simmer.
7. Cook for 20 minutes.
8. Use an immersion blender to blend.
9. Add kale and pepper and simmer for 2 minutes over low heat.
10. Ladle soup to bowls and top with sausage with pieces.
11. Serve and enjoy!

Nutrition Values:

Calories: 200
Fat: 2g
Carbohydrates: 6g
Protein:8g

360. DAZZLING PIZZA SOUP

Servings:6
Preparation Time: 5 minutes
Cooking Time: 30 minutes

Ingredients:

- 12 ounces chicken meat, sliced
- 4 ounces uncured pepperoni
- 1 can 25 ounces marinara
- 1 can 14.5 ounces fire roasted tomatoes
- 1 large onion, diced
- 15 ounces mushrooms, sliced
- 1 can 3 ounce sliced black olives
- 1tablespoon dried oregano
- 1 teaspoon garlic powder
- ½ teaspoon salt

Directions:

1. Take large sized saucepan and add in the peperoni, chicken meat, marinara, onions, tomatoes, mushroom, oregano, olives, salt and garlic powder.
2. Cook the mixture for 30 minutes over medium level heat and soften the mushroom and onions.
3. Serve hot.

Nutrition Values:

Calories: 90
Fat: 2g
Carbohydrates: 17g
Protein: 3g

361. MESMERIZING LENTIL SOUP

Servings:4
Preparation Time: 10 minutes
Cooking Time: 8 hours

Ingredients:

- 1 pound dried lentils, soaked overnight and rinsed
- 3 carrots, peeled and chopped
- 1 celery stalk, chopped
- 1 onion, chopped
- 6 cups vegetables broth
- 1 ½ teaspoons garlic powder
- 1 teaspoon ground cumin
- 1 teaspoon smoked paprika
- 1 teaspoon dried thyme
- ¼ teaspoon liquid smoke
- ¼ teaspoon salt
- ¼ teaspoon ground pepper

Directions:

1. Add listed ingredients to Slow Cooker and stir well.
2. Place lid and cook for 8 hours on LOW.
3. Stir and serve.
4. Enjoy!

Nutrition Values:
Calories: 307
Fat: 1g
Carbohydrates: 56g
Protein: 20g

362. ORGANICALLY HEALTHY CHICKEN SOUP

Servings:4
Preparation Time: 10 minutes
Cooking Time: 12-15 minutes

Ingredients:

- 2 cans (14 ounces eachlow sodium chicken broth
- 2 cups water
- 1 cup twisted spaghetti
- ¼ teaspoon pepper
- 3 cups mixed vegetables (such as broccoli, carrots etc.
- 1 and ½ cups chicken, cooked and cubed
- 1 tablespoon fresh basil, snipped
- ¼ cup parmesan, finely shredded

Directions:

1. Take a Dutch Oven and add broth, water, pepper and bring the mixture to a boil.
2. Gently stir in pasta and wait until the mixture reaches boiling point again,
3. Lower down the heat and let the mixture simmer for 5 minutes (covered).
4. Remove lid and stir in the vegetables, return the mixture boil and lower down heat once again.
5. Cover and let it simmer over low heat for 5-8 minutes until the pasta and veggies and tender and cooked.
6. Stir in cooked chicken and garnish with basil.
7. Serve with a topping of parmesan.
8. Enjoy!

Nutrition Values (Per Serving

Calories: 400
Fat: 9g
Carbohydrates: 37g
Protein: 45g[F8]

363. POTATO AND ASPARAGUS BISQUE

Servings:4
Preparation Time: 5 minutes
Cooking Time: 6 minutes

Ingredients:

- 1 ½ pound asparagus
- 2 pounds sweet potatoes
- 6 cups vegetable broth
- 1 large sized onion
- 8 cloves garlic
- 2 tablespoons dried dill
- 2 tablespoons flavored vinegar
- 3-4 cups almond milk
- 4 tablespoons Dijon mustard
- 4 tablespoons yeast

Directions:

1. Add the listed ingredients (except milk, mustard and yeastto your pot.
2. Lock the lid and cook on HIGH pressure for 6 minutes.
3. Release the pressure naturally.
4. Open the lid and add almond milk, yeast and mustard.
5. Puree using immersion blender.
6. Serve over rice.
7. Enjoy!

Nutrition Values:

Calories: 430
Fat: 12g
Carbohydrates: 77g
Protein: 6g

364. CABBAGE AND LEEK SOUP

Servings:4
Preparation Time: 10 minutes
Cooking Time: 25 minutes

Ingredients:

- 2 tablespoons coconut oil
- ½ head chopped up cabbage
- 3-4 diced ribs celery
- 2-3 carefully cleaned and chopped leeks
- 1 diced bell pepper
- 2-3 diced carrots
- 2/3 cloves minced garlic
- 4 cups chicken broth
- 1 teaspoon Italian seasoning
- 1 teaspoon Creole seasoning
- Black pepper as needed
- 2-3 cups mixed salad greens

Directions:

1. Set your pot to Sauté mode and add coconut oil.
2. Allow the oil to heat up.
3. Add the veggies (except salad greensstarting from the carrot, making sure to stir well after each vegetable addition.
4. Make sure to add the garlic last.
5. Season with Italian seasoning, black pepper and Creole seasoning.
6. Add broth and lock the lid.
7. Cook on SOUP mode for 20 minutes.
8. Release the pressure naturally and add salad greens, stir well and allow to sit for a while.
9. Allow for a few minutes to wilt the veggies.
10. Season with a bit of flavored vinegar and pepper and enjoy!

Nutrition Values:

Calories: 32
Fat: 0g
Carbohydrates: 4g

Protein: 2g

365. ONION SOUP

Servings:4
Preparation Time: 10 minutes
Cooking Time: 3 hours

Ingredients:

- 2 tablespoons avocado oil
- 5 yellow onions, cut into halved and sliced
- Black pepper to taste
- 5 cups beef stock
- 3 thyme sprigs
- 1 tablespoon tomato paste

Directions:

1. Take a pot and place it over medium high heat.
2. Add onion and thyme and stir.
3. Reduce heat to low and cook for 30 minutes.
4. Uncover pot and cook onions for 1 hour and 30 minutes more, stirring often.
5. Add tomato paste, stock and stir.
6. Simmer for 1 hour more.
7. Ladle soup into bowls and enjoy!

Nutrition Values:

Calories: 200
Fat: 4g
Carbohydrates: 6g
Protein: 8g

366. CARROT, GINGER AND TURMERIC SOUP

Servings:4
Preparation Time: 15 minutes
Cooking Time: 40 minutes

Ingredients:

- 6 cups chicken broth
- ¼ cup full fat coconut milk, unsweetened
- ¾ pound carrots, peeled and chopped
- 1 teaspoon turmeric, ground
- 2 teaspoons ginger, grated
- 1 yellow onion, chopped
- 2 garlic cloves, peeled
- Pinch of pepper

Directions:

1. Take a stockpot and add all the ingredients except coconut milk into it.
2. Place stockpot over medium heat.
3. Bring to a boil.
4. Reduce heat to simmer for 40 minutes.
5. Remove the bay leaf.
6. Blend the soup until smooth by using an immersion blender.

7. Add the coconut milk and stir.
8. Serve immediately and enjoy!

Nutrition Values:

Calories: 79
Fat: 4g
Carbohydrates: 7g
Protein: 4g

367. OFFBEAT SQUASH SOUP

Servings:4
Preparation Time: 10 minutes
Cooking Time: 50 minutes

Ingredients:

- 1 butternut squash, cut in halve lengthwise and deseeded
- 14 ounces coconut milk
- Pinch of salt
- Black pepper to taste
- Handful of parsley, chopped
- Pinch of nutmeg, ground

Directions:

1. Add butternut squash halves on a lined baking sheet.
2. Place in oven and bake for 45 minutes at 350 degrees F.
3. Leave squash to cool down and scoop out the flesh to a pot.
4. Add half of the coconut milk to the pot and blend using immersion blender.
5. Heat soup over medium-low heat and add remaining coconut milk.
6. Add a pinch of salt, black pepper to taste.
7. Add nutmeg, parsley and blend using an immersion blender once again for a few seconds.
8. Cook for 4 minutes.
9. Serve and enjoy!

Nutrition Values:

Calories: 144
Fat: 10g
Carbohydrates: 7g
Protein: 2g

368. LEEK AND CAULIFLOWER SOUP

Servings:6
Preparation Time: 10 minutes
Cooking Time: 40 minutes

Ingredients:

- 3 cups cauliflower, riced
- 1 bay leaf
- 1 teaspoon herbs de Provence
- 2 garlic cloves, peeled and diced
- ½ cup coconut milk

- 2 ½ cups vegetable stock
- 1 tablespoon coconut oil
- ½ teaspoon cracked pepper
- 1 leek, chopped

Directions:
1. Take a pot, heat oil into it.
2. Sauté the leeks in the oil for 5 minutes.
3. Add the garlic and then stir-cook for another minute.
4. Add all the remaining ingredients and mix them well.
5. Cook for 30 minutes.
6. Stir occasionally.
7. Blend the soup until smooth by using an immersion blender.
8. Serve hot and enjoy!

Nutrition Values:
Calories: 90
Fat: 7g
Carbohydrates: 4g
Protein: 2g

369. DREAMY ZUCCHINI BOWL

Servings:4
Preparation Time: 10 minutes
Cooking Time: 20 minutes

Ingredients:
- 1 onion, chopped
- 3 zucchini, cut into medium chunks
- 2 tablespoons coconut almond milk
- 2 garlic cloves, minced
- 4 cups vegetable stock
- 2 tablespoons coconut oil
- Pinch of sunflower seeds
- Black pepper to taste

Directions:
1. Take a pot and place it over medium heat.
2. Add oil and let it heat up.
3. Add zucchini, garlic, onion and stir.
4. Cook for 5 minutes.
5. Add stock, sunflower seeds, pepper and stir.
6. Bring to a boil and reduce heat.
7. Simmer for 20 minutes.
8. Remove from heat and add coconut almond milk.
9. Use an immersion blender until smooth.
10. Ladle into soup bowls and serve.
11. Enjoy!

Nutrition Values:
Calories: 160
Fat: 2g
Carbohydrates: 4g

Protein: 7g

370. COLD CRAB AND WATERMELON SOUP

Servings:4
Preparation Time: 10 minutes + chill time
Cooking Time: nil

Ingredients:
- ¼ cup basil, chopped
- 2 pounds tomatoes
- 5 cups watermelon, cubed
- ¼ cup wine vinegar
- 2 garlic cloves, minced
- 1 zucchini, chopped
- Pepper to taste
- 1 cup crabmeat

Directions:
1. Take your blender and add tomatoes, basil, vinegar, 4 cups watermelon, garlic, 1/3 cup oil, pepper and pulse well.
2. Transfer to fridge and chill for 1 hour.
3. Divide into bowls and add zucchini, crab and remaining watermelon.
4. Serve and enjoy!

Nutrition Values:
Calories: 121
Fat: 3g
Carbohydrates: 4g
Protein: 8g

371. PALEO LEMON AND GARLIC SOUP

Servings:4
Preparation Time: 10 minutes
Cooking Time: 10 minutes

Ingredients:
- 6 cups shellfish stock
- 1 tablespoon garlic, minced
- 1 tablespoon coconut oil, melted
- 2 whole eggs
- ½ cup lemon juice
- Pinch of salt
- White pepper to taste
- 1 tablespoon arrowroot powder
- Finely chopped cilantro for serving

Directions:
1. Heat up a pot with oil over medium high heat.
2. Add garlic, stir cook for 2 minutes.
3. Add stock (reserve ½ cup for later use).
4. Stir and bring mix to a simmer.
5. Take a bowl and add eggs, sea salt, pepper,

reserved stock, lemon juice and arrowroot.
6. Whisk well.
7. Pour in to the soup and cook for a few minutes.
8. Ladle soup into bowls and serve with chopped cilantro.
9. Enjoy!

Nutrition Values:
Calories: 135
Fat: 3g
Carbohydrates: 12g
Protein: 8

372. BRUSSELS SOUP

Servings:4
Preparation Time: 10 minutes
Cooking Time: 20 minutes

Ingredients:

- 2 tablespoons olive oil
- 1 yellow onion, chopped
- 2 pounds Brussels sprouts, trimmed and halved
- 4 cups chicken stock
- ¼ cup coconut cream

Directions:

1. Take a pot and place it over medium heat.
2. Add oil and let it heat up.
3. Add onion and stir-cook for 3 minutes.
4. Add Brussels sprouts and stir, cook for 2 minutes.
5. Add stock and black pepper, stir and bring to a simmer.
6. Cook for 20 minutes more.
7. Use an immersion blender to make the soup creamy.
8. Add coconut cream and stir well.
9. Ladle into soup bowls and serve.
10. Enjoy!

Nutrition Values:
Calories: 200
Fat: 11g
Carbohydrates: 6g
Protein: 11g

373. SPRING SOUP AND POACHED EGG

Servings:4
Preparation Time: 5 minutes
Cooking Time: 15 minutes

Ingredients:

- 2 whole eggs
- 32 ounces chicken broth
- 1 head romaine lettuce, chopped

Directions:

1. Bring the chicken broth to a boil.
2. Reduce the heat and poach the 2 eggs in the broth for 5 minutes.
3. Take two bowls and transfer the eggs into a separate bowl.
4. Add chopped romaine lettuce into the broth and cook for a few minutes.
5. Serve the broth with lettuce into the bowls.
6. Enjoy!

Nutrition Values:
Calories: 150
Fat: 5g
Carbohydrates: 6g
Protein: 16g

374. LOBSTER BISQUE

Servings:4
Preparation Time: 10 minutes
Cooking Time: 15 minutes

Ingredients:

- ¾ pound lobster, cooked and lobster
- 4 cups chicken broth
- 2 garlic cloves, chopped
- ¼ teaspoon pepper
- ½ teaspoon paprika
- 1 yellow onion, chopped
- ½ teaspoon salt
- 14 ½ ounces tomatoes, diced
- 1 tablespoon coconut oil
- 1 cup low fat cream

Directions:

1. Take a stockpot and add the coconut oil over medium heat.
2. Then sauté the garlic and onion for 3 to 5 minutes.
3. Add diced tomatoes, spices and chicken broth and bring to a boil.
4. Reduce to a simmer, then simmer for about 10 minutes.
5. Add the warmed heavy cream to the soup.
6. Blend the soup till creamy by using an immersion blender.
7. Stir in cooked lobster.
8. Serve and enjoy!

Nutrition Values:
Calories: 180
Fat: 11g
Carbohydrates: 6g
Protein: 16g

375. TOMATO BISQUE

Servings:4

Preparation Time: 10 minutes
Cooking Time: 40 minutes

Ingredients:

- 4 cups chicken broth
- 1 cup low fat cream
- 1 teaspoon thyme dried
- 3 cups canned whole, peeled tomatoes
- 2 tablespoons almond butter
- 3 garlic cloves, peeled
- Pepper as needed

Directions:

1. Take a stockpot and first add the butter to the bottom of a stockpot.
2. Then add all the ingredients except heavy cream into it.
3. Bring to a boil.
4. Simmer for 40 minutes.
5. Warm the heavy cream and stir into the soup.
6. Serve and enjoy!

Nutrition Values:

Calories: 141
Fat: 12g
Carbohydrates: 4g
Protein: 4g

376. CHIPOTLE CHICKEN CHOWDER

Servings:4
Preparation Time: 10 minutes
Cooking Time: 23 minutes

Ingredients:

- 1 medium onion, chopped
- 2 garlic cloves, minced
- 6 bacon slices, chopped
- 4 cups jicama, cubed
- 3 cups chicken stock
- 1 teaspoon salt
- 2 cups low-fat, cream
- 1 tablespoon olive oil
- 2 tablespoons fresh cilantro, chopped
- 1 ¼ pounds chicken, thigh boneless, cut into 1 inch chunks
- ½ teaspoon pepper
- 1 chipotle pepper, minced

Directions:

1. Heat olive oil over medium heat in a large sized saucepan, add bacon.
2. Cook until crispy, add onion, garlic, and jicama.
3. Cook for 7 minutes, add chicken stock and chicken.
4. Bring to a boil and reduce temperature to low.

5. Simmer for 10 minutes
6. Season with salt and pepper.
7. Add heavy cream and chipotle, simmer for 5 minutes.
8. Sprinkle chopped cilantro and serve, enjoy!

Nutrition Values:

Calories: 350
Fat: 22g
Carbohydrates: 8g
Protein: 22g

377. BAY SCALLOP CHOWDER

Servings:4
Preparation Time: 10 minutes
Cooking Time: 18 minutes

Ingredients:

- 1 medium onion, chopped
- 2 ½ cups chicken stock
- 4 slices bacon, chopped
- 3 cups daikon radish, chopped
- ½ teaspoon dried thyme
- 2 cups low-fat cream
- 1 tablespoon almond butter
- Pepper to taste
- 1 pound bay scallops

Directions:

1. Heat olive over medium heat in a large sized saucepan,add bacon and cook until crisp, add onion and daikon radish.
2. Cook for 5 minutes, add chicken stock.
3. Simmer for 8 minutes, season with salt and pepper, thyme.
4. Add heavy cream, bay scallops, simmer for 4 minutes
5. Serve and enjoy!

Nutrition Values:

Calories: 307
Fat: 22g
Carbohydrates: 7g
Protein: 22g

378. SALMON AND VEGETABLE SOUP

Servings:4
Preparation Time: 10 minutes
Cooking Time: 22 minutes

Ingredients:

- 2 tablespoons extra-virgin olive oil
- 1 leek, chopped
- 1 red onion, chopped
- Pepper to taste
- 2 carrots, chopped
- 4 cups low stock vegetable stock

- 4 ounces salmon, skinless and boneless, cubed
- ½ cup coconut cream
- 1 tablespoon dill, chopped

Directions:

1. Take a pan and place it over medium heat, add leek, onion, stir and cook for 7 minutes.
2. Add pepper, carrots, stock and stir.
3. Boil for 10 minutes.
4. Add salmon, cream, dill and stir.
5. Boil for 5-6 minutes.
6. Ladle into bowls and serve.
7. Enjoy!

Nutrition Values:

Calories: 240
Fat: 4g
Carbohydrates: 7g
Protein: 12g

379. GARLIC TOMATO SOUP

Servings:4
Preparation Time: 15 minutes
Cooking Time: 15 minutes

Ingredients:

- 8 Roma tomatoes, chopped
- 1 cup tomatoes, sundried
- 2 tablespoons coconut oil
- 5 garlic cloves, chopped
- 14 ounces coconut milk
- 1 cup vegetable broth
- Pepper to taste
- Basil, for garnish

Directions:

1. Take a pot, heat oil into it.
2. Sauté the garlic in it for ½ minute.
3. Mix in the Roma tomatoes and cook for 8-10 minutes.
4. Stir occasionally.
5. Add in the rest of the ingredients, except the basil, and stir well.
6. Cover the lid and cook for 5 minutes.
7. Let it cool.
8. Blend the soup until smooth by using an immersion blender.
9. Garnish with basil.
10. Serve and enjoy!

Nutrition Values:

Calories: 240
Fat: 23g
Carbohydrates: 16g
Protein: 7g

380. MELON SOUP

Servings:4

Prep Time:6 minutes
Cooking Time: Nil

Ingredients:

- 4 cups casaba melon, seeded and cubed
- 1 tablespoon fresh ginger, grated
- ¾ cup coconut milk
- Juice of 2 limes

Directions:

1. Add the lime juice, coconut milk, casaba melon, ginger and salt into your blender.
2. Blend for 1-2 minutes until you get a smooth mixture.
3. Serve and enjoy!

Nutrition Values:

Calories: 134
Fat:9g
Carbohydrates: 13g
Protein: 2g

381. COLBY AND TUNA STUFFED AVOCADO

Preparation Time: 25 minutes
Servings: 4

Nutrition Values: 286 Calories; 23.9g Fat; 6g Carbs; 11.2g Protein;

Ingredients

- 2 large-sized avocados, halved and pitted
- 4 ounces Colby cheese, freshly grated
- 2 ounces canned tuna, flaked
- 2 tablespoons scallions, chopped
- Salt and freshly ground black pepper, to taste
- 2 tablespoons fresh cilantro, chopped
- 1/2 cup radicchios, sliced

Directions

1. Begin by preheating your oven to 360 degrees F. Place the avocado halves in an ovenproof dish.
2. Now, thoroughly combine the Colby cheese, tuna, scallions, salt and pepper in a mixing bowl. Stuff the avocado halves with cheese/tuna mixture.
3. Divide the mixture among the avocado halves. Bake approximately 18 minutes and top with fresh cilantro. Garnish with radicchio and serve immediately. Bon appétit!

382. CHEESE AND SCALLION STUFFED TOMATOES

Preparation Time: 45 minutes
Servings: 5

Nutrition Values: 306 Calories; 27.5g Fat; 4.4g Carbs; 11.3g Protein;

Ingredients

- Nonstick cooking spray
- 5 vine-ripened tomatoes
- 1 cup cream cheese, at room temperature
- 1 ½ cups Monterey-Jack cheese, shredded
- 1/4 cup sour cream
- 1 egg, whisked
- 1 clove garlic, minced
- 4 tablespoons fresh scallions, chopped
- Salt and ground black pepper, to taste
- 2 teaspoons butter

Directions

1. Preheat your oven to 360 degrees F. Lightly grease a rimmed baking sheet with a nonstick cooking spray.
2. Slice the tomatoes into halves horizontally and discard the hard cores; scoop out the pulp and seeds.
3. In a mixing bowl, thoroughly combine the cheese, sour cream, egg, garlic, scallions, salt, pepper, and butter.
4. Divide the filling between the tomatoes and bake in the preheated oven for 30 to 35 minutes. Allow them to cool on a wire rack for 5 minutes; serve with fresh rocket leaves. Bon appétit!

383. CHEESE STICKS WITH ROASTED RED PEPPER DIP

Preparation Time: 40 minutes
Servings: 8

Nutrition Values: 200 Calories; 16.9g Fat; 3.7g Carbs; 9.4g Protein;

Ingredients

- 2 (8-ouncepackages Monterey Jack cheese with jalapeno peppers
- 3/4 cup Parmigiano-Reggiano cheese, grated
- 2 tablespoons almond flour
- 1 tablespoon flax meal
- 1 teaspoon baking powder
- Salt and red pepper flakes, to serve
- 1/3 teaspoon cumin powder
- 1/2 teaspoon dried oregano
- 1/3 teaspoon dried rosemary
- 2 eggs

For Roasted Red Pepper Dip:

- 1 cup cream cheese
- 1/3 cup Greek yogurt
- 3/4 cup jarred fire-roasted red peppers, drained and chopped
- 1 tablespoon Dijon mustard
- 1 chili pepper, deveined and minced
- 2 garlic cloves, chopped
- Sea salt and pepper to taste

Directions

1. Cut the cheese crosswise into sticks.
2. In a shallow bowl, combine the dry ingredients. In another bowl, whisk the eggs.
3. Dip each stick into the eggs, and then roll in the dry mixture. Place the cheese sticks on a wax paper-lined baking sheet; place in your freezer for about 30 minutes.
4. Deep fry the cheese sticks until the coating is

golden brown and crisp about 5 minutes. Transfer to pepper towels to drain the excess oil.

5. Then, make the dipping sauce by mixing all ingredients for the roasted red pepper dip. Bon appétit!

384. CURRIED PICKLED EGGS

Preparation Time: 20 minutes
Servings: 5

Nutrition Values: 145 Calories; 9g Fat; 2.8g Carbs; 11.4g Protein;

Ingredients

- 10 eggs
- 1/2 cup onions, sliced
- 3 cardamom pods
- 1 tablespoon yellow curry powder
- 1 teaspoon yellow mustard seeds
- 2 clove garlic, sliced
- 1 cup cider vinegar
- 1 ¼ cups water
- 1 tablespoon salt

Directions

1. Boil the eggs until hard-cooked; peel them and rinse under cold, running water. Add the peeled eggs to a large-sized jar.
2. Add all remaining ingredients to a pan that is preheated over a moderately high heat; bring to a rapid boil.
3. Now, turn the heat to medium-low; let it simmer for 6 minutes. Spoon this mixture into the jar.
4. Keep in your refrigerator for 2 to 3 weeks. Bon appétit!

385. EASY AND YUMMY SCOTCH EGGS

Preparation Time: 20 minutes
Servings: 8

Nutrition Values: 247 Calories; 11.4g Fat; 0.6g Carbs; 33.7g Protein;

Ingredients

- 8 eggs
- 1 ½ pounds ground beef
- 1/2 cup parmesan cheese, freshly grated
- 1 teaspoon granulated garlic
- 1/2 teaspoon shallot powder
- 1/2 teaspoon cayenne pepper
- 1 teaspoon dried rosemary, chopped
- Salt and pepper to taste

Directions

1. Boil the eggs until hard-cooked; peel them and rinse under cold, running water. Set aside.
2. In a mixing bowl, thoroughly combine the other ingredients. Divide the meat mixture among 8 balls; flatten each ball and place a boiled egg on it.
3. Shape the meat mixture around the eggs by using your fingers.
4. Add the balls to a baking pan that is previously greased with a nonstick cooking spray.
5. Bake in the preheated oven, at 360 degrees F for 18 minutes, until crisp and golden. Bon appétit!

386. TRADITIONAL EGG SOUP WITH TOFU

Preparation Time: 15 minutes
Servings: 3

Nutrition Values: 153 Calories; 9.8g Fat; 2.7g Carbs; 15g Protein;

Ingredients

- 2 cups homemade chicken stock
- 1 tablespoon tamari sauce
- 1 teaspoon coconut oil, softened
- 2 eggs, beaten
- 1/2 teaspoon turmeric powder
- 1-inch knob of ginger, grated
- Salt and ground black ground, to taste
- 1/4 teaspoon paprika
- 1/2 pound extra-firm tofu, cubed

Directions

1. In a pan that is preheated over a moderately high heat, whisk the stock, tamari sauce and coconut oil; bring to a rolling boil.
2. Stir in the eggs, whisking constantly, until it is well incorporated.
3. Now, turn the heat to medium-low and season with the turmeric, ginger, salt, black pepper and paprika.
4. Add the tofu and let it simmer another 1 to 2 minutes
5. Ladle into individual soup bowls and eat warm. Bon appétit!

387. ZUCCHINI BOATS WITH SAUSAGE AND EGGS

Preparation Time: 35 minutes
Servings: 3

Nutrition Values: 506 Calories; 41g Fat; 4.5g Carbs; 27.5g Protein;

Ingredients

- 3 medium-sized zucchinis, cut into halves
- 1 tablespoon deli mustard
- 2 sausages, cooked and crumbled
- 6 eggs
- Salt, to taste
- 1/4 teaspoon black pepper, or more to taste
- 1/4 teaspoon dried dill weed

Directions

1. Scoop the flesh from each zucchini half to make the shells; place the zucchini boats on a baking pan.
2. Spread the mustard on the bottom of each zucchini half. Divide the crumbled sausage among the zucchini boats.
3. Crack an egg in each zucchini half, sprinkle with salt, pepper, and dill.
4. Bake in the preheated oven at 400 degrees F for 30 minutes or until zucchini boats are tender. Bon appétit!

388. CREAMY GRUYÈRE EGG BITES

Preparation Time: 20 minutes
Servings: 5

Nutrition Values: 177 Calories; 12.7g Fat; 4.6g Carbs; 11.4g Protein;

Ingredients

- 10 eggs
- 1/4 cup mayonnaise
- 1 tablespoon tomato paste
- 2 tablespoons celery, finely chopped
- 2 tablespoons carrot, finely chopped
- 2 tablespoons scallion, minced
- 2 tablespoons Gruyère cheese, grated
- 1/2 teaspoon paprika
- Salt and black pepper, to taste

Directions

1. Place the eggs in a wide pot; cover with cold water by 1 inch. Bring to a rapid boil. Now, turn the heat to medium-low; let the eggs simmer for a further 10 minutes.
2. Peel the eggs and rinse them under running water.
3. Slice each egg in half lengthwise and remove the yolks. Thoroughly combine the yolks with the remaining ingredients.
4. Divide the mixture among the egg whites and arrange the deviled eggs on a nice serving platter. Bon appétit!

389. CLASSIC EGG SALAD

Preparation Time: 20 minutes
Servings: 4

Nutrition Values: 284 Calories; 21.3g Fat; 6.8g Carbs; 16.7g Protein;

Ingredients

- 8 eggs
- 1/3 cup mayonnaise
- 1 tablespoon minced shallot
- 1/2 teaspoon brown mustard
- 1 ½ teaspoons lime juice
- Salt and black pepper, to taste
- 10 lettuce leaves
- 1/2 cup bacon crumbs

Directions

1. Place the eggs in a single layer in a pan; cover with 2 inches of water.
2. Bring to a boil over a high heat; now, reduce the heat and cook, covered, for 1 minute.
3. Remove from the heat and leave your eggs for 15 minutes; rinse. Peel and chop the eggs.
4. Transfer them to a mixing bowl along with the mayonnaise, shallots, mustard, lime juice, salt and black pepper.
5. Mound on fresh lettuce leaves; sprinkle with bacon crumbs and serve.

390. MOM'S PEPPER JACK CHEESE SOUP

Preparation Time: 20 minutes
Servings: 4

Nutrition Values: 296 Calories; 14.1g Fat; 6.4g Carbs; 14.2g Protein;

Ingredients

- 2 tablespoons ghee
- 1/2 cup scallions, chopped
- 1 celery stalk, chopped
- 1 jalapeno pepper, finely chopped
- 1 teaspoon garlic paste
- 1 ½ tablespoons flaxseed meal
- 2 cups water
- 1 ½ cups milk
- 6 ounces Pepper Jack cheese, shredded
- Salt and black pepper, to taste
- A pinch of paprika, to garnish

Directions

1. Warm the ghee in a deep pan over a moderately high heat.
2. Now, sauté the scallions, celery and jalapeno until they are softened and aromatic.
3. Add the garlic paste, flaxseed meal, water, and milk and reduce the heat to medium-low. Let it simmer, partially covered, 10 minutes more or until thoroughly cooked.

4. Afterwards, fold in the shredded cheese, heat off and stir until the cheese has melted and everything is homogenous. Season with salt and pepper to taste.
5. Taste and adjust the seasonings. Ladle into individual bowls, sprinkle with paprika and serve. Eat warm.

391. ALFREDO, KALE AND CHEESE DIP
Preparation Time: 30 minutes
Servings: 12

Nutrition Values: 154 Calories; 13g Fat; 3.3g Carbs; 6.2g Protein;

Ingredients
- 2 tablespoons butter
- 6 ounces heavy cream
- Salt and ground black pepper, to taste
- 2 egg yolks
- 2 cloves garlic, chopped
- 1 ½ cups kale, chopped
- 3/4 cup sour cream
- 1/2 cup Swiss cheese, grated
- 1 cup Cottage cheese, softened
- 1/2 cup smoked ham, roughly chopped

Directions
1. To make an Alfredo-style sauce, melt the butter in a pan over medium heat. Now, cook the heavy cream, stirring constantly. Add the salt and pepper; whisk in the egg yolks.
2. Turn the heat to medium-low; cook for a further 4 minutes, stirring continuously. Transfer to a casserole dish.
3. Add the remaining ingredients and stir to combine well.
4. Bake in the preheated oven at 360 degrees F, approximately 25 minutes. Bon appétit!

392. ITALIAN SALAMI AND CHEESE CASSEROLE
Preparation Time: 1 hour
Servings: 4

Nutrition Values: 334 Calories; 23g Fat; 6.2g Carbs; 25.5g Protein;

Ingredients
- Nonstick cooking spray
- 8 eggs
- Coarse salt, to taste
- 1 cup Mozzarella cheese, grated
- 1/2 cup Ricotta cheese
- 1 bell pepper, chopped
- 1 poblano pepper, deveined and chopped
- 1/2 teaspoon dried dill weed
- 1 teaspoon Dijon mustard
- 4 slices pepperoni, chopped
- 4 slices pancetta, chopped

Directions
1. Begin by preheating your oven to 360 degrees F. Generously grease a casserole dish with a nonstick cooking spray.
2. Beat the eggs, salt and cheese on medium-high speed until everything is well incorporated. Spoon the mixture into the casserole dish.
3. Add the remaining ingredients; gently stir with a spoon. Place a roasting pan with 6 cups of hot water in the middle of the preheated oven. Lower the casserole dish into the roasting pan.
4. Bake about 1 hour. Allow it to cool down for a couple of minutes before cutting it into squares. Serve warm and enjoy!

393. PANNA COTTA WITH ROASTED CARTOS AND BASIL
Preparation Time: 40 minutes
Servings: 8

Nutrition Values: 155 Calories; 12.7g Fat; 6.2g Carbs; 4.6g Protein;

Ingredients
- 4 large carrots, sliced
- 1 tablespoon coconut oil, melted
- 1/4 cup fresh basil, chopped
- 1 cup heavy cream
- 1/2 cup cremefraiche
- 1 cup Ricotta cheese
- 2 teaspoons powdered unflavored gelatin
- 2-inchsection of fresh rosemary stem, chopped
- Celery salt, to taste
- 1/4 teaspoon onion flakes
- 1/2 teaspoon fennel seeds
- 1/2 teaspoon mixed peppercorns, crushed
- 1/2 teaspoon cayenne pepper

Directions
1. Drizzle the carrot slices with the melted coconut oil. Roast the carrots in the preheated oven approximately 30 minutes, stirring once.
2. Transfer the carrots to a blender. Pulse until creamy and smooth.
3. Meanwhile, heat a saucepanover low heat; cook the fresh basil with the creamfor 4 minutes. Add the remaining ingredients and cook until completely melted, 4 to 6 minutes longer.

4. Fold in the pureed carrots and stir to combine well. Spoon mixture into 8 ramekins. Transfer to your refrigerator and let it sit overnight or until set.
5. Run a thin knife around the edge of each panna cotta; flip the ramekin onto serving plate. Bon appétit!

394. STUFFED PEPPERS WITH CHEESE AND PORK RINDS

Preparation Time: 45 minutes
Servings: 4

Nutrition Values: 359 Calories; 29.7g Fat; 6.7g Carbs; 17.7g Protein;

Ingredients
- 4 bell peppers
- 6 ounces cream cheese, room temperature
- 6 ounces blue cheese, crumbled
- 1/2 cup pork rinds, crushed
- 2 cloves garlic, smashed
- 1 ½ cups pureed tomatoes
- 1/2 teaspoon dried oregano
- 1 teaspoon dried basil
- Salt and ground black pepper, to taste
- 1/2 teaspoon cayenne pepper

Directions
1. Parboil the peppers in salted water for 4 to 6 minutes.
2. Preheat the oven to 360 degrees F. Lightly grease the sides and bottom of a casserole dish with a nonstick cooking spray.
3. In a mixing bowl, thoroughly combine the cream cheese, blue cheese, pork rinds, and garlic.
4. Stuff the peppers and transfer to the prepared casserole dish.
5. Then, mix the pureed tomatoes with the oregano, basil, salt, black pepper and cayenne pepper. Pour the tomato mixture over the stuffed pepper; cover the dish with foil.
6. Bake for 40 minutes and serve warm. Bon appétit!

395. FLAVORED ASIAGO CHEESE CHIPS

Preparation Time: 18 minutes
Servings: 2

Nutrition Values: 100 Calories; 8g Fat; 0g Carbs; 7g Protein;

Ingredients
- 3 cups Asiago cheese, freshly grated
- 1/3 teaspoon salt

- 1/2 teaspoon garlic powder
- 1/2 teaspoon cayenne pepper
- ½ teaspoon dried rosemary
- 1/3 teaspoon chili powder

Directions
1. Preheat your oven to 420 degrees F. Now, line a baking sheet with parchment paper.
2. Then, thoroughly combine the grated Asiago cheese with the spices.
3. Then, form 2 tablespoons of the cheese mixture into small mounds on the baking sheet.
4. Bake approximately 15 minutes; your chips will start to get hard as they cool.

396. KETO MAC AND CHEESE

Preparation Time: 15 minutes
Servings: 4

Nutrition Values: 357 Calories; 32.5g Fat; 6.9g Carbs; 8.4g Protein;

Ingredients
- 1 large-sized head cauliflower, broken into florets
- 2 tablespoons butter
- Salt and pepper, to taste
- 1/2 cup milk
- 1/2 cup heavy whipping cream
- 1 cup cream cheese
- 1/2 teaspoon turmeric powder
- 1 teaspoon garlic paste
- 1/2 teaspoon onion flakes

Directions
1. Begin by preheating your oven to 450 degrees F. Brush a baking sheet with a nonstick cooking spray.
2. Toss the cauliflower florets with the melted butter, salt, and pepper. Place the cauliflower florets on the prepared baking sheet; roast about 13 minutes.
3. Heat the remaining ingredients in a heavy-bottomed saucepan, stirring frequently. Simmer over medium-low heat until cooked through.
4. Toss the cauliflower with the creamy cheese sauce and eat warm.

397. VEGETABLE AND CHEESEBURGER QUICHE

Preparation Time: 45 minutes
Servings: 6

Nutrition Values: 310 Calories; 18.3g Fat; 3.8g Carbs; 30.7g Protein;

Ingredients

- 1 pound ground beef
- 1 onion, chopped
- 1 garlic clove, chopped
- 1 bell pepper, chopped
- 1/2 teaspoon coarse salt
- 1/4 teaspoon black pepper, or more to taste
- 2 zucchinis, thinly sliced
- 2 tomatoes, thinly sliced
- 1/4 cup whipping cream
- 8 eggs
- 1/2 cup Cheddar cheese, grated

Directions

1. Preheat an oven to 360 degrees F. Brush a baking dish with a nonstick cooking spray.
2. Then, in a heavy-bottomed skillet, brown the ground beef along with the onion, garlic and bell pepper. Season with salt and pepper.
3. Spread the meat layer on the bottom of the baking dish. Layer the zucchini slices on top. Top with tomato slices.
4. After that, whisk the whipping cream, eggs and cheese in a mixing bowl. Spoon this creamy mixture on the top of the vegetables.
5. Bake for 40 to 45 minutes, until it is browned around the edges. Bon appétit!

398. FRENCH-STYLE EGGS WITH APPENZELLER CHEESE

Preparation Time: 20 minutes
Servings: 5

Nutrition Values: 444 Calories; 35.3g Fat; 2.7g Carbs; 29.8g Protein;

Ingredients

- 1 tablespoon olive oil
- 4 slices Jambon de Bayonne, chopped
- 1/2 cup scallions, chopped
- 1/2 cup broccoli, chopped
- 1 clove garlic, minced
- 1 teaspoon fines herbes
- 1/4 cup chicken broth
- 5 eggs
- 1 ½ cups Appenzeller cheese, shredded

Directions

1. Heat the oil in a nonstick frying pan; cook the Jambon de Bayonne about 4 minutes, until browned and crisp; set it aside.
2. In the same pan, cook the scallions in the pan drippings. Add the broccoli and garlic and continue to cook, stirring periodically, until they are softened. Add the fines herbes and

chicken broth and cook an additional 6 minutes.
3. Now, make 5 holes in the vegetable mixture to reveal the bottom of your pan. Crack an egg into each hole.
4. Scatter the shredded cheese over the top and cook an additional 6 minutes. Remove from the heat and top with the reserved Jambon de Bayonne.

399. TWO-CHEESE AND WALNUT LOGS

Preparation Time: 10 minutes + chilling time
Servings: 15

Nutrition Values: 209 Calories; 18.9g Fat; 3.7g Carbs; 6.6g Protein;

Ingredients

- 14 ounces cream cheese, at room temperature
- 14 ounces sharp American cheese
- 1/2 cup full-fat mayonnaise
- 1 (1-ouncepackage ranch dressing mix
- 1 teaspoon lime juice
- 1/2 cup walnuts, finely chopped

Directions

1. Combine the cream cheese and sharp cheese with an electric mixer.
2. Stir in the mayonnaise, ranch dressing mix, and lime juice; mix well. Place in your refrigerator for 3 to 4 hours or until solid and firm.
3. When firm, shape the mixture into two logs; roll in walnuts. Serve well-chilled.

400. OMELET WITH BACON AND BLUE CHEESE

Preparation Time: 10 minutes
Servings: 2

Nutrition Values: 431 Calories; 33.1g Fat; 2.7g Carbs; 30.3g Protein;

Ingredients

- 4 slices cooked bacon, crumbled
- 4 eggs, beaten
- 1 teaspoon rosemary, chopped
- 1 teaspoon parsley, chopped
- Sea salt and black pepper
- 4 ounces blue cheese

Directions

1. Add the bacon to the frying pan; cook until sizzling.
2. Then, mix in the eggs, rosemary, parsley, salt, and black pepper.
3. Crumble the cheese over the eggs; fold in

half. Cook an additional 1 to 2 minutes or until everything is heated through.

401. MINI HAM FRITTATAS WITH SWISS CHEESE

Preparation Time: 40 minutes
Servings: 5

Nutrition Values: 261 Calories; 16g Fat; 6.6g Carbs; 21.1g Protein;

Ingredients

- 1 tablespoon avocado oil
- 1 red onion, chopped
- 1 bell pepper, chopped
- 1 cup mustard greens
- 6 slices ham, chopped
- 8 eggs, whisked
- 1 cup Swiss cheese, shredded
- Salt and pepper, to taste
- 1/4 teaspoon tarragon
- 1/2 teaspoon ancho powder
- 1/2 teaspoon Korean red pepper flakes
- 1 tablespoon fresh parsley, chopped

Directions

1. Start by preheating your oven to 390 degrees F. Add cupcake liners to your muffin pan.
2. Heat the avocado oil in nonstick skillet and sweat the onions for 5 to 6 minutes. Add the bell pepper and mustard greens, and continue to cook an additional 4 minutes, stirring frequently.
3. Add the ham and cook an additional 3 minutes. Stir in the remaining ingredients; stir until everything is well incorporated.
4. Transfer the mixture to the lined muffin pan and bake for 23 minutes or until set. Allow the muffins to cool for a couple of minutes before removing them from the cups. Enjoy!

402. SALAMI AND CHEESE BALLS

Preparation Time: 15 minutes
Servings: 8

Nutrition Values: 168 Calories; 13g Fat; 2.5g Carbs; 10.3g Protein;

Ingredients

- 1 egg
- 6 slices Genoa salami, chopped
- 6 ounces Ricotta cheese
- 6 ounces Colby cheese
- Salt and ground black pepper, to taste
- 1/4 cup almond flour
- 1 teaspoon baking powder

- 1 teaspoon garlic powder
- 1 teaspoon Italian seasoning

Directions

1. Begin by preheating an oven to 420 degrees F.
2. Whisk the eggs vigorously; add the remaining ingredients and mix to combine well.
3. Divide the mixture into 16 balls; arrange the balls on a baking sheet lined with parchment paper or a silicone mat.
4. Bake approximately 13 minutes or until they are crisp and golden brown.

SMOOTHIES

403. NUTTY CHOCO MILK SHAKE

Preparation Time: 5 minutes
Cooking Time: 0 minutes
Servings: 1

Ingredients:
- ¼ cup whole milk
- 1 tbsp cocoa powder
- 1 packet Stevia, or more to taste
- ¼ cup pecans
- 1 tbsp macadamia oil
- 1 ½ cups water

Directions:
1. Add all ingredients in blender.
2. Blend until smooth and creamy.
3. Serve and enjoy.

Nutrition Values:
Calories: 358; Fat: 34.0g; Carbs: 15.5g; Protein: 5.1g

404. STRAWBERRY-CHOCOLATE YOGURT SHAKE

Preparation Time: 5 minutes
Cooking Time: 0 minutes
Servings: 1

Ingredients:
- ½ cup whole milk yogurt
- ½ cup strawberries, chopped
- 1 tbsp cocoa powder
- 1 tbsp coconut oil
- 1 tbsp pepitas
- 1 ½ cups water
- 1 packet Stevia, or more to taste

Directions:
1. Add all ingredients in blender.
2. Blend until smooth and creamy.
3. Serve and enjoy.

Nutrition Values:
Calories: 269; Fat: 7.9g; Carbs: 16.5g; Protein: 33.0g

405. LEMONY-AVOCADO CILANTRO SHAKE

Preparation Time: 5 minutes
Cooking Time: 0 minutes
Servings: 1

Ingredients:
- ½ cup whole milk yogurt
- 1 packet Stevia, or more to taste
- 1 whole avocado
- 1 tbsp chopped cilantro
- 1 ½ cups water

Directions:
1. Add all ingredients in blender.
2. Blend until smooth and creamy.
3. Serve and enjoy.

Nutrition Values:
Calories: 397; Fat: 33.4g; Carbs: 23.4g; Protein: 8.3g

406. BERRY-CHOCO GOODNESS SHAKE

Preparation Time: 5 minutes
Cooking Time: 0 minutes
Servings: 1

Ingredients:
- ½ cup whole milk yogurt
- ¼ cup raspberries
- ¼ cup Blackberry
- ¼ cup strawberries, chopped
- 1 tbsp avocado oil
- 1 packet Stevia, or more to taste
- 1 tbsp cocoa powder
- 1 ½ cups water

Directions:
1. Add all ingredients in blender.
2. Blend until smooth and creamy.
3. Serve and enjoy.

Nutrition Values:
Calories: 255; Fat: 19.2g; Carbs: 20.2g; Protein: 6.4g

407. COCONUT-MELON YOGURT SHAKE

Preparation Time: 5 minutes
Cooking Time: 0 minutes
Servings: 1

Ingredients:
- ¼ cup whole milk yogurt
- 1 tbsp coconut oil
- ½ cup melon, slices
- 1 tbsp coconut flakes, unsweetened
- 1 tbsp chia seeds
- 1 ½ cups water
- 1 packet Stevia, or more to taste

Directions:
1. Add all ingredients in blender.
2. Blend until smooth and creamy.
3. Serve and enjoy.

Nutrition Values:
Calories: 278; Fat: 21.6g; Carbs: 19.8g; Protein: 5.4g

408. STRAWBERRY-COCONUT SHAKE

Preparation Time: 5 minutes
Cooking Time: 0 minutes
Servings: 1

Ingredients:

- ½ cup whole milk yogurt
- 1 tbsp MCT oil
- ¼ cup strawberries, chopped
- 1 tbsp coconut flakes, unsweetened
- 1 tbsp hemp seeds
- 1 ½ cups water
- 1 packet Stevia, or more to taste

Directions:

1. Add all ingredients in blender.
2. Blend until smooth and creamy.
3. Serve and enjoy.

Nutrition Values:
Calories: 282; Fat: 23.7g; Carbs: 14.0g; Protein: 6.5g

409. BLACKBERRY-CHOCOLATE SHAKE

Preparation Time: 5 minutes
Cooking Time: 0 minutes
Servings: 1

Ingredients:

- ½ cup whole milk yogurt
- ¼ cup blackberries
- 1 tbsp MCT oil
- 1 tbsp Dutch-processed cocoa powder
- 2 tbsp Macadamia nuts, chopped
- 1 ½ cups water
- 1 packet Stevia, or more to taste

Directions:

1. Add all ingredients in blender.
2. Blend until smooth and creamy.
3. Serve and enjoy.

Nutrition Values:
Calories: 463; Fat: 43.9g; Carbs: 17.9g; Protein: 8.5g

410. LETTUCE GREEN SHAKE

Preparation Time: 5 minutes
Cooking Time: 0 minutes
Servings: 1

Ingredients:

- ¾ cup whole milk yogurt
- 2 cups 5-lettuce mix salad greens
- 1 tbsp MCT oil
- 1 tbsp chia seeds
- 1 ½ cups water
- 1 packet Stevia, or more to taste

Directions:

1. Add all ingredients in blender.
2. Blend until smooth and creamy.
3. Serve and enjoy.

Nutrition Values:
Calories: 320; Fat: 24.2g; Carbs: 19.1g; Protein: 10.4g

411. ITALIAN GREENS AND YOGURT SHAKE

Preparation Time: 5 minutes
Cooking Time: 0 minutes
Servings: 1

Ingredients:

- 1 cup whole milk yogurt
- 1 cup Italian greens
- 1 packet Stevia, or more to taste
- 1 tbsp hemp seeds
- 1 tbsp olive oil
- 1 cup water

Directions:

1. Add all ingredients in blender.
2. Blend until smooth and creamy.
3. Serve and enjoy.

Nutrition Values:
Calories: 333; Fat: 25.9g; Carbs: 17.2g; Protein: 11.2g

412. GARDEN GREENS & YOGURT SHAKE

Preparation Time: 5 minutes
Cooking Time: 0 minutes
Servings: 1

Ingredients:

- 1 cup whole milk yogurt
- 1 cup Garden greens
- 1 tbsp MCT oil
- 1 tbsp flaxseed, ground
- 1 cup water
- 1 packet Stevia, or more to taste

Directions:

1. Add all ingredients in blender.
2. Blend until smooth and creamy.
3. Serve and enjoy.

Nutrition Values:
Calories: 334; Fat: 26.0g; Carbs: 17.2g; Protein: 11.2g

413. HAZELNUT-LETTUCE YOGURT SHAKE

Preparation Time: 5 minutes
Cooking Time: 0 minutes
Servings: 1

Ingredients:

- 1 cup whole milk yogurt
- 1 cup lettuce chopped
- 3 tbsp Hazelnut chopped
- 1 packet Stevia, or more to taste
- 1 tbsp olive oil
- 1 cup water

Directions:

1. Add all ingredients in blender.
2. Blend until smooth and creamy.
3. Serve and enjoy.

Nutrition Values:

Calories: 412; Fat: 34.7g; Carbs: 17.2g; Protein: 12.5g

414. NUTTY ARUGULA YOGURT SMOOTHIE

Preparation Time: 5 minutes
Cooking Time: 0 minutes
Servings: 1

Ingredients:

- 1 cup whole milk yogurt
- 1 cup baby arugula
- 1 tbsp avocado oil
- 2 tbsps.macadamia nuts
- 1 cup water
- 1 packet Stevia, or more to taste

Directions:

1. Add all ingredients in blender.
2. Blend until smooth and creamy.
3. Serve and enjoy.

Nutrition Values:

Calories: 399; Fat: 34.8g; Carbs: 15.5g; Protein: 10.3g

415. BABY KALE AND YOGURT SMOOTHIE

Preparation Time: 5 minutes
Cooking Time: 0 minutes
Servings: 1

Ingredients:

- 1 cup whole milk yogurt
- 1 cup baby kale greens
- 1 packet Stevia, or more to taste
- 1 tbsp MCT oil
- 1 tbsp sunflower seeds
- 1 cup water

Directions:

1. Add all ingredients in blender.
2. Blend until smooth and creamy.
3. Serve and enjoy.

Nutrition Values:

Calories: 329; Fat: 26.2g; Carbs: 15.6g; Protein: 11.0g

416. MINTY-COCO AND GREENS SHAKE

Preparation Time: 5 minutes
Cooking Time: 0 minutes
Servings: 1

Ingredients:

- ½ cup coconut milk
- 2 peppermint leaves
- 2 packets Stevia, or as needed
- 1 cup 50/50 salad mix
- 1 tbsp coconut oil
- 1 ½ cups water

Directions:

1. Add all ingredients in blender.
2. Blend until smooth and creamy.
3. Serve and enjoy.

Nutrition Values:

Calories: 344; Fat: 37.8g; Carbs: 5.8g; Protein: 2.7g

417. AVOCADO AND GREENS SMOOTHIE

Preparation Time: 5 minutes
Cooking Time: 0 minutes
Servings: 1

Ingredients:

- ½ cup coconut milk
- ½ Avocado fruit
- 1 cup Spring mix greens
- 1 tbsp avocado oil
- 1 ½ cups water
- 2 packets Stevia, or as needed

Directions:

1. Add all ingredients in blender.
2. Blend until smooth and creamy.
3. Serve and enjoy.

Nutrition Values:

Calories: 439; Fat: 43.4g; Carbs: 16.1g; Protein: 6.5g

418. BLUEBERRY AND GREENS SMOOTHIE

Preparation Time: 5 minutes
Cooking Time: 0 minutes
Servings: 1

Ingredients:

- ½ cup coconut milk
- ½ cup blueberries
- 1 cup arugula
- 1 tbsp hemp seeds
- 2 packets Stevia, or as needed

- 1 ½ cups water

Directions:
1. Add all ingredients in blender.
2. Blend until smooth and creamy.
3. Serve and enjoy.

Nutrition Values:
Calories: 321; Fat: 29.0g; Carbs: 18.4g; Protein: 5.2g

419. BOYSENBERRY AND GREENS SHAKE

Preparation Time: 5 minutes
Cooking Time: 0 minutes
Servings: 1

Ingredients:
- ½ cup coconut milk
- ½ cup Boysenberry
- 2 packets Stevia, or as needed
- 1 cup Baby Kale salad mix
- 1 tbsp MCT oil
- 1 ½ cups water

Directions:
1. Add all ingredients in blender.
2. Blend until smooth and creamy.
3. Serve and enjoy.

Nutrition Values:
Calories: 381; Fat: 38.0g; Carbs: 14.6g; Protein: 3.7g

420. RASPBERRY-COFFEE CREAMY SMOOTHIE

Preparation Time: 5 minutes
Cooking Time: 0 minutes
Servings: 1

Ingredients:
- ½ cup coconut milk
- 1 ½ cups brewed coffee, chilled
- ¼ cup Raspberries
- ¼ avocado fruit
- 1 tsp chia seeds
- 2 packets Stevia or more to taste

Directions:
1. Add all ingredients in blender.
2. Blend until smooth and creamy.
3. Serve and enjoy.

Nutrition Values:
Calories: 346; Fat: 33.2g; Carbs: 15.2g; Protein: 4.9g

421. RASPBERRY-FLAVORED CHAI SMOOTHIE

Preparation Time: 5 minutes
Cooking Time: 0 minutes
Servings: 1

Ingredients:
1 black tea bag
- ¼ tsp ginger
- ¼ tsp cardamom powder
- ¾ cup coconut milk
- ¼ cup raspberries
- 2 packets Stevia or as desired
- 1 ¼ cups boiling water
- ¼ tsp cinnamon

Directions:
1. Add all ingredients in blender.
2. Blend until smooth and creamy.
3. Serve and enjoy.

Nutrition Values:
Calories: 357; Fat: 36.4g; Carbs: 12.4g; Protein: 3.9g

422. CHAI TEA SMOOTHIE

Preparation Time: 5 minutes
Cooking Time: 0 minutes
Servings: 1

Ingredients:
- 1 black tea bag
- ¼ tsp ginger
- ¼ tsp cinnamon
- ¼ tsp cardamom powder
- 1 cup coconut milk
- 1 cup boiling water
- 2 packets Stevia or as desired

Directions:
1. Add all ingredients in blender.
2. Blend until smooth and creamy.
3. Serve and enjoy.

Nutrition Values:
Calories: 453; Fat: 48.3g; Carbs: 10.3g; Protein: 4.7g

423. COCO-LOCO CREAMY SHAKE

Preparation Time: 5 minutes
Cooking Time: 0 minutes
Servings: 1

Ingredients:
- ½ cup coconut milk
- 2 tbsp Dutch-processed cocoa powder, unsweetened
- 1 cup brewed coffee, chilled
- 1 tbsp hemp seeds
- 1-2 packets Stevia

Directions:
1. Add all ingredients in blender.
2. Blend until smooth and creamy.
3. Serve and enjoy.

Nutrition Values:

Calories: 354; Fat: 34.6g; Carbs: 16.2g; Protein: 6.8g

424. CARDAMOM-CINNAMON SPICED COCO-LATTE

Preparation Time: 5 minutes
Cooking Time: 0 minutes
Servings: 1

Ingredients:

- ½ cup coconut milk
- ¼ tsp cardamom powder
- 1 tbsp chocolate powder
- 1 ½ cups brewed coffee, chilled
- 1 tbsp coconut oil
- ¼ tsp cinnamon
- ¼ tsp nutmeg

Directions:

1. Add all ingredients in blender.
2. Blend until smooth and creamy.
3. Serve and enjoy.

Nutrition Values:

Calories: 362; Fat: 38.7g; Carbs: 7.5g; Protein: 3.8g

425. HAZELNUT AND COCONUT SHAKE

Preparation Time: 5 minutes
Cooking Time: 0 minutes
Servings: 1

Ingredients:

- ½ cup coconut milk
- ¼ cup hazelnut, chopped
- 1 ½ cups water
- 1 packet Stevia, optional

Directions:

1. Add all ingredients in blender.
2. Blend until smooth and creamy.
3. Serve and enjoy.

Nutrition Values:

Calories: 457; Fat: 46.1g; Carbs: 12.5g; Protein: 7.0g

SALAD

426. SPRING SALAD

Servings:2
Preparation Time: 10-15 minutes
Cooking Time: 0 minutes

Ingredients:

- 2 ounces mixed green vegetables
- 3 tablespoons roasted pine nuts
- 2 tablespoons 5 minute 5 Keto Raspberry Vinaigrette
- 2 tablespoons shaved Parmesan
- 2 slices bacon
- Pepper as required

Directions:

1. Take a cooking pan and add bacon, cook the bacon until crispy.
2. Take a bowl and add the salad ingredients and mix well, add crumbled bacon into the salad.
3. Mix well.
4. Dress it with your favorite dressing.
5. Enjoy!

Nutrition Values:

Calories: 209
Fat: 17g
Net Carbohydrates: 10g
Protein: 4g

427. HEARTY ORANGE AND ONION SALAD

Servings:2
Preparation Time: 10 minutes
Cooking Time: nil

Ingredients:

- 6 large oranges
- 3 tablespoons red wine vinegar
- 6 tablespoons olive oil
- 1 teaspoon dried oregano
- 1 red onion, thinly sliced
- 1 cup olive oil
- ¼ cup fresh chives, chopped
- Ground black pepper

Directions:

1. Peel orange and cut into 4-5 crosswise slices.
2. Transfer orange to shallow dish.
3. Drizzle vinegar, olive oil on top.
4. Sprinkle oregano.
5. Toss well to mix.
6. Chill for 30 minutes and arrange sliced onion and black olives on top.

7. Sprinkle more chives and pepper.
8. Serve and enjoy!

Nutrition Values:

Calories: 120
Fat: 6g
Carbohydrates: 20g
Protein: 2g

428. GROUND BEEF BELL PEPPERS

Servings:3
Preparation Time: 10 minutes
Cooking Time: 10 minutes

Ingredients:

- 1 onion, chopped
- 2 tablespoons coconut oil
- 1 pound ground beef
- 1 red bell pepper, diced
- 2 cups spinach, chopped
- Pepper to taste

Directions:

1. Take a skillet and place it over medium heat.
2. Add onion and cook until slightly browned.
3. Add spinach and ground beef.
4. Stir fry until done.
5. Take the mixture and fill up the bell peppers.
6. Serve and enjoy!

Nutrition Values:

Calories: 350
Fat: 23g
Carbohydrates: 4g
Protein: 28g

429. HEALTHY MEDITERRANEAN LAMB CHOPS

Servings:4
Preparation Time: 10 minutes
Cooking Time: 10 minute

Ingredients:

- 4 lamb shoulder chops, 8 ounces each
- 2 tablespoons Dijon mustard
- 2 tablespoons Balsamic vinegar
- ½ cup olive oil
- 2 tablespoons shredded fresh basil

Directions:

1. Pat your lamb chops dry using a kitchen towel and arrange them on a shallow glass baking dish.
2. Take a bowl and whisk in Dijon mustard, balsamic vinegar, pepper and mix them well.

3. Whisk in the oil very slowly into the marinade until the mixture is smooth.
4. Stir in basil.
5. Pour the marinade over the lamb chops and stir to coat both sides well .
6. Cover the chops and allow them to marinate for 1-4 hours (chilled.
7. Take the chops out and let them rest for 30 minutes to allow the temperature to reach a normal level.
8. Pre-heat your grill to medium heat and add oil to the grate.
9. Grill the lamb chops for 5-10 minutes per side until both sides are browned.
10. Once the center reads 145 degrees F, the chops are ready, serve and enjoy!

Nutrition Values:
Calories: 521
Fat: 45g
Carbohydrates: 3.5g
Protein: 22g

430. A TURTLE FRIEND SALAD

Servings:6
Preparation Time: 5 minutes
Cooking Time: 5 minutes

Ingredients:

- 1 Romaine lettuce, chopped
- 3 Roma tomatoes, diced
- 1 English cucumber, diced
- 1 small red onion, diced
- ½ cup parsley, chopped
- 2 tablespoons virgin olive oil
- ½ large lemon, juice
- 1 teaspoon garlic powder
- Sunflower seeds and pepper to taste

Directions:

1. Wash the vegetables thoroughly under cold water.
2. Prepare them by chopping, dicing or mincing as needed.
3. Take a large salad bowl and transfer the prepped veggies.
4. Add vegetable oil, olive oil, lemon juice, and spice.
5. Toss well to coat.
6. Serve chilled if preferred.
7. Enjoy!

Nutrition Values:
Calories: 200
Fat: 8g
Carbohydrates: 18g
Protein: 10g

431. AVOCADO AND CILANTRO MIX

Servings:2
Preparation Time: 10 minutes
Cooking Time: nil

Ingredients:

- 2 avocados, peeled, pitted and diced
- 1 sweet onion, chopped
- 1 green bell pepper, chopped
- 1 large ripe tomato, chopped
- ¼ cup of fresh cilantro, chopped
- ½ lime, juiced
- Sunflower seeds and pepper as needed

Directions:

1. Take a medium sized bowl and add onion, tomato, avocados, bell pepper, lime and cilantro.
2. Give the whole mixture a toss.
3. Season accordingly and serve chilled.
4. Enjoy!

Nutrition Values:
Calories: 126
Fat: 10g
Carbohydrates: 10g
Protein: 2g

432. EXCEPTIONAL WATERCRESS AND MELON SALAD

Servings:4
Preparation Time: 15 minutes
Cooking Time: 20 minutes

Ingredients:

- 3 tablespoons lime juice
- 1 teaspoon date paste
- 1 teaspoon fresh ginger root, minced
- ¼ cup vegetable oil
- 2 bunch watercress, chopped
- 2 ½ cups watermelon, cubed
- 2 ½ cups cantaloupe, cubed
- 1/3 cup almonds, toasted and sliced

Directions:

1. Take a large sized bowl and add lime juice, ginger, date paste.
2. Whisk well and add oil.
3. Season with pepper and sunflower seeds.
4. Add watercress, watermelon.
5. Toss well
6. Transfer to a serving bowl and garnish with sliced almonds.
7. Enjoy!

Nutrition Values:
Calories: 274

Fat: 20g

Carbohydrates: 21g

Protein: 7g

433. ZUCCHINI AND ONIONS PLATTER

Servings:4

Preparation Time: 15 minutes

Cooking Time: 45 minutes

Ingredients:

- 3 large zucchini, julienned
- 1 cup cherry tomatoes, halved
- ½ cup basil
- 2 red onions, thinly sliced
- ¼ teaspoon sunflower seeds
- 1 teaspoon cayenne pepper
- 2 tablespoons lemon juice

Directions:

1. Create zucchini Zoodles by using a vegetable peeler and shaving the zucchini with peeler lengthwise until you get to the core and seeds.
2. Turn zucchini and repeat until you have long strips.
3. Discard seeds.
4. Lay strips in cutting board and slice lengthwise to your desired thickness.
5. Mix Zoodles in a bowl alongside onion, basil, tomatoes and toss.
6. Sprinkle sunflower seeds and cayenne pepper on top.
7. Drizzle lemon juice.
8. Serve and enjoy!

Nutrition Values:

Calories: 156

Fat: 8g

Carbohydrates: 6g

Protein: 7g

434. TENDER WATERMELON AND RADISH SALAD

Servings:4

Preparation Time: 15 minutes

Cooking Time: 25 minutes

Ingredients:

- 10 medium beets, peeled and cut into 1-inch chunks
- 1 teaspoon extra virgin olive oil
- 4 cups seedless watermelon, diced
- 1 tablespoon fresh thyme, chopped
- 1 lemon, juiced
- 2 cups kale, torn
- 3 cups radish, diced

- Sunflower seeds, to taste
- Pepper, to taste

Directions:

1. Pre-heat your oven to 350 degrees F.
2. Take a small bowl and add beets, olive oil and toss well to coat the beets.
3. Roast beets for 25 minutes until tender.
4. Transfer to large bowl and cool them.
5. Add watermelon, kale, radishes, thyme, lemon juice, and toss.
6. Season sea sunflower seedsand pepper.
7. Serve and enjoy!

Nutrition Values:

Calories: 178

Fat: 2g

Carbohydrates: 39g

Protein: 6g

435. FIERY TOMATO SALAD

Servings:4

Preparation Time: 10 minutes

Cooking Time: 25 minutes

Ingredients:

- ½ cup scallions, chopped
- 1 pound cherry tomatoes
- 3teaspoons olive oil
- Sea sunflower seeds and freshly ground black pepper, to taste
- 1 tablespoon red wine vinegar

Directions:

1. Season tomatoes with spices and oil.
2. Heat your oven to 450 degrees F.
3. Take a baking sheet and spread the tomatoes.
4. Bake for 15 minutes.
5. Stir and turn the tomatoes.
6. Then, bake again for 10 minutes.
7. Take a bowl and mix the roasted tomatoes with all the remaining ingredients.
8. Serve and enjoy!

Nutrition Values:

Calories: 115

Fat: 10.4g

Carbohydrates: 5.4g

Protein: 12g

436. HEALTHY CAULIFLOWER SALAD

Servings:4

Preparation Time: 10 minutes

Cooking Time: nil

Ingredients:

- 1 head cauliflower, broken into florets
- 1 small onion, chopped
- 1/8 cup extra virgin olive oil

- ¼ cup apple cider vinegar
- ½ teaspoon sea salt
- ½ teaspoon black pepper
- ¼ cup dried cranberries
- ¼ cup pumpkin seeds

Directions:

1. Wash the cauliflower thoroughly and break down into florets.
2. Transfer the florets to a bowl.
3. Take another bowl and whisk in oil, salt, pepper and vinegar.
4. Add pumpkin seeds, cranberries to the bowl with dressing.
5. Mix well and pour dressing over cauliflower florets.
6. Toss well.
7. Add onions and toss.
8. Chill and serve.
9. Enjoy!

Nutrition Values:

Calories: 163
Fat: 11g
Carbohydrates: 16g
Protein: 3g

437. CHICKPEA SALAD

Servings:4
Preparation Time: 6 minutes
Cooking Time: Nil

Ingredients:

- 1 cup canned chickpeas, drained and rinsed.
- 2 spring onions, thinly sliced.
- 1 small cucumber, diced.
- 2 green bell peppers, chopped.
- 2 tomatoes, diced.
- 2 tablespoons fresh parsley, chopped.
- 1 teaspoon capers, drained and rinsed.
- Half a lemon, juiced.
- 2 tablespoons sunflower oil.
- 1 tablespoon red wine vinegar.
- Pinch of dried oregano.
- Sunflower seeds and pepper to taste

Directions:

1. Take a medium sized bowl and add chickpeas, spring onions, cucumber, bell pepper, tomato, parsley and capers.
2. Take another bowl and mix in the rest of the ingredients, pour mixture over chickpea salad and toss well.
3. Coat and serve, enjoy!

Nutrition Values:

Calories: 74

Fat: 0.7g
Carbohydrates: 16g
Protein: 2g

438. DASHING BOK CHOY SAMBA

Servings:3
Preparation Time: 5 minutes
Cooking Time: 15 minutes

Ingredients:

- 4 bokchoy,sliced
- 1 onion, sliced
- ½ cup Parmesan cheese, grated
- 4teaspoons coconut cream
- Sunflower seeds and freshly ground black pepper, to taste

Directions:

1. Mix bokchoy with black pepper and sunflower seeds.
2. Take a cooking pan, heat the oil and to sauté sliced onion for 5 minutes.
3. Then add cream and seasoned bokchoy.
4. Cook for 6 minutes.
5. Stir in Parmesan cheese and cover with a lid.
6. Reduce the heat to low and cook for 3 minutes.
7. Serve warm and enjoy!

Nutrition Values:

Calories: 112
Fat: 4.9g
Carbohydrates: 1.9g
Protein: 3g

439. SIMPLE AVOCADO CAPRESE SALAD

Servings:6
Preparation Time: 15 minutes
Cooking Time: 29 minutes

Ingredients:

- 2 avocados, cubed
- 1 cup cherry tomatoes, halved
- 8 ounces mozzarella balls, halved
- 2 tablespoons finely chopped fresh basil
- 2 tablespoons olive oil
- 2 tablespoons balsamic vinegar
- 1 tablespoon sunflower seeds
- Fresh ground black pepper

Directions:

1. Take a bowl and add the listed ingredients, toss them well until thoroughly mixed.
2. Season with pepper according to your taste.
3. Serve and enjoy!

Nutrition Values:

Calories: 358
Fat: 30g
Carbohydrates: 9g
Protein: 14g

440. THE RUTABAGA WEDGE DISH

Servings:4
Preparation Time: 15 minutes
Cooking Time: 45 minutes

Ingredients:

- 2 medium rutabagas, medium, cleaned and peeled
- 4 tablespoons almond butter
- ½ teaspoon sunflower seeds
- ½ teaspoon onion powder
- 1/8 teaspoon black pepper
- ½ cup buffalo wing sauce
- ¼ cup blue cheese dressing, low fat and low sodium
- 2 green onions, chopped

Directions:

1. Pre-heat your oven to 400 degrees F.
2. Line a baking sheet with parchment paper.
3. Wash and peel rutabagas, clean and peel them, and cut into wedge shapes.
4. Take a skillet and place it over low heat, add almond butter and melt.
5. Stir in onion powder, sunflower seeds, onion, black pepper.
6. Use seasoned almond butter to coat wedges.
7. Arrange wedges in a single layer on the baking sheet.
8. Bake for 30 minutes.
9. Remove and coat in buffalo sauce and return to oven.
10. Bake for 15 minutes more.
11. Place wedges on serving plate and trickle with blue cheese dressing.
12. Garnish with chopped green onion and enjoy!

Nutrition Values:

Calories: 235
Fat: 15g
Carbohydrates: 10g
Protein: 2.5g

441. RED COLESLAW

Servings:4
Preparation Time: 10 minutes
Cooking Time: 0 minutes

Ingredients:

- 1 2/3 pounds red cabbage
- 2 tablespoons ground caraway seeds
- 1 tablespoon whole grain mustard

- 1 1/4 cups mayonnaise
- Sunflower seeds and black pepper

Directions:

1. Take a large bowl and all the remaining ingredients.
2. Mix it well and let it sit for 10 minutes.
3. Serve and enjoy!

Nutrition Values:

Calories: 406
Fat: 40.8g
Carbohydrates: 10g
Protein: 2.2g

442. CLASSIC TUNA SALAD

Servings:4
Preparation Time: 10 minutes
Cooking Time: Nil

Ingredients:

- 12 ounces white tuna, in water
- ½ cup celery, diced
- 2 tablespoons fresh parsley, chopped
- 2 tablespoons low-calorie mayonnaise, low fat and low sodium
- ½ teaspoon Dijon mustard
- ½ teaspoon sunflower seeds
- ¼ teaspoon fresh ground black pepper

Direction

1. Take a medium sized bowl and add tuna, parsley, and celery.
2. Mix well and add mayonnaise and mustard.
3. Season with pepper and sunflower seeds.
4. Stir and add olives, relish, chopped pickle, onion and mix well.
5. Serve and enjoy

Nutrition Values:

Calories: 137
Fat: 5g
Carbohydrates: 1g
Protein: 20g

443. GREEK SALAD

Servings:4
Preparation Time: 6 minutes
Cooking Time: Nil

Ingredients:

- 2 cucumbers, diced
- 2 tomatoes, sliced
- 1 green lettuce, cut into thin strips
- 2 red bell peppers, cut
- ½ cup black olives pitted
- 3 ½ ounces feta cheese, cut
- 1 red onion, sliced

- 2 tablespoons olive oil
- 2 tablespoons lemon juice
- Sunflower seeds and pepper to taste

Direction

1. Dice cucumbers and slice up the tomatoes.
2. Tear the lettuce and cut it into thin strips.
3. De-seed and cut the peppers into strips.
4. Take a salad bowl and mix in all the listed vegetables, add olives and feta cheese (cut into cubes).
5. Take a small cup and mix in olive oil and lemon juice, season with sunflower seeds and pepper.
6. Pour mixture into the salad and toss well, enjoy!

Nutrition Values:
Calories: 132
Fat: 4g
Carbohydrates: 3g
Protein: 5g

444. FANCY GREEK ORZO SALAD

Servings:4
Preparation Time: 5 minutes and 24 hours chill time
Cooking Time: 10 minutes

Ingredients:

- 1 cup orzo pasta, uncooked
- ½ cup fresh parsley, minced
- 6 teaspoons olive oil
- 1 onion, chopped
- 1 ½ teaspoons oregano

Directions:

1. Cook the orzo and drain them.
2. Add to a serving dish.
3. Add 2 teaspoons of oil.
4. Take another dish and add parsley, onion, remaining oil and oregano.
5. Season with sunflower seeds, pepperaccording to your taste.
6. Pour the mixture over the orzo and let it chill for 24 hours.
7. Serve and enjoy at lunch!

Nutrition Values:
Calories: 399
Fat: 12g
Carbohydrates: 55g
Protein:16g

445. HOMELY TUSCAN TUNA SALAD

Servings:4
Preparation Time: 5-10 minutes
Cooking Time: Nil

Ingredients:

- 15 ounces small white beans
- 6 ounces drained chunks of light tuna
- 10 cherry tomatoes, quartered
- 4 scallions, trimmed and sliced
- 2 tablespoons lemon juice

Directions:

1. Add all of the listed ingredients to a bowl and gently stir.
2. Season with sunflower seeds and pepper accordingly, enjoy!

Nutrition Values:
Calories: 322
Fat: 8g
Carbohydrates: 32g
Protein:30g

446. ASPARAGUS LOADED LOBSTER SALAD

Servings:4
Preparation Time: 10 minutes
Cooking Time: Nil
Smart Points: 5

Ingredients:

- 8 ounces lobster, cooked and chopped
- 3 ½ cups asparagus, chopped and steamed
- 2 tablespoons lemon juice
- 4 teaspoons extra virgin olive oil
- ¼ teaspoon kosher sunflower seeds
- Pepper
- ½ cup cherry tomatoes halved
- 1 basil leaf, chopped
- 2 tablespoons red onion, diced

Directions:

1. Whisk in lemon juice, sunflower seeds, pepper in a bowl and mix with oil.
2. Take a bowl and add the rest of the ingredients.
3. Toss well and pour dressing on top.
4. Serve and enjoy!

Nutrition Values:
Calories: 247
Fat: 10g
Carbohydrates: 14g
Protein: 27g

447. TASTY YOGURT AND CUCUMBER SALAD

Servings:4
Preparation Time: 10 minutes
Cooking Time: Nil

Ingredients:

- 5-6 small cucumbers, peeled and diced
- 1 (8 ouncescontainer plain Greek yogurt
- 2 garlic cloves, minced
- 1 tablespoon fresh mint, minced
- Sea sunflower seeds and fresh black pepper

Directions:
1. Take a large bowl and add cucumbers, garlic, yogurt, mint.
2. Season with sunflower seeds and pepper.
3. Refrigerate the salad for 1 hour and serve.
4. Enjoy!

Nutrition Values:
Calories: 74
Fat: 0.7g
Carbohydrates: 16g
Protein: 2g

448. UNIQUE EGGPLANT SALAD

Servings:3
Preparation Time: 10 minutes
Cooking Time: 30 minutes

Ingredients:
- 2 eggplants, peeled and sliced
- 2 garlic cloves
- 2 green bell pepper, sliced, seeds removed
- ½ cup fresh parsley
- ½ cup mayonnaise, low fat, low sodium
- Sunflower seeds and black pepper

Directions:
1. Preheat your oven to 480 degrees F.
2. Take a baking pan and add eggplant, bell peppers and season with black pepper to it.
3. Bake for about 30 minutes.
4. Flip the vegetables after 20 minutes.
5. Then, take a bowl, add baked vegetables and all the remaining ingredients.
6. Mix well.
7. Serve and enjoy!

Nutrition Values:
Calories: 196
Fat: 108.g
Carbohydrates: 13.4g
Protein: 14.6g

449. ZUCCHINI PESTO SALAD

Servings:4
Preparation Time: 10 minutes
Cooking Time: 10 minutes

Ingredients:
- 2 cups spiral pasta
- 2 zucchini, sliced and halved
- 4 tomatoes, cut

- 1 cup white mushrooms, cut
- 1 small red onion, chopped
- 2 tablespoons fresh basil leaves, chopped
- 2 tablespoons sunflower oil
- 1 tablespoon lemon juice
- Pepper and sunflower seeds to taste

Directions:
1. Cook the pasta according to the package instructions, drain and rinse under cold water.
2. Take a large bowl and add zucchini, tomatoes, mushrooms, onion, and pasta.
3. Mix well,
4. In a food processor, add oil, lemon juice, basil, blue cheese, black, and process well.
5. Pour the mixture over the salad and toss well.
6. Serve and enjoy!

Nutrition Values:
Calories: 301
Fat: 25g
Net Carbohydrates: 7g
Protein: 10g

450. WHOLESOME POTATO AND TUNA SALAD

Servings:4
Preparation Time: 10 minutes
Cooking Time: nil

Ingredients:
- 1 pound baby potatoes, scrubbed, boiled
- 1 cup tuna chunks, drained
- 1 cup cherry tomatoes, halved
- 1 cup medium onion, thinly sliced
- 8 pitted black olives
- 2 medium hard-boiled eggs, sliced
- 1 head Romaine lettuce
- ¼ cup olive oil
- 2 tablespoons lemon juice
- 1 tablespoon Dijon mustard
- 1 teaspoon dill weed, chopped
- Pepper as needed

Directions:
1. Take a small glass bowl and mix in your olive oil, lemon juice, Dijon mustard and dill.
2. Season the mix with pepper and salt.
3. Add in the tuna, baby potatoes, cherry tomatoes, red onion, green beans, black olives and toss everything nicely.
4. Arrange your lettuce leaves on a beautiful serving dish to make the base of your salad.
5. Top them with your salad mixture and place the egg slices.

6. Drizzle with the previously prepared Salad Dressing.
7. Serve hot

Nutrition Values:
Calories: 406
Fat: 22g
Carbohydrates: 28g
Protein: 26g

451. BABY SPINACH SALAD

Servings:2
Preparation Time: 10 minutes
Cooking Time: nil

Ingredients:
- 1 bag baby spinach, washed and dried
- 1 red bell pepper, cut in slices
- 1 cup cherry tomatoes, cut in halves
- 1 small red onion, finely chopped
- 1 cup black olives, pitted

For dressing:
- 1 teaspoon dried oregano
- 1 large garlic clove
- 3 tablespoons red wine vinegar
- 4 tablespoons olive oil
- Sunflower seeds and pepper to taste

Directions:
1. Prepare the dressing by blending in garlic, olive oil, vinegar in a food processor.
2. Take a large salad bowl and add spinach leaves, toss well with the dressing.
3. Add remaining ingredients and toss again, season with sunflower seeds and pepper and enjoy!

Nutrition Values:
Calories: 126
Fat: 10g
Carbohydrates: 10g
Protein: 2g

452. ELEGANT CORN SALAD

Servings:6
Preparation Time: 10 minutes
Cooking Time: 2 hours

Ingredients:
- 2 ounces prosciutto, cut into strips
- 1 teaspoon olive oil
- 2 cups corn
- 1/2 cup salt-free tomato sauce
- 1 teaspoon garlic, minced
- 1 green bell pepper, chopped

Directions:
1. Grease your Slow Cooker with oil.

2. Add corn, prosciutto, garlic, tomato sauce, bell pepper to your Slow Cooker.
3. Stir and place lid.
4. Cook on HIGH for 2 hours.
5. Divide between serving platters and enjoy!

Nutrition Values:
Calories: 109
Fat: 2g
Carbohydrates: 10g
Protein: 5g

453. ARABIC FATTOUSH SALAD

Servings:4
Preparation Time: 15 minutes
Cooking Time: 2-3 minutes

Ingredients:
- 1 whole wheat pita bread
- 1 large English cucumber, diced
- 2 cup grape tomatoes, halved
- ½ medium red onion, finely diced
- ¾ cup fresh parsley, chopped
- ¾ cup mint leaves, chopped
- 1 clove garlic, minced
- ¼ cup fat free feta cheese, crumbled
- 1 tablespoon olive oil
- 1 teaspoon ground sumac
- Juice from ½ a lemon
- Salt and pepper as needed

Directions:
1. Mist pita bread with cooking spray.
2. Season with salt.
3. Toast until the breads are crispy.
4. Take a large bowl and add the remaining ingredients and mix (except feta).
5. Top the mix with diced toasted pita and feta.
6. Serve and enjoy!

Nutrition Values:
Calories: 86
Fat: 3g
Carbohydrates: 9g
Protein: 9g

454. CHEESE BURGER MUFFINS

Preparation Time: 40 minutes
Servings: 9

Ingredients:

- 1/2 cup flaxseed meal
- 1 teaspoon baking powder
- 1/4 cups sour cream
- 1/2 cup almond flour
- 2 eggs
- Salt and black pepper to the taste.
- For the filling:
- 1/2 teaspoon onion powder
- 2 tablespoons tomato paste
- 1/2 teaspoon garlic powder
- 1/2 cup cheddar cheese, grated
- 16 ounces beef, ground
- 2 tablespoons mustard
- Salt and black pepper to the taste.

Directions:

1. In a bowl, mix almond flour with flaxseed meal, salt, pepper and baking powder and whisk.
2. Add eggs and sour cream and stir very well.
3. Divide this into a greased muffin pan and press well using your fingers
4. Heat up a pan over medium high heat; add beef; stir and brown for a few minutes
5. Add salt, pepper, onion powder, garlic powder and tomato paste and stir well.
6. Cook for 5 minutes more and take off heat.
7. Fill cupcakes crusts with this mix, introduce in the oven at 350 degrees F and bake for 15 minutes
8. Spread cheese on top, introduce in the oven again and bake muffins for 5 minutes more
9. Serve with mustard and your favorite toppings on top.

Nutrition Values: Calories: 245; Fat: 16; Fiber: 6; Carbs: 2; Protein: 14

455. ONION AND CAULIFLOWER DIP

Preparation Time: 40 minutes
Servings: 24

Ingredients:

- 1 cauliflower head, florets separated
- 1½ cups chicken stock
- 1/2 teaspoon chili powder
- 1/2 teaspoon garlic powder
- 1/4 cup mayonnaise
- 1/2 cup yellow onion, chopped.
- 1/2 teaspoon cumin, ground
- ¾ cup cream cheese
- Salt and black pepper to the taste.

Directions:

1. Put the stock in a pot, add cauliflower and onion, heat up over medium heat and cook for 30 minutes
2. Add chili powder, salt, pepper, cumin and garlic powder and stir.
3. Also add cream cheese and stir a bit until it melts
4. Blend using an immersion blender and mix with the mayo.
5. Transfer to a bowl and keep in the fridge for 2 hours before you serve it.

Nutrition Values: Calories: 60; Fat: 4; Fiber: 1; Carbs: 1; Protein: 1

456. KETO MARINATED EGGS

Preparation Time: 2 hours 17 minutes
Servings: 4

Ingredients:

- 1/4 cup unsweetened rice vinegar
- 4 ounces cream cheese
- 6 eggs
- 2 garlic cloves, minced
- 1 teaspoon stevia
- 1 tablespoon chives, chopped.
- 1¼ cups water
- 2 tablespoons coconut aminos
- Salt and black pepper to the taste.

Directions:

1. Put the eggs in a pot, add water to cover, bring to a boil over medium heat; cover and cook for 7 minutes
2. Rinse eggs with cold water and leave them aside to cool down.
3. In a bowl, mix 1 cup water with coconut aminos, vinegar, stevia and garlic and whisk well.
4. Put the eggs in this mix, cover with a kitchen towel and leave them aside for 2 hours rotating from time to time
5. Peel eggs, cut in halves and put egg yolks in a bowl.
6. Add 1/4 cup water, cream cheese, salt, pepper and chives and stir well.

7. Stuff egg whites with this mix and serve them.

Nutrition Values: Calories: 210; Fat: 3; Fiber: 1; Carbs: 3; Protein: 12

457. KETO TORTILLA CHIPS

Preparation Time: 24 minutes
Servings: 6

Ingredients:

For the tortillas:

- 2 teaspoons olive oil
- 2 tablespoons psyllium husk powder
- 1/4 teaspoon xanthan gum
- 1/2 teaspoon curry powder
- 3 teaspoons coconut flour
- 1 cup flax seed meal
- 1 cup water

For the chips:

- 6 flaxseed tortillas
- 3 tablespoons vegetable oil
- Fresh salsa for serving
- Sour cream for serving
- Salt and black pepper to the taste.

Directions:

1. In a bowl, mix flaxseed meal with psyllium powder, olive oil, xanthan gum, water and curry powder and mix until you obtain an elastic dough.
2. Spread coconut flour on a working surface
3. Divide dough into 6 pieces, place each piece on the working surface and roll into a circle and cut each into 6 pieces
4. Heat up a pan with the vegetable oil over medium high heat; add tortilla chips, cook for 2 minutes on each side and transfer to paper towels
5. Put tortilla chips in a bowl, season with salt and pepper and serve with some fresh salsa and sour cream on the side

Nutrition Values: Calories: 30; Fat: 3; Fiber: 1.2; Carbs: 0.5; Protein: 1

458. ARTICHOKE DIP

Preparation Time: 25 minutes
Servings: 16

Ingredients:

- 28 ounces canned artichoke hearts, chopped.
- 1/4 cup sour cream
- 1/4 cup heavy cream
- 1/4 cup mayonnaise
- 1/4 cup shallot, chopped.
- 1/2 cup parmesan cheese, grated
- 1 cup mozzarella cheese, shredded

- 4 ounces feta cheese, crumbled
- 1 tablespoon balsamic vinegar
- 10 ounces spinach, chopped.
- 1 tablespoon olive oil
- 2 garlic cloves, minced
- 4 ounces cream cheese
- Salt and black pepper to the taste.

Directions:

1. Heat up a pan with the oil over medium heat; add shallot and garlic; stir and cook for 3 minutes
2. Add heavy cream and cream cheese and stir.
3. Also add sour cream, parmesan, mayo, feta cheese and mozzarella cheese; stir and reduce heat.
4. Add artichoke, spinach, salt, pepper and vinegar; stir well, take off heat and transfer to a bowl.
5. Serve as a tasty keto dip.

Nutrition Values: Calories: 144; Fat: 12; Fiber: 2; Carbs: 5; Protein: 5

459. KETO CHIA SEEDS SNACK

Preparation Time: 45 minutes
Servings: 36

Ingredients:

- 1/2 cup chia seeds, ground
- 1/4 teaspoon oregano, dried
- 1/4 teaspoon garlic powder
- 1/4 teaspoon sweet paprika
- 3 ounces cheddar, cheese, grated
- 1/4 teaspoon xanthan gum
- 1/4 teaspoon onion powder
- 1¼ cup ice water
- 2 tablespoons olive oil
- 2 tablespoons psyllium husk powder
- Salt and black pepper to the taste.

Directions:

1. In a bowl, mix chia seeds with xanthan gum, psyllium powder, oregano, garlic and onion powder, paprika, salt and pepper and stir.
2. Add oil and stir well.
3. Add ice water and stir until you obtain a firm dough.
4. Spread this on a baking sheet, introduce in the oven at 350 degrees F and bake for 35 minutes
5. Leave aside to cool down, cut into 36 crackers and serve them as a keto snack.

Nutrition Values: Calories: 50; Fat: 3; Fiber: 1; Carbs: 0.1; Protein: 2

460. KETO MAPLE AND PECAN BARS

Preparation Time: 35 minutes
Servings: 12

Ingredients:

- 2 cups pecans, toasted and crushed.
- 1 cup almond flour
- 1/4 teaspoon stevia
- 1/2 cup coconut, shredded
- 1/2 cup coconut oil
- 1/2 cup flaxseed meal
- 1/4 cup "maple syrup"

For the maple syrup:

- 2 teaspoons maple extract
- 1/2 teaspoon vanilla extract
- 1 tablespoon ghee
- ¾ cup water
- 1/4 teaspoon xanthan gum
- 1/4 cup erythritol
- 2 ¼ teaspoons coconut oil

Directions:

1. In a heatproof bowl, mix ghee with 2¼ teaspoons coconut oil and xanthan gum; stir, introduce in your microwave and heat up for 1 minute
2. Add erythritol, water, maple and vanilla extract; stir well and heat up in the microwave for 1 minute more
3. In a bowl, mix flaxseed meal with coconut and almond flour and stir.
4. Add pecans and stir again.
5. Add 1/4 cup "maple syrup", stevia and 1/2 cup coconut oil and stir well.
6. Spread this in a baking dish, press well, introduce in the oven at 350 degrees F and bake for 25 minutes
7. Leave aside to cool down, cut into 12 bars and serve as a keto snack.

Nutrition Values: Calories: 300; Fat: 30; Fiber: 12; Carbs: 2; Protein: 5

461. KETO PEPPER NACHOS

Preparation Time: 30 minutes
Servings: 6

Ingredients:

- 1 pound mini bell peppers, cut in halves
- 1 pound beef meat, ground
- 1 teaspoon cumin, ground
- 1/2 cup tomato, chopped.
- 1 teaspoon garlic powder
- 1 teaspoon sweet paprika
- 1/2 teaspoon oregano, dried
- 1/4 teaspoon red pepper flakes
- 1½ cups cheddar cheese, shredded
- 1 tablespoons chili powder
- Sour cream for serving
- Salt and black pepper to the taste.

Directions:

1. In a bowl, mix chili powder with paprika, salt, pepper, cumin, oregano, pepper flakes and garlic powder and stir.
2. Heat up a pan over medium heat; add beef; stir and brown for 10 minutes
3. Add chili powder mix; stir and take off heat.
4. Arrange pepper halves on a lined baking sheet, stuff them with the beef mix, sprinkle cheese, introduce in the oven at 400 degrees F and bake for 10 minutes
5. Take peppers out of the oven, sprinkle tomatoes and divide between plates and serve with sour cream on top.

Nutrition Values: Calories: 350; Fat: 22; Fiber: 3; Carbs: 6; Protein: 27

462. DELIGHTFUL BOMBS

Preparation Time: 10 minutes
Servings: 6

Ingredients:

- 8 black olives, pitted and chopped.
- 4 ounces cream cheese
- 1 tablespoons basil, chopped.
- 2 tablespoons sun-dried tomato pesto
- 14 pepperoni slices, chopped.
- Salt and black pepper to the taste.

Directions:

1. In a bowl, mix cream cheese with salt, pepper, pepperoni, basil, sun dried tomato pesto and black olives and stir well.
2. Shape balls from this mix, arrange on a platter and serve

Nutrition Values: Calories: 110; Fat: 10; Fiber: 0; Carbs:1.4; Protein: 3

463. KETO BROCCOLI AND CHEDDAR BISCUITS

Preparation Time: 35 minutes
Servings: 12

Ingredients:

- 4 cups broccoli florets
- 1½ cup almond flour
- 2 eggs
- 1/2 teaspoon apple cider vinegar
- 1/2 teaspoon baking soda

- 1 teaspoon paprika
- 1/4 cup coconut oil
- 2 cups cheddar cheese, grated
- 1 teaspoon garlic powder
- Salt and black pepper to the taste.

Directions:

1. Put broccoli florets in your food processor, add some salt and pepper and blend well.
2. In a bowl, mix almond flour with salt, pepper, paprika, garlic powder and baking soda and stir.
3. Add cheddar cheese, coconut oil, eggs and vinegar and stir everything.
4. Add broccoli and stir again.
5. Shape 12 patties, arrange on a baking sheet, introduce in the oven at 375 degrees F and bake for 20 minutes
6. Turn the oven to broiler and broil your biscuits for 5 minutes more
7. Arrange on a platter and serve

Nutrition Values: Calories: 163; Fat: 12; Fiber: 2; Carbs: 2; Protein: 7

464. ZUCCHINI CHIPS

Preparation Time: 3 hours 10 minutes
Servings: 8

Ingredients:

- 3 zucchinis, very thinly sliced
- 2 tablespoons balsamic vinegar
- 2 tablespoons olive oil
- Salt and black pepper to the taste.

Directions:

1. In a bowl, mix oil with vinegar, salt and pepper and whisk well.
2. Add zucchini slices, toss to coat well and spread on a lined baking sheet, introduce in the oven at 200 degrees F and bake for 3 hours
3. Leave chips to cool down and serve them as a keto snack.

Nutrition Values: Calories: 40; Fat: 3; Fiber: 7; Carbs: 3; Protein: 7

465. KETO AVOCADO DIP

Preparation Time: 3 hours 20 minutes
Servings: 4

Ingredients:

- 2 avocados, pitted, peeled and cut into slices
- 1/2 cup cilantro, chopped.
- 1 cup coconut milk
- 1/4 cup erythritol powder
- 1/4 teaspoon stevia

- Juice and zest of 2 limes

Directions:

1. Place avocado slices on a lined baking sheet, squeeze half of the lime juice over them and keep in your freezer for 3 hours
2. Heat up the coconut milk in a pan over medium heat.
3. Add lime zest; stir and bring to a boil.
4. Add erythritol powder; stir, take off heat and leave aside to cool down a bit.
5. Transfer avocado to your food processor, add the rest of the lime juice and the cilantro and pulse well.
6. Add coconut milk mix and stevia and blend well.
7. Transfer to a bowl and serve right away.

Nutrition Values: Calories: 150; Fat: 14; Fiber: 2; Carbs: 4; Protein: 2

466. KETO TACO CUPS

Preparation Time: 50 minutes
Servings: 30

Ingredients:

- 1 pound beef, ground
- 2 cups cheddar cheese, shredded
- 2 tablespoons cumin
- 2 tablespoons chili powder
- 1/4 cup water
- Pico de gallo for serving
- Salt and black pepper to the taste.

Directions:

1. Divide spoonful of parmesan on a lined baking sheet, introduce in the oven at 350 degrees F and bake for 7 minutes
2. Leave cheese to cool down for 1 minute, transfer them to mini cupcake molds and shape them into cups
3. Meanwhile; heat up a pan over medium high heat; add beef; stir and cook until it browns
4. Add the water, salt, pepper, cumin and chili powder; stir and cook for 5 minutes more
5. Divide into cheese cups, top with pico de gallo, transfer them all to a platter and serve

Nutrition Values: Calories: 140; Fat: 6; Fiber: 0; Carbs: 6; Protein: 15

467. KETO MUFFINS SNACK

Preparation Time: 25 minutes
Servings: 20

Ingredients:

- 3 hot dogs, cut into 20 pieces
- 1/2 cup flaxseed meal

- 1/2 cup almond flour
- 1/4 cup coconut milk
- 1/3 cup sour cream
- 3 tablespoons swerve
- 1 tablespoon psyllium powder
- 1/4 teaspoon baking powder
- 1 egg
- Cooking spray
- A pinch of salt

Directions:
1. In a bowl, mix flaxseed meal with flour, psyllium powder, swerve, salt and baking powder and stir.
2. Add egg, sour cream and coconut milk and whisk well.
3. Grease a muffin tray with cooking oil, divide the batter you've just make, stick a hot dog piece in the middle of each muffin, introduce in the oven at 350 degrees F and bake for 12 minutes
4. Broil in preheated broil for 3 minutes more, divide on a platter and serve

Nutrition Values: Calories: 80; Fat: 6; Fiber: 1; Carbs: 1; Protein: 3

468. KETO PUMPKIN MUFFINS

Preparation Time: 25 minutes
Servings: 18

Ingredients:
- 1/4 cup sunflower seed butter
- 3/4 cup pumpkin puree
- 1/2 teaspoon nutmeg, ground
- 1/2 teaspoon baking soda
- 1 egg
- 1/2 teaspoon baking powder
- 1 teaspoon cinnamon, ground
- 2 tablespoons flaxseed meal
- 1/4 cup coconut flour
- 1/2 cup erythritol
- A pinch of salt

Directions:
1. In a bowl, mix butter with pumpkin puree and egg and blend well.
2. Add flaxseed meal, coconut flour, erythritol, baking soda, baking powder, nutmeg, cinnamon and a pinch of salt and stir well.
3. Spoon this into a greased muffin pan, introduce in the oven at 350 degrees F and bake for 15 minutes
4. Leave muffins to cool down and serve them as a snack.

Nutrition Values: Calories: 50; Fat: 3; Fiber: 1; Carbs: 2; Protein: 2

469. FRIED QUESO SNACK

Preparation Time: 20 minutes
Servings: 6

Ingredients:
- 5 ounces queso Blanco, cubed and freeze for a couple of minutes
- 1 ½ tablespoons olive oil
- 2 ounces olives, pitted and chopped.
- A pinch of red pepper flakes

Directions:
1. Heat up a pan with the oil over medium high heat; add queso cubes and cook until the bottom melts a bit.
2. Flip cubes with a spatula and sprinkle black olives on top.
3. Leave cubes to cook a bit more, flip and sprinkle red pepper flakes and cook until they are crispy.
4. Flip, cook on the other side until it's crispy as well, transfer to a cutting board, cut into small blocks and then serve as a snack.

Nutrition Values: Calories: 500; Fat: 43; Fiber: 4; Carbs: 2; Protein: 30

470. KETO PESTO CRACKERS

Preparation Time: 27 minutes
Servings: 6

Ingredients:
- 1/2 teaspoon baking powder
- 1/4 teaspoon basil, dried
- 1¼ cups almond flour
- 1 garlic clove, minced
- 2 tablespoons basil pesto
- A pinch of cayenne pepper
- 3 tablespoons ghee
- Salt and black pepper to the taste.

1. **Directions:**
2. In a bowl, mix salt, pepper, baking powder and almond flour.
3. Add garlic, cayenne and basil and stir.
4. Add pesto and whisk.
5. Also add ghee and mix your dough with your finger.
6. Spread this dough on a lined baking sheet, introduce in the oven at 325 degrees F and bake for 17 minutes
7. Leave aside to cool down, cut your crackers and serve them as a snack.

Nutrition Values: Calories: 200; Fat: 20; Fiber:

1; Carbs: 4; Protein: 7

471. KETO PIZZA DIP

Preparation Time: 30 minutes
Servings: 4

Ingredients:

- 4 ounces cream cheese, soft
- 1/2 cup tomato sauce
- 1/4 cup mayonnaise
- 1/2 cup mozzarella cheese
- 6 pepperoni slices, chopped.
- 1/2 teaspoon Italian seasoning
- 1/4 cup sour cream
- 1/4 cup parmesan cheese, grated
- 1 tablespoon green bell pepper, chopped.
- 4 black olives, pitted and chopped.
- Salt and black pepper to the taste.

Directions:

1. In a bowl, mix cream cheese with mozzarella, sour cream, mayo, salt and pepper and stir well.
2. Spread this into 4 ramekins, add a layer of tomato sauce, then layer parmesan cheese, top with bell pepper, pepperoni, Italian seasoning and black olives
3. Introduce in the oven at 350 degrees F and bake for 20 minutes Serve warm.

Nutrition Values: Calories: 400; Fat: 34; Fiber: 4; Carbs: 4; Protein: 15

472. YUMMY SPINACH BALLS

Preparation Time: 22 minutes
Servings: 30

Ingredients:

- 4 tablespoons melted ghee
- 2 eggs
- 1 cup almond flour
- 16 ounces spinach
- 1/3 cup feta cheese, crumbled
- 1/4 teaspoon nutmeg, ground
- 1/3 cup parmesan, grated
- 1 tablespoon onion powder
- 3 tablespoons whipping cream
- 1 teaspoon garlic powder
- Salt and black pepper to the taste.

Directions:

1. In your blender, mix spinach with ghee, eggs, almond flour, feta cheese, parmesan, nutmeg, whipping cream, salt, pepper, onion and garlic pepper and blend very well.
2. Transfer to a bowl and keep in the freezer for 10 minutes
3. Shape 30 spinach balls, arrange on a lined baking sheet, introduce in the oven at 350 degrees F and bake for 12 minutes
4. Leave spinach balls to cool down and serve as a party appetizer.

Nutrition Values: Calories: 60; Fat: 5; Fiber: 1; Carbs: 0.7; Protein: 2

473. JALAPENO BALLS

Preparation Time: 20 minutes
Servings: 3

Ingredients:

- 3 bacon slices
- 3 ounces cream cheese
- 1/2 teaspoon parsley, dried
- 1/4 teaspoon garlic powder
- 1/4 teaspoon onion powder
- 1 jalapeno pepper, chopped.
- Salt and black pepper to the taste.

Directions:

1. Heat up a pan over medium high heat; add bacon, cook until it's crispy, transfer to paper towels, drain grease and crumble
2. Reserve bacon fat from the pan.
3. In a bowl, mix cream cheese with jalapeno pepper, onion and garlic powder, parsley, salt and pepper and stir well.
4. Add bacon fat and bacon crumbles; stir gently, shape balls from this mix and serve

Nutrition Values: Calories: 200; Fat: 18; Fiber: 1; Carbs: 2; Protein: 5

474. KETO SAUSAGE AND CHEESE DIP

Preparation Time: 2 hours 20 minutes
Servings: 28

Ingredients:

- 1 pound Italian sausage, ground
- 8 ounces cream cheese
- 15 ounces canned tomatoes mixed with habaneros
- 16 ounces sour cream
- 8 ounces pepper jack cheese, chopped.
- A pinch of salt and black pepper
- 1/4 cup green onions, chopped.

Directions:

1. Heat up a pan over medium heat; add sausage; stir and cook until it browns
2. Add tomatoes mix; stir and cook for 4 minutes more
3. Add a pinch of salt, pepper and the green onions; stir and cook for 4 minutes

4. Spread pepper jack cheese on the bottom of your slow cooker.
5. Add cream cheese, sausage mix and sour cream, cover and cook on High for 2 hours
6. Uncover your slow cooker; stir dip, transfer to a bowl and serve

Nutrition Values: Calories: 144; Fat: 12; Fiber: 1; Carbs: 3; Protein: 6

475. KETO BREAD STICKS

Preparation Time: 25 minutes
Servings: 24

Ingredients:

- 2 cups mozzarella cheese, melted for 30 seconds in the microwave
- 1 teaspoon baking powder
- 1 teaspoon onion powder
- 1 egg
- 2 tablespoons Italian seasoning
- 3 tablespoons cream cheese, soft
- 1 tablespoon psyllium powder
- ¾ cup almond flour
- 3 ounces cheddar cheese, grated
- Salt and black pepper to the taste.

Directions:

1. In a bowl, mix psyllium powder with almond flour, baking powder, salt and pepper and whisk.
2. Add cream cheese, melted mozzarella and egg and stir using your hands until you obtain a dough.
3. Spread this on a baking sheet and cut into 24 sticks
4. Sprinkle onion powder and Italian seasoning over them.
5. Top with cheddar cheese, introduce in the oven at 350 degrees F and bake for 15 minutes
6. Serve them as a keto snack!

Nutrition Values: Calories: 245; Fat: 12; Fiber: 5; Carbs: 3; Protein: 14

476. TOMATO TARTS

Preparation Time: 1 hour 20 minutes
Servings: 12

Ingredients:

- 2 tomatoes, sliced
- 1/4 cup olive oil
- Salt and black pepper to the taste.

For the base:

- 5 tablespoons ghee
- 1 tablespoon psyllium husk
- 1/2 cup almond flour
- 2 tablespoons coconut flour
- A pinch of salt

For the filling:

- 3 ounces goat cheese, crumbled
- 1 small onion, thinly sliced
- 3 teaspoons thyme, chopped.
- 2 tablespoons olive oil
- 2 teaspoons garlic, minced

Directions:

1. Spread tomato slices on a lined baking sheet, season with salt and pepper, drizzle 1/4 cup olive oil, introduce in the oven at 425 degrees F and bake for 40 minutes
2. Meanwhile; in your food processor mix almond flour with psyllium husk, coconut flour, salt, pepper and cold butter and stir until you obtain a dough.
3. Divide this dough into silicone cupcake molds, press well, introduce in the oven at 350 degrees F and bake for 20 minutes
4. Take cupcakes out of the oven and leave aside
5. Also take tomato slices out of the oven and cool them down a bit.
6. Divide tomato slices on top of cupcakes
7. Heat up a pan with 2 tablespoons olive oil over medium high heat; add onion; stir and cook for 4 minutes
8. Add garlic and thyme; stir, cook for 1 minute more and take off heat.
9. Spread this mix on top of tomato slices
10. Sprinkle goat cheese, introduce in the oven again and cook at 350 degrees F for 5 minutes more
11. Arrange on a platter and serve

Nutrition Values: Calories: 163; Fat: 13; Fiber: 1; Carbs: 3; Protein: 3

477. KETO MUSHROOMS APPETIZER

Preparation Time: 30 minutes
Servings: 5

Ingredients:

- 24 ounces white mushroom caps
- 1/4 cup mayo
- 1/4 cup sour cream
- 1/2 cup Mexican cheese, shredded
- 1 teaspoon garlic powder
- 1 small yellow onion, chopped.
- 1 teaspoon curry powder
- 4 ounces cream cheese, soft
- 1 cup shrimp, cooked, peeled, deveined and chopped.

- Salt and black pepper to the taste.

Directions:

1. In a bowl, mix mayo with garlic powder, onion, curry powder, cream cheese, sour cream, Mexican cheese, shrimp, salt and pepper to the taste. and whisk well.
2. Stuff mushrooms with this mix, place on a baking sheet and cook in the oven at 350 degrees F for 20 minutes
3. Arrange on a platter and serve

Nutrition Values: Calories: 244; Fat: 20; Fiber: 3; Carbs: 7; Protein: 14

478. PROSCIUTTO AND SHRIMP APPETIZER

Preparation Time: 30 minutes
Servings: 16

Ingredients:

- 11 prosciutto sliced
- 10 ounces already cooked shrimp, peeled and deveined
- 2 tablespoons olive oil
- 1/3 cup blackberries, ground
- 1/3 cup red wine
- 1 tablespoons mint, chopped.
- 2 tablespoons erythritol

Directions:

1. Wrap each shrimp in prosciutto slices, arrange on a lined baking sheet, drizzle the olive oil over them, introduce in the oven at 425 degrees F and bake for 15 minutes
2. Heat up a pan with ground blackberries over medium heat; add mint, wine and erythritol; stir, cook for 3 minutes and take off heat.
3. Arrange shrimp on a platter, drizzle blackberries sauce over them and serve

Nutrition Values: Calories: 245; Fat: 12; Fiber: 2; Carbs: 1; Protein: 14

479. AVOCADO SALSA

Preparation Time: 10 minutes
Servings: 4

Ingredients:

- 2 avocados, pitted, peeled and chopped.
- 1/2 tomato, chopped.
- 1 small red onion, chopped.
- 3 jalapeno pepper, chopped.
- 2 tablespoons cumin powder
- 2 tablespoons lime juice
- Salt and black pepper to the taste.

Directions:

1. In a bowl, mix onion with avocados, peppers, salt, black pepper, cumin, lime juice and tomato pieces and stir well.
2. Transfer this to a bowl and serve with toasted baguette slices as a keto appetizer.

Nutrition Values: Calories: 120; Fat: 2; Fiber: 2; Carbs: 0.4; Protein: 4

480. COCONUT BARS

Preparation time: 10 minutes
Cooking time: 2 hours and 30 minutes
Servings: 12

Ingredients:

- 2 egg whites
- ¼ cup coconut oil, melted
- 1 cup coconut sugar
- ½ teaspoon vanilla extract
- 1/2 teaspoon baking soda
- 3 tablespoons lemon juice
- 1 ½ cups coconut flour
- ½ cup coconut flakes
- Olive oil

Directions:

1. In a bowl, mix all the ingredients except the olive oil and stir.
2. Line your slow cooker with parchment paper and grease it with olive oil. Add the cookie mixture to the slow cooker, press it on the bottom of the pot, cover and cook on low for 2 hours and 30 minutes.
3. Take the cookie sheet out of the slow cooker, cut into bars and serve.

Nutrition Values: Calories 541, fat 28,5, fiber 3,8, carbs 73,3, protein 4

481. MAPLE WALNUTS

Preparation time: 10 minutes
Cooking time: 2 hours
Servings: 5

Ingredients:

- 3 cups walnuts
- ¼ cup maple syrup
- 1 tablespoon coconut oil, melted

Directions:

1. In your slow cooker, combine all the ingredients, cover, cook on low for 2 hours, divide into cups and serve.

Nutrition Values: Calories 528, fat 47, fiber 5,1, carbs 18, protein 18,1

482. ORANGE PLUMS

Preparation time: 10 minutes
Cooking time: 4 hours

Servings: 4

Ingredients:

- 1 pound plums, stones removed and halved
- 2 cups orange juice
- ¼ cup maple syrup

Directions:

1. In your slow cooker, combine all the ingredients, cover and cook on low for 4 hours.
2. Divide into bowls and serve.

Nutrition Values: Calories 115, fat 0,3, fiber 0,5, carbs 28,1, protein 1

483. FLAVORED NECTARINES

Preparation time: 4 minutes
Cooking time: 3 hours
Servings: 4

Ingredients:

- 1 pound nectarines, stones removed and halved
- 1/3 cup coconut sugar
- 1 teaspoon fresh grated ginger
- 2 teaspoons lemon zest
- ½ teaspoon ground cinnamon
- 1 tablespoon lemon juice
- 1 tablespoon coconut oil
- ½ cup water

Directions:

1. In your slow cooker, combine all the ingredients, cover and cook on low for 3 hours.
2. Divide into bowls and serve cold.

Nutrition Values: Calories 118, fat 3,8, fiber 2,2, carbs 22,3, protein 1,3

484. SIMPLE CAKE

Preparation time: 5 minutes
Cooking time: 2 hours and 30 minutes
Servings: 10

Ingredients:

- 1 cup almond flour
- ½ cup coconut sugar
- ½ teaspoons baking soda
- 3 tablespoons lemon juice
- 3 eggs, whisked
- 4 tablespoons coconut oil, melted
- ¾ teaspoon vanilla extract
- 2/3 cup almond milk
- 1/3 cup cocoa powder
- 2 tablespoons cocoa butter

Directions:

1. In a bowl, mix all the ingredients and stir well.
2. Pour this into a slow cooker lined with parchment paper and cook on low for 2 hours and 30 minutes.
3. Leave the cake to cool down, slice and serve it.

Nutrition Values: Calories 194, fat 15,7, fiber 1,5, carbs 13,3, protein 3,2

485. PEANUT BUTTER CAKE

Preparation time: 5 minutes
Cooking time: 2 hours and 30 minutes
Servings: 10

Ingredients:

- ½ teaspoons baking soda
- 3 tablespoons lemon juice
- 2 cups coconut flour
- ¼ teaspoon ground nutmeg
- 1 ½ teaspoons ground cinnamon
- 1 tablespoon coconut oil, melted
- 1 egg white
- 1 tablespoon vanilla extract
- 1 cup pumpkin puree
- 1/3 cup peanut butter, soft
- 1 teaspoon lime juice
- Olive oil

Directions:

1. In a bowl, mix all the ingredients except the olive oil and stir well.
2. Grease your slow cooker with olive oil, line it with parchment paper and pour the cake batter on top. Spread the batter evenly in the slow cooker, cover and cook on low for 2 hours and 30 minutes.
3. Cool the cake down, sliced and serve it.

Nutrition Values: Calories 103, fat 7,6, fiber 2,5, carbs 6, protein 3,2

486. PECAN PUDDING

Preparation time: 5 minutes
Cooking time: 4 hours
Servings: 4

Ingredients:

- Olive oil
- 1/3 teaspoon baking soda
- 2 tablespoons lemon juice
- 1 cup coconut flour
- 1 cup date sugar
- 3 tablespoons coconut oil, melted
- 1 cup almond milk
- 1 ½cup chopped pecans
- 1 Tbsp lemon zest

- ¾ cup orange juice

Directions:

1. In a bowl, combine all the ingredients except the olive oil, and stir well.
2. Grease the slow cooker with the olive oil, pour the pecans mixture, spread, cover and cook on low for 4 hours.
3. Divide into dessert bowls and serve.

Nutrition Values: Calories 499, fat 46,2, fiber 6,2, carbs 22,3, protein 5,1

487. SPICY PINEAPPLE

Preparation time: 5 minutes
Cooking time: 4 hours
Servings: 8

Ingredients:

- 2 teaspoons lemon juice
- 3 tablespoons coconut sugar
- ¼ teaspoon fresh grated ginger
- 3 cups pineapple chunks
- 1/8 teaspoon ground nutmeg
- ¼ teaspoon ground cinnamon
- ¼ cup coconut oil, melted

Directions:

1. In your slow cooker, combine all the ingredients, cover and cook on low for 4 hours.
2. Divide into bowls and serve.

Nutrition Values: Calories 104, fat 6,9, fiber 0,9, carbs 12, protein 0,4

488. STRAWBERRY PIE

Preparation time: 5 minutes
Cooking time: 2 hours and 30 minutes
Servings: 4

Ingredients:

- 2 pounds strawberries, chopped
- ¾ cup water
- 1 cup coconut sugar
- 1 cup coconut flour
- 1/2 teaspoon baking soda
- 3 tablespoons lemon juice
- 1/3 cup almond milk
- 1 egg, whisked
- 1 teaspoon lime zest
- 3 tablespoons coconut oil, melted

Directions:

1. In a bowl, combine all the ingredients and stir well.
2. Line the slow cooker with parchment paper, spread the strawberry mix on top of the

parchment, cover, cook on low for 2 hours and 30 minutes, divide into dessert bowls and serve.

Nutrition Values: Calories 428, fat 17,3, fiber 6,3, carbs 70,9, protein 4

489. HONEY BALLS

Preparation time: 5 minutes
Cooking time: 2 hours
Servings: 10

Ingredients:

- 1/3 cup almond flour
- ½ teaspoon baking soda
- 2 tablespoons lemon juice
- 3 eggs, whisked
- 5 tablespoons coconut oil, melted
- 2 tablespoons honey
- For dipping:
- 4 tablespoons coconut oil, melted
- 1 cup honey

Directions:

1. In a bowl, mix the flour with baking soda, lemon juice, eggs, 5 tablespoons oil and 2 tablespoons honey, stir well until you obtain a nice smooth dough. Shape 10 balls out of the dough.
2. In a bowl, mix the 4 tablespoons oil with 1 cup honey.
3. Dip the balls into this mix then arrange them in your slow cooker lined with parchment paper, cover and cook on low for 2 hours.

Nutrition Values: Calories 265, fat 15, fiber 0,4, carbs 34,3, protein 2,4

490. STRAWBERRY CAKE

Preparation time: 5 minutes
Cooking time: 3 hours
Servings: 6

Ingredients:
For the crust:

- ½ cup dates, pitted
- 1 tablespoon almond milk
- ½ teaspoon vanilla extract
- ½ cup almonds, chopped

For the cake:

- 2 ½ cups cashews, soaked for 8 hours
- 1 cup strawberries
- ¾ cup honey
- 1 tablespoon coconut oil, melted

Directions:

1. In your food processor, mix dates with the almond milk, vanilla and almonds and pulse

well. Flatten this mix on the bottom of the slow cooker lined with parchment paper.

2. In a blender, mix the cashews with strawberries, honey and the oil and pulse well.
3. Spread the strawberry mix evenly on the crust, cover the pot, and cook on low for 3 hours.
4. Slice the cake, divide between plates and serve.

Nutrition Values: Calories 578, fat 33,4, fiber 4,5, carbs 68,4, protein 11,1

491. PEACH AND CREAM

Preparation time: 5 minutes
Cooking time: 2 hours
Servings: 2

Ingredients:

- 1 pound peaches, stones removed and chopped
- 2 cups coconut cream

Directions:

1. In the slow cooker, combine the peaches with the cream, cover, and cook on low for 2 hours.
2. Blend using an immersion blender, divide into bowls and serve.

Nutrition Values: Calories 582, fat 57,4, fiber 6,4, carbs 20,3, protein 6,2

492. MAPLE FIGS

Preparation time: 5 minutes
Cooking time: 3 hours
Servings: 4

Ingredients:

- 2 tablespoons coconut butter
- 12 figs, halved
- ¼ cup maple syrup

Directions:

1. In your slow cooker, combine all the ingredients, cover and cook on low for 3 hours.
2. Divide into bowls and serve cold.

Nutrition Values: Calories 286, fat 9,6, fiber 8,1, carbs 53,1, protein 2,9

493. APPLE CAKE

Preparation time: 10 minutes
Cooking time: 30 minutes
Servings: 4

Ingredients:

- 1 ½ cups coconut flour
- 1 teaspoon ground cinnamon
- 1/3 teaspoon baking soda

- 2 tablespoons lemon juice
- 1 teaspoon baking soda
- ¾ cup maple syrup
- 1 cup chopped apples
- ½ cup coconut oil, melted

Directions:

1. In a bowl, mix all the ingredients and whisk them well.
2. Pour this into a slow cooker lined with parchment paper, spread, cover and cook on low for 3 hours.
3. Slice the cake, divide between plates and serve.

Nutrition Values: Calories 444, fat 28,3, fiber 3,6, carbs 51, protein 1

494. PEAR BUTTER

Preparation time: 5 minutes
Cooking time: 3 hours
Servings: 4

Ingredients:

- 4 pears, cored and chopped
- ½ cup coconut cream
- 1 tablespoon pure maple syrup
- ½ teaspoon ground cinnamon
- 2 tablespoons coconut sugar
- ½ teaspoon vanilla extract

Directions:

1. In your slow cooker, combine all the ingredients, cover and cook on low for 3 hours.
2. Blend the mix using an immersion blender, divide into jars and use cold.

Nutrition Values: Calories 222, fat 7,5, fiber 7,3, carbs 41,6, protein 1,5

495. MINTY GRAPEFRUIT MIX

Preparation time: 5 minutes
Cooking time: 2 hours
Servings: 4

Ingredients:

- 1 cup water
- 1 cup maple syrup
- ½ cup chopped mint
- 2 cups grapefruits, cut into segments

Directions:

1. In your slow cooker, combine all the ingredients, cover and cook on low for 2 hours.
2. Divide into cups and serve cold.

Nutrition: 247, fat 0,4, carbs 2,1, fiber 63,1,

protein 1,1

496. MAPLE MANGO MIX

Preparation time: 5 minutes
Cooking time: 2 hours
Servings: 6

Ingredients:

- 4 cups peeled, cubed mango
- 2 tablespoons lemon juice
- 6 tablespoons maple syrup

Directions:

1. In your slow cooker, combine all the ingredients, cover and cook on low for 2 hours.
2. Divide into bowls and serve.

Nutrition Values: Calories 161, fat 3, fiber 2, carbs 8, protein 1

497. COCOA PLUM JAM

Preparation time: 5 minutes
Cooking time: 2 hours
Servings: 4

Ingredients:

- ½ cup cocoa powder
- 1 cup chopped, pitted plums
- ¼ cup maple syrup
- 1 cup water

Directions:

1. In the slow cooker, combine all the ingredients, cover and cook on high for 2 hours.
2. Stir the mix well, divide into cups and use once cooled.

Nutrition Values: Calories 89, fat 0,2, fiber 1, carbs 22,9, protein 0,2

498. BASIL STRAWBERRY STEW

Preparation time: 5 minutes
Cooking time: 2 hours and 30 minutes
Servings: 4

Ingredients:

- 2 tablespoons lime juice
- 1 ½ tablespoons maple syrup
- 1 tablespoon coconut oil, melted
- 1 pound strawberries, halved
- ¼ cup chopped basil leaves

Directions:

1. In your slow cooker, combine all the ingredients, cover and cook on low for 2 hours and 30 minutes.
2. Divide the stew into bowls and serve.

Nutrition Values: Calories 87, fat 3,8, fiber

2,3, carbs 14,3, protein 0,8

499. LEMON PUDDING

Preparation time: 5 minutes
Cooking time: 2 hours and 30 minutes
Servings: 6

Ingredients:

- 1 cup homemade lemon curd
- Lemon zest from 1 lemon
- ½ cup maple syrup
- 3 eggs, whisked
- 2 ounces coconut oil, melted
- 3 ½ ounces coconut milk
- ½ cup almond flour
- ½ teaspoon baking soda
- 3 tablespoons lemon juice

Directions:

1. In your slow cooker, combine all the ingredients, cover and cook on low for 2 hours and 30 minutes.
2. Divide the pudding into bowls and serve cold.

Nutrition Values: Calories 375, fat 30,4, fiber 1,4, carbs 27,6, protein 6,9

FAVORITES

500. FALL CABBAGE SOUP

Preparation Time: 25 minutes
Servings: 4

Nutrition Values: 185 Calories; 16.6g Fat; 2.4g Carbs; 2.9g Protein;

Ingredients

- 1 ½ tablespoons butter, melted
- 1 leek, chopped
- 2 garlic cloves, minced
- 2 carrots, chopped
- 1 cup cabbage, shredded
- 1 green pepper, chopped
- 4 cups water
- 2 bouillon cubes
- 1 cup sour cream
- Fresh tarragon sprigs, for garnish

Directions

1. Warm the butter in a large pot over a medium flame. Sauté the leeks until just tender and fragrant. Now, add the remaining vegetables and cook for 5 to 7 minutes, stirring periodically.
2. Add the water andbouillon cubes; cover partially and cook an additional 13 minutes.
3. Blend the mixture until creamy, uniform and smooth. Stir in the sour cream; gently heat, stirring continuously, until your soup is hot.
4. Ladle into individual bowls and serve garnished with fresh tarragon. Bon appétit!

501. FRENCH STYLE VEGETABLES

Preparation Time: 15 minutes
Servings: 4

Nutrition Values: 318 Calories; 24.3g Fat; 5.1g Carbs; 15.4g Protein;

Ingredients

- 2 tablespoons olive oil
- 2 garlic cloves, minced
- 1/2 cup red onion, chopped
- 1/2 pound button mushrooms, chopped
- 1 cup cauliflower, cut into small florets
- 1 medium-sized eggplant, chopped
- 1 teaspoon dried basil
- 1 teaspoon dried oregano
- 1 rosemary sprig, leaves picked
- 1 thyme sprig, leaves picked
- 1/2 cup tomato sauce

- 1/4 cup dry white wine
- 8 ounces Halloumi cheese, cubed

Directions

1. Heat the olive oil in a saucepan over a moderately high heat. Now, sauté the garlic for 1 to 1½ minutes.
2. Now, stir in the onion, mushrooms, cauliflower, and eggplant; cook an additional 5 minutes, stirring periodically.
3. Add the seasonings, tomato sauce, and wine; continue to cook for 4 more minutes. Remove from the heat and divide among individual plates.
4. Serve topped with Halloumi cheese and enjoy!

502. ASPARAGUS WITH FETA CHEESE

Preparation Time: 15 minutes
Servings: 6

Nutrition Values: 128 Calories; 9.4g Fat; 2.9g Carbs; 6.4g Protein;

Ingredients

- 1 ½ pounds asparagus spears
- 2 tablespoons butter, melted
- 2 green onions, chopped
- 2 garlic cloves, minced
- Salt and black pepper, to the taste
- 1 cup feta cheese, crumbled
- 1/2 cup fresh parsley, roughly chopped

Directions

1. Preheat an oven to 420 degrees F.
2. Drizzle the asparagus with the melted butter. Toss with the green onions, garlic, salt, and black pepper.
3. Place the asparagus on a lightly-greased baking pan in a single layer. Roast for about 14 minutes.
4. Scatter the crumbled feta over the warm asparagus spears. Serve garnished with fresh parsley.

503. YUMMY GREEK SALAD

Preparation Time: 15 minutes + chilling time
Servings: 4

Nutrition Values: 318 Calories; 24.3g Fat; 4.1g Carbs; 15.4g Protein;

Ingredients

- 1 cup Greek-style yogurt
- 1 teaspoon garlic, minced

- 1 tablespoon fresh lime juice
- 1 teaspoon fresh or dried rosemary, minced
- 2 green onions, thinly sliced
- 4 cucumbers, sliced
- 6 radishes, sliced
- Sea salt and ground black pepper, to taste
- 4 Boston lettuce leaves

Directions

1. In a mixing bowl, thoroughly whisk the Greek-style yogurt, garlic, lime juice and rosemary.
2. Toss the green onions, cucumbers, and radishes with prepared yogurt dressing; season with salt and pepper to taste and toss to coat well.
3. Divide the Boston lettuce leaves among four serving plates. Mound well-chilled salad onto each lettuce leaf and serve.Bon appétit!

504. NUTTY COLESLAW

Preparation Time: 10 minutes + chilling time
Servings: 4

Nutrition Values: 242 Calories; 20.5g Fat; 6.2g Carbs; 1g Protein;

Ingredients

- 3/4 pound Napa cabbage, cored and shredded
- 1 large-sized carrot, shredded
- 1 cup mayonnaise
- 1 teaspoon coarse ground mustard
- 1/2 cup fresh parsley leaves, loosely packed and coarsely chopped
- 1 teaspoon celery seeds
- Salt and ground pepper, to taste
- 2 tablespoons sunflower seeds

Directions

1. Add the cabbage and carrots to your salad bowl. Now, stir in the mayonnaise, mustard, parsley, celery seeds, salt, and pepper.
2. Gently stir to combine all ingredients. Allow it to sit for 3 hours in the refrigerator. Serve sprinkled with sunflower seeds.

505. HOT VEGETARIAN DELIGHT

Preparation Time: 15 minutes
Servings: 4

Nutrition Values: 290 Calories; 21.7g Fat; 6.5g Carbs; 10.6g Protein;

Ingredients

- 2 tablespoons olive oil
- 2 small-sized shallots, chopped
- 1 garlic clove, minced

- 1 pound cremini mushroom, sliced
- 1/2 teaspoon salt
- 1/2 teaspoon ground black pepper
- 1 cup tomatillo, chopped
- 4 eggs
- 1/4 cup enchilada sauce
- 1 medium-sized avocado, pitted and mashed

Directions

1. Heat the olive oil in a saucepan over a moderate flame. Now, cook the shallot and garlic until just tender and fragrant.
2. Now, add the mushrooms and stir until they're tender. Season with salt and pepper; stir in the chopped tomatillo.
3. Stir in the eggs and scramble them well. Top with the enchilada sauce; serve warm with avocado slices.

506. CHEESE BALLS WITH FRESH CUCUMBER

Preparation Time: 25 minutes
Servings: 2

Nutrition Values: 133 Calories; 9.9g Fat; 6.8g Carbs; 6g Protein;

Ingredients

- 1 ounce blue cheese
- 1 ounce Neufchatel
- 1 medium-sized cucumber, chopped
- 1 tablespoon fresh parsley, chopped
- 2 tablespoons walnuts, chopped

Directions

1. Drop the chopped cucumbers into a colander; sprinkle with a pinch of salt. Let it stand for 20 minutes in the sink; press your cucumber firmly to drain away the excess liquid.
2. Thoroughly mix the cheese, cucumber, and parsley in a bowl.
3. Shape into 4 balls and roll them in chopped walnuts. Refrigerate until ready to serve.

507. TASTY OVEN-ROASTED ASPARAGUS

Preparation Time: 20 minutes
Servings: 4

Nutrition Values: 48 Calories; 1.6g Fat; 4.4g Carbs; 5.5g Protein;

Ingredients

- 1 pound asparagus spears
- Salt and freshly ground black pepper, to your liking
- 1 teaspoon onion powder
- 1/4 teaspoon cumin powder

- 1/2 teaspoon dried thyme
- 4 tablespoons bacon bits

Directions

1. Start by preheating your oven to 460 degrees F.
2. Toss the asparagus spears with the salt, black pepper, onion powder, cumin powder, and thyme. Arrange them on a baking sheet.
3. Spritz with a nonstick cooking spray. Bake for 8 to 10 minutes; turn them over and bake an additional 8 minutes.
4. Serve garnished with bacon bits and enjoy!

508. YUMMY VEGETABLES WITH HOT DIP

Preparation Time: 45 minutes
Servings: 4
Nutrition Values: 357 Calories; 35.8g Fat; 5.2g Carbs; 3.4g Protein;
Ingredients

- 2 carrots, cut into sticks
- 1 celery stalk, cut into sticks
- 1 red bell pepper, sliced
- 1 green bell pepper, sliced
- 1 red onion, sliced into rings
- 1/4 cup olive oil
- 1 garlic clove, minced
- 1 tablespoon fresh parsley, minced
- 1/2 teaspoon paprika

For the Spicy Sour Cream Dip:

- 1 ½ cups sour cream
- 2 tablespoons mayonnaise
- 3/4 teaspoon Dijon mustard
- 1 jalapeño pepper, finely minced
- 1 tablespoon lime juice
- Salt and black pepper, to taste
- 2 tablespoons sage leaves, chopped

Directions

1. Preheat your oven to 390 degrees F. Line a baking sheet with parchment paper.
2. In a mixing dish, toss the carrots, celery, bell pepper, onion, olive oil, garlic, parsley, and paprika.
3. Arrange the vegetables on the baking sheet and roast about 40 minutes; be sure to stir halfway through.
4. Combine all ingredients for the sour cream dip; whisk until everything is well incorporated. Serve with the roasted vegetables and enjoy!

509. STUFFED CHANTERELLES WITH PROSCIUTTO

Preparation Time: 25 minutes
Servings: 6
Nutrition Values: 98 Calories; 5.8g Fat; 3.9g Carbs; 8.4g Protein;
Ingredients

- 6 medium-sized Chanterelles, stems removed
- 3 teaspoons sesame oil
- 1 tablespoon Worcestershire sauce
- Coarse salt and ground black pepper, to your liking
- 3 slices of prosciutto, finely chopped
- 2 tablespoons fresh cilantro, minced
- 1 teaspoon fresh rosemary, minced
- 2 ounces Asiago cheese, grated

Directions

1. Start by preheating your oven to 355 degrees F. Line a baking sheet with a piece of parchment paper.
2. Rub the sesame oil and Worcestershire sauce on the mushroom caps. Season them with salt and pepper.
3. Now, combine the prosciutto, cilantro, rosemary and cheese; mix well. Stuff the mushroom caps and bake for 18 to 22 minutes.
4. Adjust the seasonings and serve immediately. Bon appétit!

510. GREEN BEANS WITH TAPENADE

Preparation Time: 15 minutes
Servings: 4
Nutrition Values: 183 Calories; 16.1g Fat; 4.4g Carbs; 3.2g Protein;
Ingredients

- 1 pound green beans
- 1 tablespoon sesame oil
- 1 celery stalk, shredded
- 1 garlic clove, smashed
- 1/2 teaspoon smoked paprika
- Flaky sea salt and ground black pepper, to taste

For Tapenade:

- 1/2 cup Kalamata olives
- 1 ½ tablespoons capers
- 2 anchovy fillets
- 1 tablespoon fresh lemon juice
- 3 tablespoons extra-virgin olive oil

Directions

1. Put the green beans in a steamer basket over boiling water; steam approximately 4 minutes or until crisp-tender.
2. Heat the sesame oil in a sauté pan over a

moderate flame. Add the celery and garlic; sauté an additional 4 minutes, stirring periodically.

3. Season with paprika, salt, and black pepper.
4. Puree all the ingredients for the tapenade in your food processor. Serve immediately with the sautéed green beans. Bon appétit!

511. SPINACH WITH COTTAGE CHEESE

Preparation Time: 10 minutes
Servings: 4
Nutrition Values: 208 Calories; 13.5g Fat; 6g Carbs; 14.5g Protein;
Ingredients
- 1/2 stick butter
- 2 garlic cloves, minced
- 2 pounds spinach leaves, rinsed and torn into pieces
- 1 teaspoon salt
- 1/2 teaspoon cayenne pepper
- 1/4 teaspoon turmeric powder
- 1 cup cottage cheese

Directions
1. Melt the butter in a Dutch oven and sauté the garlic until it's just browned.
2. Add the spinach leaves, salt, cayenne pepper, and turmeric powder; cook another 2 to 3 minutes over a moderate heat, adding a splash of warm water if needed.
3. Next, turn the heat on high, and cook for 1 to 2 minutes more, stirring often. Taste and adjust the seasonings.
4. Serve topped with cottage cheese.

512. FAMILY VEGETABLE PATTIES

Preparation Time: 15 minutes
Servings: 6
Nutrition Values: 153 Calories; 11.8g Fat; 6.6g Carbs; 6.4g Protein;
Ingredients
- 2 medium-sized zucchinis,shredded
- 2 carrots,shredded
- 1 small-sized celery stalk, shredded
- 2 tablespoons parsley,chopped
- 1 white onion, finely chopped
- 1 garlic clove, finely minced
- 1 cup cheddar cheese, grated
- 2 tablespoons olive oil
- 1 egg yolk
- Salt and black pepper, to taste
- Lemon wedges, to serve

Directions
1. Start by preheating your oven to 360 degrees

F. Line a baking sheet with parchment paper.
2. Now, press the shredded vegetables firmly to drain away the excess liquid. Then, thoroughly combine all ingredients, except for the lemon wedges, in a mixing bowl.
3. Shape the mixture into 12 patties and bake for 5 minutes per side. Serve with fresh lemon wedges and enjoy!

513. PORK AND CHEESE SAUSAGE BALLS

Preparation Time: 15 minutes + chilling time
Servings: 6
Nutrition Values: 353 Calories; 30.7g Fat; 3g Carbs; 16.1g Protein;
Ingredients
- 1 tablespoon olive oil
- 1/2 pound pork sausage, ground
- 1 tomato, pureed
- 1 teaspoon garlic paste
- 2 tablespoons onion, minced
- 4 ounces Neufchatel cheese, room temperature
- 1/4 teaspoon kosher salt
- 1/4 teaspoon ground black pepper
- 4 ounces chive & onion cream cheese
- 4 ounces fontina cheese, crumbled
- 2 tablespoons flaxseed meal

Directions
1. Heat the oil in a skillet that is preheated over moderate heat. Now, brown the sausage for 3 to 4 minutes, stirring periodically.
2. Add the tomatoes, garlic paste, and onion; cook for a further 5 minutes. Add the other ingredients and mix well to combine.
3. Place the mixture in your refrigerator to harden. Shape the mixture into bite-sized balls. Serve well-chilled.

514. BRIE-STUFFED MEATBALLS

Preparation Time: 25 minutes
Servings: 5
Nutrition Values: 302 Calories; 17.3g Fat; 1.9g Carbs; 33.4g Protein;
Ingredients
- 1 pound ground pork
- 1/3 cup heavy cream
- 2 eggs, beaten
- 1 tablespoon fresh cilantro
- 2 tablespoons shallots, minced
- 2 cloves garlic, minced
- 1 teaspoon kosher salt
- 1/2 teaspoon ground black pepper

- 1 teaspoon dried thyme
- 10 (1-inchcubes of brie

Directions
1. Combine all ingredients, except for the cubes of brie, in a mixing bowl.
2. Then, shape the mixture into 10 patties by using oiled hands. Now, place a piece of brie in the center of each patty and roll into a ball.
3. Preheat your oven to 390 degrees F. Arrange the meatballs on a foil-lined baking pan. Bake for 20 to 22 minutes.
4. Serve with mustard or low-carb salsa. Enjoy!

515. YUMMY MUFFINS WITH GROUND PORK

Preparation Time: 25 minutes
Servings: 6
Nutrition Values: 479 Calories; 42g Fat; 5.8g Carbs; 17.9g Protein;
Ingredients
- 1 tablespoon canola oil
- 1 ½ cups ground pork
- Salt and cayenne pepper, to your liking
- 1 stick butter
- 3 ½ cups almond flour
- 1/2 teaspoon baking powder
- 1/2 teaspoon baking soda
- 3 large eggs, lightly beaten
- 2 tablespoons full-fat milk
- 1/2 teaspoon ground cloves
- 1/2 teaspoon dried oregano

Directions
1. Heat the oil in a frying pan over medium heat. Now, cook the ground pork until the juices run clear, about 4 to 5 minutes.
2. Then, preheat your oven to 360 degrees F.
3. Add the remaining ingredients to a mixing dish, in the order listed above. Thoroughly combine until everything is well incorporated.
4. Divide the mixture among 12 muffin cups. Bake in the preheated oven for 15 to 18 minutes.
5. Allow your muffins to cool down before removing from the baking tin. Serve with full-fat sour cream. Bon appétit!

516. PORK SHOULDER WITH BLUE CHEESE SAUCE

Preparation Time: 30 minutes
Servings: 6
Nutrition Values: 495 Calories; 36.9g Fat; 3.6g Carbs; 33.4g Protein;
Ingredients

- 1 ½ pounds pork shoulder, boneless and cut into 6 pieces
- Salt and freshly cracked black peppercorns, to taste
- 1 teaspoon dried thyme
- 1 tablespoon butter
- 1 onion, chopped
- 2 garlic cloves, chopped
- 1/3 cup dry sherry wine
- 1/3 cup broth, preferably homemade
- 1 teaspoon dried hot chile flakes
- 1 tablespoon soy sauce
- 6 ounces blue cheese
- 1/3 cup double cream

Directions
1. Rub each piece of the pork shoulder with salt, black peppercorns, and thyme.
2. Now, warn the butter in a sauté pan over a moderately high heat. Then, brown the pork on all sides about 18 minutes; reserve.
3. Next, sauté the onions and garlic until the onions are caramelized. Add the wine and broth and stir, scraping up any brown bits from the bottom.
4. Turn the heat to medium and add the other ingredients; continue to simmer until the desired thickness is reached by evaporation.
5. Serve the reserved pork with the sauce on the side.Bon appétit!

517. MEAT LOAF AND CARROT MUFFINS

Preparation Time: 35 minutes
Servings: 6
Nutrition Values: 220 Calories; 6.3g Fat; 5.4g Carbs; 33.8g Protein;
Ingredients
- 1 pound pork, ground
- 1/2 pound turkey, ground
- 1 cup carrots, shredded
- 2 ripe tomatoes, pureed
- 1 ounce envelope onion soup mix
- 1 tablespoon Worcestershire sauce
- 1 tablespoon Dijon mustard
- 1/2 teaspoon dry basil
- 1 teaspoon dry oregano
- Kosher salt and ground black pepper, to taste
- 2 cloves of garlic, minced
- 1 eggs, whisked
- 1 cup mozzarella cheese, shredded

Directions
1. Start by preheating your oven to 350 degrees

2. Then, thoroughly combine all ingredients until everything is blended.
3. Spoon the mixture into a muffin tin that is previously coated with a nonstick cooking spray.
4. Bake for 30 minutes; allow them to cool slightly before removing from the tin. Bon appétit!

518. PORK SOUP WITH AVOCADO

Preparation Time: 20 minutes
Servings: 6
Nutrition Values: 423 Calories; 31.8g Fat; 6g Carbs; 25.9g Protein;
Ingredients
- 2 tablespoons lard
- 1 medium-sized yellow onion, peeled and chopped
- 2 cloves garlic, peeled and minced
- 1 teaspoon Mezzeta pepper, seeded and minced
- 1 celery, chopped
- 1 ¼ pounds pork shoulder, cut into chunks
- 3 cups beef broth, less-sodium
- Sea salt and ground black pepper, to taste
- A pinch of dried basil
- 2 ripe tomatoes, undrained
- 1/4 cup fresh parsley, roughly chopped
- 1 medium-sized avocado, pitted and sliced

Directions
1. Melt the lard in a large-sized stock pot over a moderate flame. Next, sauté the onion, garlic, Mezzeta pepper and celery for 2 to 3 minutes or until the onion is translucent.
2. Stir in the pork chunks and continue cooking for 4 minutes more, stirring continuously. Add the other ingredients.
3. Now, lower the heat and simmer for 10 minutes, partially covered; make sure to stir periodically.
4. Serve topped with fresh parsley leaves and sliced avocado.

519. HOT SAUERKRAUT WITH BEEF

Preparation Time: 20 minutes
Servings: 4
Nutrition Values: 330 Calories; 12.2g Fat; 4.7g Carbs; 44.4g Protein;
Ingredients
- 1 tablespoon tallow, melted
- 2 onions, chopped
- 2 garlic cloves, smashed
- 1 ¼ pounds ground beef
- 18 ounces sauerkraut, rinsed and well drained
- 1 teaspoon chili pepper flakes
- 1 teaspoon mustard powder
- 1 bay leaf
- Sea salt and ground black pepper, to taste

Directions
1. Heat a saucepan over a moderately high heat. Now, warm the tallow and cook the onions and garlic until aromatic.
2. Stir in the ground beef and cook until it is slightly browned.
3. Add the remaining ingredients. Reduce the heat to medium. Cook about 6 minutes or until everything is thoroughly cooked. Bon appétit!

520. YUMMY CHEESEBURGER SOUP

Preparation Time: 20 minutes
Servings: 4
Nutrition Values: 326 Calories; 20.5g Fat; 4.5g Carbs; 26.8g Protein;
Ingredients
- 2 tablespoons coconut oil
- 1/2 pound ground beef
- 1 cup shallots, chopped
- 1 celery stalk, chopped
- 1 tablespoon celery leaves, chopped
- 1 tablespoon fresh cilantro, chopped
- 4 cups beef bone broth
- 1/2 cup full-fat milk
- 1 cup pepper jack cheese, shredded
- 1 tablespoon rice vinegar

Directions
1. Melt the coconut oil in a stock pot that is preheated over a moderate heat. Now, cook the ground beef until it is no longer pink; reserve.
2. Add the shallots and chopped celery stalk; cook an additional 2 minutes, stirring continuously. Add a splash of broth if needed.
3. Add the celery leaves, cilantro and broth and bring to a boil; cook another 10 minutes, partially covered.
4. Gradually add the milk to the soup, stirring often. Reduce the heat and let it simmer an additional 5 minutes. Fold in the cheese and remove from the heat.
5. Add the vinegar and stir until the cheese is completely melted. Bon appétit!

521. BEEF STEAKS WITH SOUR CREAM-MUSTARD SAUCE

Preparation Time: 20 minutes

Servings: 4

Nutrition Values: 321 Calories; 13.7g Fat; 1g Carbs; 45g Protein;

Ingredients

- 1/3 cup sour cream
- 1 tablespoon stone-ground mustard
- 1 ½ tablespoons flat-leaf parsley, finely chopped
- 4 (1 ½-inch thick filet mignon steaks
- 1/2 teaspoon seasoned salt
- 1/4 teaspoon ground black pepper
- 2 sprigs thyme, chopped
- 1 sprig rosemary, chopped
- 1 tablespoon vegetable oil

Directions

1. In a mixing bowl, whisk together the sour cream, mustard, and parsley. Keep in your refrigerator until ready to serve.
2. Then, season the filet mignon steaks with salt, pepper, thyme, and rosemary.
3. Heat the oil in a pan that is preheated over moderately high heat for 4 minutes on each side. Serve with the prepared mustard sauce and enjoy!

522. JUICY BEEF SHORT LOIN

Preparation Time: 2 hours

Servings: 4

Nutrition Values: 238 Calories; 9.2g Fat; 6.3g Carbs; 27.4g Protein;

Ingredients

- 1 tablespoon olive oil
- 1 pound beef short loin, thinly sliced
- 1 leek, sliced
- 1 parsnip, chopped
- 3 garlic cloves, thinly sliced
- 1/2 teaspoon grated nutmeg
- 1 teaspoon lemon zest
- 1/2 teaspoon red pepper flakes, crushed
- 1/3 cup red wine
- 2 tablespoons Worcestershire sauce
- 1 ½ cups beef stock

Directions

1. Heat the oil in a heavy-bottomed skillet that is preheated over a moderate heat. Sear the beef short loin for 10 to 13 minutes; reserve.
2. Then, in the same skillet, cook the leeks, parsnip and garlic for 3 to 4 minutes, stirring constantly.
3. Add the remaining ingredients and bring to a rapid boil. Then, turn the heat to a simmer.

Cook for 1 ½ to 2 hours. Bon appétit!

523. TRADITIONAL BEEF STEW

Preparation Time: 40 minutes

Servings: 6

Nutrition Values: 259 Calories; 10.1g Fat; 4.1g Carbs; 35.7g Protein;

Ingredients

- 1 tablespoon tallow, at room temperature
- 1 ½ pounds beef stew meat, cubed
- 1 cup leeks, thinly sliced
- 2 garlic cloves, chopped
- 1 tablespoon cremini mushrooms, thinly sliced
- Salt and black pepper, to taste
- 1 teaspoon dried marjoram
- 1 teaspoon cayenne pepper
- 1/4 teaspoon smoked paprika
- 1 bay leaf
- 4 cubes beef bouillon, crumbled
- 4 cups water
- 1 egg, lightly whisked

Directions

1. Melt the tallow in your pot that is preheated over a moderate flame.
2. Now, sear the beef until it's just browned; make sure to stir periodically. Set aside.
3. In pan drippings, cook the leeks and garlic for 1 minute to 90 seconds or until aromatic. Stir in the mushrooms; cook until they're tender and fragrant.
4. Add the remaining ingredients, cover and cook for 30 to 40 minutes. Add the whisked egg in the hot soup and stir for 1 minute. Serve in individual bowls and enjoy!

21-DAYS MEAL PLAN

DAY	BREAKFAST	MAIN DISH	SNACK/DESSERT
1	Mushroom and Chorizo Mix	Masala Chicken	Cheese Burger Muffins
2	Smoked Ham and Baby Spinach Mix	Pork Strips and Sweet Potatoes	Onion And Cauliflower Dip
3	Apples and Walnut Bowls	Sweet Potato Chili	Keto Marinated Eggs
4	Leek and Turkey Breakfast Mix	Carrots and Celery Stew	Keto Tortilla Chips
5	Banana Porridge	Cinnamon Pork Stew	Keto Maple And Pecan Bars
6	Cocoa Cherry Bowls	Tomato Pork Chops	Keto Chia Seeds Snack
7	Cardamom Carrots Mix	Tomato Shrimp	Delightful Bombs
8	Cinnamon Cauliflower Rice	Clam Soup	Artichoke Dip
9	Apple Cauliflower Rice	Asian Tofu Bites	Keto Pepper Nachos
10	Almond Strawberry Mix	Rice Bowl	Yummy Spinach Balls
11	Nuts and Pears Breakfast Mix	Balsamic Shrimp	Keto Pizza Dip
12	Mushroom and Kale Frittata	Clam Bowls	Keto Pesto Crackers
13	Spiced Beef Breakfast Bowls	Broccoli Cream Soup	Keto Pumpkin Muffins
14	Baked Eggs with Bacon and Double Cheese	Shrimp Curry	Fried Queso Snack
15	Breakfast Beef Meatloaf	Cod and Fennel	Keto Broccoli And Cheddar Biscuits
16	Beef Casserole	Eggplant Soup	Zucchini Chips
17	Okra Breakfast Mix	Cod and Bell Peppers	Keto Avocado Dip
18	Garlic and Leek Omelet	Salmon and Spring Onions	Jalapeno Balls
19	Mushrooms Omelet	Lemony Shrimp	Maple Walnuts
20	Sweet Potato and Spring Onions Bowls	Tomato Halibut Mix	Keto Taco Cups
21	Delicious Turkey and Cauliflower Mix	Cod and Asparagus Mix	Keto Muffins Snack

CONCLUSION

There you have it – the ketogenic diet. At this point, you already know what it is, why it's good for you, how to implement or introduce the ketogenic diet, how to tell if you've already reached a state of ketosis. You also have sample meal plans, tips for staying ketogenic while eating out, and delicious recipes to try at home. You know enough about the ketogenic diet to start enjoying its benefits.

The power behind the Ketogenic diet's ability to help you lose weight and have better health comes from one simple action that the diet initiates in your body once you start following it. This simple action is how the keto diet changes your metabolism from burning carbohydrates for energy to burning fats for energy.

If you do follow the ketogenic diet as recommended, you'll get a lean and toned physique in no time. You'll also calm your cravings, have a consistent source of energy, and won't feel fatigued throughout the day as you usually would.

Enjoy!

Printed in Great Britain
by Amazon